MEET THE MERTZES

Frawley, Vance, Lucille Ball, and Desi Arnez at the Radio-TV Mirror awards. With them are Marc Daniels, and Jess Oppenheimer. (PHOTO COURTESY OF GREGG OPPENHEIMER)

Meet the Mertzes

THE LIFE STORIES OF *I LOVE LUCY*'S OTHER COUPLE

ROB EDELMAN and
AUDREY KUPFERBERG

RENAISSANCE BOOKS
Los Angeles

For Vivian Vance and William Frawley,
who filled our lives with laughter

Library of Congress Cataloging-in-Publication Data
Edelman, Rob.
    Meet the Mertzes : the life stories of I love lucy's other couple
    / Rob Edelman and Audrey Kupferberg.
        p. cm.
    Includes bibliographical references and index.
    ISBN 1-58063-095-2 (alk. paper)
    1. Frawley, William, 1887–1966. 2. Vance, Vivian.
I. Kupferberg, Audrey E. II. Title.
    PN2287.F674E34   1999
    791.45'028'092273—dc21
    [B]   99-37037
                                                             CIP

10 9 8 7 6 5 4 3 2 1

Design by Jesus Arellano and Lisa-Theresa Lenthall

Published by Renaissance Books
Distributed by St. Martin's Press
Manufactured in the United States of America
First Edition

CONTENTS

Acknowledgments

We offer our heartfelt thanks to every person listed below for taking the time to respond to our queries or to reminisce, offer opinions and anecdotes, and, in quite a few cases, set the record straight.

The following individuals, culled from the worlds of show business and baseball, were especially kind to us: Elden Auker, Yogi Berra, Frenchy Bordagaray, Jim Bouton, Dann Cahn, Gary Collins, Tim Considine, Emily Daniels, Cliff Dapper, Dom DiMaggio, Walter Doniger, Robert Douglas, Dale Evans, Charles Forsythe, Jimmy Garrett, Paul Michael Glaser, Don Grady, Edmund Hartmann, Gloria Henry, Gene Karst, Irma Kusely, Marc Lawrence, Art Linkletter, Barry Livingston, Stanley Livingston, Marjorie Lord, Tony Lupien, Meredith MacRae, Sheila MacRae, Sylvia Miles, Tom Naud, Patricia Neal, Irv Noren, Hugh O'Brian, the late Samson Raphaelson, Rhodes Reason, Elliott Reid, Gene Reynolds, Robert Rockwell, the late Roy Rowan, Jay Sandrich, Bob Schiller, John Stephens, Chuck Stevens, Roslyn Targ, Keith Thibodeaux, Bob Weiskopf, Ted Williams, and William Windom. Extra special thanks go to Considine, Garrett, Grady, Stanley

Livingston, Lord, Meredith and Sheila MacRae, Miles, Reason, Reynolds, Sandrich, Schiller, Stephens, Stevens, and Weiskopf for the generosity of their time and their extensive, detailed recollections.

Happily, we were able to track down a number of Vivian Vance's and William Frawley's relatives, friends, and hometown natives. Dorothy Jones O'Neal (Vance's younger sister), Imogene Littell (whose father was Vance's first cousin), Edward Dailey (Frawley's distant cousin), Dan and Millie Bied, Burton Prugh Jr., and Lloyd Maffitt all were kind enough to speak with us.

A few of those who worked with Vance and Frawley, including Barbara Feldon, Sherwood Schwartz, Elena Verdugo, and Margaret Whiting, expressed their enthusiasm for the project. Here is where an additional dilemma in researching events that unfolded several decades earlier comes into play. For example, comedy-writer maven Sherwood Schwartz co-authored a Thanksgiving 1958 edition of TV's *Red Skelton Show* in which Frawley appeared as a guest. "Sorry, I don't remember Frawley on the *Skelton* show . . . ," Schwartz declared. "Hell, I don't even remember what I had for breakfast today."

Still others were gracious enough to respond to our queries: Steve Allen, Donald L. Burrows (son of the late Mary Jane Walsh), Hume Cronyn, Fred DeCordova, Jim Delsing, Victoria Enos (daughter of the late Vic Lombardi), Carl Erskine, Nina Foch, Joe Garagiola, Bert Granet, Kitty Carlisle Hart, Clyde King, Ruta Lee, Gavin MacLeod, Walter Parker (administrator of the estate of Willard Parker), Hugh Rawson, Mike Sandlock, Robert Stack, Don Taylor, Harry Walker, Max Wilk, and Don Zimmer.

Additionally, a book such as *Meet the Mertzes* would be impossible to complete without the assistance of librarians and archivists. The following individuals and institutions offered invaluable assistance: Maryann Chach of the Shubert Archive; Joan Clawson of the Albuquerque (New Mexico) Little Theater; Laurel E. Drew and Gail Rasmussen, librarians, Albuquerque/Bernalillo (New Mexico) County Library System; Dan Einstein, television archivist at the UCLA Film and Television Archive; Jim Gates, Greg Harris, Corey Seeman, and Helen Stiles of the National Baseball

Hall of Fame and Museum; Susie Guest of the Burlington (Iowa) Public Library; Rosemary Hanes and Madeline Matz, reference librarians, Motion Picture, Broadcasting and Recorded Sound Division, Library of Congress; Patricia King Hanson, the American Film Institute Catalog of Feature Films; Ron Hutchinson of the Vitaphone Project; Karol Kennedy of the Dubuque County Recorder's Office; Deb Kolz-Olson of the Des Moines County Historical Society; Jessie Lickteig, librarian, Cherryvale (Kansas) Public Library; Howard Prouty, archivist, Margaret Herrick Library, Center for Motion Picture Study, Academy of Motion Picture Arts and Sciences; the New York Public Library at Lincoln Center; Ron Simon of the Museum of Television and Radio in New York City; and Janice Weir, library director, Independence (Kansas) Community College.

The following also came through when help was needed: David Bartholomew, Jim Beaver, Dick Beverage, the Bohman-Fannings, Ross Boissoneau, C. Douglas Bredt, John Cocchi, Stephen Cole, Rush Dudley, Geoffrey Mark Fidelman, R. Hall, Joanne Lawson, Michael Luders, Leonard Maltin, Phil Nichols, Art Pierce, David Pietrusza, Rhonda Revercomb, Tom Shieber, the Society for American Baseball Research, Thomas P. Syzdek, and our agent, Andy Zack.

A special acknowledgment is earned by Gregg Oppenheimer for allowing us access to letters, photographs, and other very special material. And finally, extra-special thanks go to our all-knowing and ever helpful editor, James Robert Parish, whose endless stream of information and suggestions is much appreciated.

On Sunday, October 3, 1954, Lucille Ball, Desi Arnaz, William Frawley, and Vivian Vance were guests on Ed Sullivan's weekly CBS-TV variety show, *Toast of the Town*.

At one point, in a skit in which all five appeared as themselves, Sullivan asked Ball, "By the way, could you tell me how to get hold of the Mertzes?"

Lucy responded, "You mean Vivian Vance and William Frawley?"

Ed said, "I always forget. . . . I always think of them as the Mertzes."

And Lucy responded, "Yeah, well, everybody does."

By the early 1950s, television rapidly was replacing the movies and radio as America's number one source of leisure-time entertainment. On October 15, 1951, a legendary half-hour comedy show initially was broadcast into homes across the country: *I Love Lucy*, starring Lucille Ball as wacky Manhattan housewife Lucy Ricardo and Desi Arnaz as her Cuban-born bandleader husband, Ricky Ricardo. The supporting players on this CBS-TV series were William Frawley and Vivian Vance, cast as Fred and Ethel Mertz, the Ricardos' landlords and best pals.

I Love Lucy, of course, became an immediate smash hit. At the end of its first season, it was the most popular sitcom in the nation. By then, more than eleven million American households were tuning in each Monday night to laugh at the antics of Lucy and Ricky Ricardo—and Fred and Ethel Mertz. For almost an entire decade, their capers delighted audiences in 179 half-hour shows and 13 hour-long programs, most of which have been spinning along in reruns for more than forty years.

The life stories of Lucille Ball and Desi Arnaz have been celebrated in dozens of biographies, autobiographies, histories, documentaries, and made-for-TV movies. However, what of William Frawley (1887–1966) and Vivian Vance (1909–1979), those indispensable second bananas?

As *I Love Lucy* remains fresh and funny, and is certain to be aired somewhere on planet Earth every day until the end of time, the personages of Fred and Ethel Mertz have become larger than the actors who played them. In the 1997 big-screen thriller *Conspiracy Theory*, taxi driver Mel Gibson, in describing the picture of Benjamin Franklin on the newly minted $100 bill, cracks, "He looks like the love child of Fred Mertz and Rosie O'Donnell." Younger viewers, who had yet to be born when Frawley last played Mertz in 1960, may be familiar enough with the character to connect with the reference. But how many of them would have appreciated the joke if Frawley's name had been inserted in place of Mertz's?

Yet without Frawley and Vance, there would be no Fred and Ethel as we know them. Certainly, the multitude of die-hard *I Love Lucy* fans need not be convinced that the contributions of these two wonderful, versatile performers were integral to the sitcom's enduring success.

The lives and careers of Frawley and Vance were multifaceted, and transcended *I Love Lucy*. Even today, however, relatively little is known about them beyond the oft-repeated anecdotes concerning how they came to be cast in the show and their legendary disdain for one another on and off the set. There is, however, much more to their stories, and many intriguing questions to be answered about them.

What Frawley and Vance do share are Midwestern roots—he hailed from Burlington, Iowa, while she was born in Cherryvale, Kansas—as well as families (and, specifically, mothers) who were dead-set against their pursuing careers as actors.

Beyond that, their backgrounds were markedly dissimilar. Until they were cast as the Mertzes, Frawley and Vance had not crossed paths professionally or personally. Prior to *I Love Lucy*, Frawley had been a beer-and-pretzels vaudevillian who appeared on Broadway during the 1920s and made scores of Hollywood films in the 1930s and 1940s. At the time he was hired for *I Love Lucy*, he was sixty-four years old and his career was definitely on the wane. The seven-year Paramount Pictures stock-player contract he signed in 1933 had long since expired and, as the Hollywood studio system was in the process of being dismantled, no such security would be forthcoming for any screen performer, let alone an aging and relative unknown.

Furthermore, Frawley's irascible personality, his insistence on offering a profanity-spewn opinion even in the presence of major studio executives, and his propensity for too frequently savoring alcoholic beverages, had caused his acting career to slump badly. The screen roles that were to sustain similar character/supporting types were quickly dwindling for the veteran actor.

It has been written that, when he was imbibing, Frawley became downright mean. However, the truth of the matter was that even when stone-cold sober, he was perfectly capable of expressing himself loudly and for any and all to hear in language spiced with raw, salty expletives. If he felt so inclined, Frawley would label a producer or director or studio head an idiot (to use a gentler term), or an actor a ham, or an actress an egomaniac. He cared little about the company he was in or who heard him.

The manner in which Frawley conducted himself was not politic for any person in any business. And once too often, his intake of alcohol was used as an excuse for his less-than-solicitous, often politically incorrect behavior.

Nonetheless, those who knew him were well aware that Frawley essentially was a harmless old Irishman who loved drinking, and talking sports, and singing with his buddies, barbershop-quartet style. His zest for life bursts forth from a birthday poem he composed for Jess Oppenheimer, one of the creative forces behind *I Love Lucy*. He signed it "F. Mertz," and it began, "Dear Jess— . . . Let's cheer n' drink some beer" and ends with "I hope you live forever."

Despite her list of professional stage credits, Vivian Vance had enjoyed only limited show-business acclaim. She was a former Broadway showgirl who between 1932 and 1947 appeared mostly, with varying degrees of success, in stylish New York–staged musicals and comedies. While she worked with dozens of Broadway and Hollywood luminaries—the list just begins with Ethel Merman, Gertrude Lawrence, Bob Hope, Danny Kaye, Jimmy Durante, and Alfred Drake—she never had approached their stardom and fame. Just prior to being signed to play Ethel Mertz in 1951, Vance made her screen debut, appearing in two films, *The Secret Fury* (1950) and *The Blue Veil* (1951). Yet at age forty-two, she was not on the list of hot new screen personalities.

Vance's personal life had not progressed to that point without plenty of melodrama. To the world, her then husband, actor Philip Ober, was her first. However, hidden in her past were two early marriages, which she preferred to overlook. Additionally, just a few years before *I Love Lucy*, Vance had undergone a major nervous breakdown. She had been playing Olive Lashbrooke in a 1945 Chicago production of the hit Broadway comedy *The Voice of the Turtle* when her psychological problems first manifested themselves, leading to a full-scale mental collapse. When she was first considered for the role of Ethel Mertz six years later, she was replaying Olive Lashbrooke at the La Jolla Playhouse near San Diego. While this was not her first stage appearance following her breakdown, Vance had to be coaxed by her actor/director friend Mel Ferrer away from the New Mexico home she shared with Ober and persuaded to take the part.

So beyond their roots, Frawley and Vance also were united by a lack of major success in their chosen profession. Had they not been cast as Fred and Ethel Mertz, they would stand shoulder-to-shoulder with thousands of long-forgotten actors. At best, they would be recalled—somewhat dimly— by musical-theater historians and, in the case of Frawley, old-movie buffs who specialize in pointing out the faces of venerable character actors. Once they became TV's Fred and Ethel, however, they were fated to be recognized throughout the world as two of the medium's most beloved second bananas.

During the years (1951–60) *I Love Lucy* was in production, a rosy view of the manner in which the show's cast members related was presented to the public—even in its final years, when the marriage of Lucille Ball and Desi Arnaz was fast disintegrating.

By then, the legions of *I Love Lucy* fans had come not only to view Fred and Ethel as America's favorite sitcom neighbors, but to admire the talents of the actors who played them. Then, few outside the program's inner circle knew that Frawley and Vance had taken an almost instant and irreversible dislike to one another.

To some of those in the know, the Frawley-Vance hatred was little more than a case of sticks-and-stones. "They'd talk about each other away from each other, which is about the worst that I can say about them," explains Bob Schiller, one of the regular *I Love Lucy* writers.

If their on-screen characters constantly made cracks about each other's idiosyncrasies—Fred would subject Ethel to fat jokes, while Ethel would offer comical references to Fred's penny-pinching ways and bald pate—the off-the-record remarks the actors would utter were at best unkind, and at worst, X-rated. If in Vance's eyes Frawley was an "old poop"—her words—Frawley was ever willing to describe Vance as "old fat-ass," a "bitch," and a "miserable cunt"—his words. Eventually, their animosity would become so strong that it would actually impede their future as television costars.

Adding to the situation was the reality that, to the outside world, they *were* Fred and Ethel Mertz, the married neighbors of Lucy and Ricky Ricardo. A fan running into Frawley or Vance on a street corner or in a restaurant would more than likely greet each with a hearty "Hiya, Fred. How's Ethel?" or "Hello, Ethel. Where's Fred?"

Who knew that Frawley actually was a confirmed bachelor who had been divorced from his first and only wife for over a quarter century? Who knew that Vance had been wed to Phil Ober for well over a decade? When they met, both were married—Vance was then the wife of husband number two, a musician named George Koch—and their extramarital affair had led to scandalous headlines in the New York tabloids.

Yet never once did Frawley or Vance allow their mutual disregard to show up on-screen; to one and all they were Fred and Ethel. And when they were in character and the cameras started rolling, they *never, ever* gave anything less than their very best.

Without discounting their differences, what William Frawley and Vivian Vance ultimately share is an enormous and everlasting popularity among generations of audiences and, within the Hollywood community, a respect for their talents.

Art Linkletter, whose fame as a television personality was concurrent with that of *I Love Lucy*, recalls only "meeting them once when I was guesting with Lucille." Still, he aptly sums up their status among their peers when he adds, "That both Bill Frawley and Vivian Vance were lovely to me will be no surprise as they were both tremendously well liked in this 'back-biting' industry. . . ."

"Half of Hollywood must have worked with them . . . the older half," notes veteran actor William Windom, who appeared with Vance on *The Lucy Show* (1962–68), the TV-comedy follow-up to *I Love Lucy*. "They were well-armed and well-preserved straight men for my generation. I can only hope to be half as well remembered."

Of Vance, actress Marjorie Lord (costar of TV's classic *The Danny Thomas Show*, 1957–64), her longtime pal, declares, "I watch her now on the reruns and I really appreciate how talented she was." Lord cites Vance's "comedy and her timing, and her whole personality, how she took all the edge off so it was always fun—which is not easy when you're playing a role like [Ethel Mertz]."

Gene Reynolds worked in front of the camera as a guest on *I Love Lucy* and went on to direct *My Three Sons* (1960–72), Frawley's subsequent TV series. He observes, "I think that Vivian, for Lucy, was just a blessing. Lucy had someone there who was encouraging, and worked with her beautifully.

"Lucy was a perfectionist," he continued. "She needed to have people around her who were disciplined. Frawley was *not* disciplined, but he was gold. But Vivian, I think, was a marvelous partner for Lucy. So much of that show was them plotting things out and getting in trouble together. So much of the success of that show, I think, was Vivian."

Frawley, meanwhile, was an accomplished character actor. Actress Sheila MacRae cites him along with such Hollywood Golden Age veterans as Edgar Kennedy, William Demarest, James Gleason, Edgar Buchanan, Billy Gilbert, and Edward Everett Horton. "It didn't matter what they wore, or what century they played in," explains MacRae, who with her husband, Gordon MacRae, socialized with Lucille Ball and Desi Arnaz and were their neighbors in Palm Springs, California. "Their types would fit in anywhere. They're identifiable people, all wonderful characters."

Gene Reynolds describes Frawley as "an incredible guy. He was one of these naturally funny people, without trying to be funny. He would arrive in the morning and say 'Good morning, good morning'"—and, here, Reynolds apes the actor's gruff voice, as did so many of those interviewed who knew Frawley—"and that was funny. He just was a natural."

Once the cameras stopped rolling, Frawley was a hard egg to crack if he did not take to someone. "He wasn't just your ordinary person," explains Tim Considine, who played Mike, the eldest son on *My Three Sons*. "He had a personality that was very strong and a little off-center. He could be a lot of fun and very amusing, or he could be tough."

In the end, whatever their faults, flaws, and problems, or their likes and dislikes, Bill Frawley and Vivian Vance both were wonderful actors, and masters of their craft. Scripter Bob Schiller, who observed the duo day in and day out as they brought the Mertzes to TV life, pays them both a deserved, high compliment—praise that cannot be offered about too many a pampered television actor or arrogant movie star.

"They both were pros," he says.

Part One

WILLIAM FRAWLEY
BEFORE FRED

Frawley in *Harmony Lane,* circa 1935.

Frawley as a detective in *The Inner Circle,* circa 1946.

Chapter One

YOUNG BILL FRAWLEY

Blue-eyed, sandy-haired William Clement Frawley was born on February 26, 1887, in Burlington, Iowa, located in the southeastern corner of the state along the banks of the Mississippi.

"We are a small town of about thirty thousand," explains Deb Kolz-Olson of the Des Moines County Historical Society, located in Burlington. "[Gossip columnist] Louella Parsons also is from here. Elliot Roosevelt [the son of President Franklin Delano Roosevelt] was married here. And of course, William Frawley is from here, too."

William was of Irish stock, and was born to M. A. "Mike" Frawley, a prominent local businessman, and the former Mary Ellen Brady. Records from St. Paul's Catholic Church in Burlington note that baby Bill was baptized on March 6, 1887. His baptismal sponsors were J. H. and Lizzie Gillespie and Clement Lowery, the church's pastor, from whom William derived his middle name.

After working for the Burlington Insurance Company, Mike Frawley established his own insurance/real-estate agency in 1891. It was located on the second floor of the J. J. Curran building on the southeast corner of Jefferson and Fourth Streets. Mike Frawley also served a term as surveyor of United States Customs for the port of Burlington.

Upon his death at age fifty in 1907, Mike Frawley was described in one local obituary as being "recognized as one of the best insurance men in the state," and as an "energetic citizen and essentially a self-made man. Whatever success he achieved in business was the result of his untiring progressiveness and he was always in the forefront in any enterprise that would help Burlington. He took a pride in Burlington and never tired of proclaiming its merits."

Another posthumous tribute characterized Mike Frawley as "an enthusiastic member of the Democratic Party" and "a man whom almost everybody knew and whom all liked." Mike was outlived by his mother, Bridget, who would later be described in her obituary as "a pioneer resident of Burlington."

Mike and Mary Ellen Frawley raised four children in their spacious one-story house at 1203 North Sixth, located on the northwest corner of North and Sixth Streets. In addition to William there was an older brother, John Joseph (who was nicknamed Jay), along with a third brother, Paul Bernard, and the youngest of the quartet, a sister named Mary.

During the course of Bill's life, six years were shaved off his age. For decades, it was written that William Frawley's year of birth was 1893. The 1949–50 *International Motion Picture Almanac* lists his birth date as February 26, 1893, and the same was reported at the time of the *I Love Lucy* premiere in October 1951. This same birth date was also listed on an ABC-TV network "biography" of Frawley, released as he entered his final season as a regular on *My Three Sons* in 1964. The same natal information appears in the edition of *Who Was Who in America* published after Frawley's death in 1966.

And so, upon Bill Frawley's demise, his *New York Times* obituary listed his age as seventy-two, while a UPI news item noted that he was seventy-three. Actually, at his death, on March 3, 1966, he was five days past his seventy-ninth birthday. According to the United States Government Social Security Death Index, William Frawley—Social Security Number: 562-05-1177—was born on "26 Feb 1887."

As he aged, Frawley himself was uncertain of his exact birth year. A year before he died, he even wrote the clerk of the Des Moines County District Court to seek verification of his birth date for a passport.

♥

Although his hair was destined to thin early in his adult life, Frawley was said to have had a thick head of golden curls as a youngster. His mother delighted in Bill's tresses, but the rough-and-tumble youngster preferred that they be shorn, as he feared his neighborhood pals would label him a pantywaist.

One of Frawley's favorite youthful hangouts was the Sutter Drug Store—and, specifically, the emporium's soda fountain. In a 1953 profile published in the *Burlington* (Iowa) *Hawk-Eye*, Tom Green, the actor's cousin, who then was a retired local newspaperman, recalled that, as youngsters, Jay, Bill, and Paul Frawley also "carried the old *Gazette* on a near North Hill route, beginning on Main Street and progressing north on Third, Fourth, Fifth, and Sixth. This route was at one time covered by Len [Leonard] McKitterick, who later accumulated a million dollars in various enterprises in New York City, one of which was Philip Morris." Well over a half century later, the Philip Morris Tobacco Company would be the initial sponsor of *I Love Lucy*. And in winter 1955, when told of the subzero Burlington temperatures by a *Des Moines Sunday Register* reporter, Frawley cracked, "Well, I know a lot about that. I used to carry the *Burlington Gazette* and sometimes those drifts on North Hill were as high as I was."

Tom Green remembered "the time when [Bill] and his brother, Paul, rollicked in the Murray Iron Works boiler shop, under the watchful eye of John A. Dailey, another cousin, and superintendent of that department. And one summer the boys served as timekeepers for contractor John McKee, during the brick paving of several blocks of Mount Pleasant Street."

Frawley's parents stressed a solid Catholic upbringing for their children. During the school year, young Bill attended Lourdes Academy. He and Paul also sang in the choir at the local St. Paul's Church.

While in school, Frawley played baseball and football, and it was as a youngster that he developed what would be a lifelong obsession with sports. In 1942, nine years after coming to Hollywood, Bill was cast in Errol Flynn's *Gentleman Jim*, one of his many sports-related movies, a biography of James J. Corbett (1866–1933), the San Francisco bank clerk who became heavyweight boxing champ. Frawley's colorful role was Billy Delaney, the fighter's first manager and trainer. "Each summer," noted the actor in the Warner Bros. publicity material for the movie, "[the prizefighting Corbett] used to make a tour of cities in the minor leagues, playing first base for the home team for three or four innings and picking himself up a neat bit of change. He came to my hometown of Burlington, Iowa, one summer, and my father, who knew him slightly, took me to see the game and to meet the champion."

Between 1895 and 1900, Corbett was in the box scores of twenty-nine official bush-league contests, appearing as a gate attraction and batting .274. In 1897, the year Frawley celebrated his tenth birthday, Corbett was in twenty-one of them—and pocketed $17,000.

"He was a pretty hammy first-baseman," declared Frawley (who is described as "a connoisseur of things athletic"), who "always fancied himself a pretty good ballplayer. In fact, [Corbett's] brother, Joe, was good enough to play in the big leagues and the champ thought he was just as good.

"He was a nice guy," Frawley added of the fighter, who was to become one of the actor's many sports-world cronies. The film player then displayed his well-honed baseball expertise when he described Corbett as being "no Hal Chase around that first cushion."

Although agriculture has played a significant role in Burlington and Des Moines County life, the development of the railroad is as much a key to understanding the area's history. More to the point, the railroad was destined to play a primary role in Frawley's early life.

As young Bill Frawley came of age, it appeared that he was headed for a straight-arrow, nine-to-five career as a railroad employee. This in fact was

Mike Frawley's wish for his middle son. In 1939, six years after coming to Hollywood, Bill declared, "By right, I should now be in the railroad business. You see, my dad was a railroad man"—for some reason, Frawley felt compelled to state that his dad was in the transportation profession, rather than the more stodgy insurance business—"and, as soon as I started wearing long pants, he saw to it that I got a job with the railroad company.

"So, after I left high school, I found myself traffic inspector for the Burlington Railroad." According to Thomas F. Dailey, a Burlington resident who appeared on a *This Is Your Life* TV tribute to Frawley in 1961, the actor-to-be also worked for a while as a salesman for the National Biscuit Company.

But the young man's career interests lay elsewhere. For one thing, he savored performing. For another, he was blessed with a distinct and sweet-sounding Irish tenor voice. "He was always a great one for theatricals," Dailey would recall in the 1960s. "He used to put on shows for me when I was operating a dance school here in Burlington."

"When the Elks gave a show in town," Frawley remembered late in life, "I was always singing and dancing. And when they needed extras in the local opera house, I was in that."

Young Bill knew that he wanted to channel his extroverted personality into a profession and a lifestyle that would suit his demeanor. That profession would prove to be the theater, and that lifestyle would encompass the late-to-bed, late-to-rise existence of a typical actor. Even in his youth, it was clear that pear-shaped Bill lacked the looks to be a conventional leading man. Yet surely his gregarious personality and his performing abilities, his dancing Irish eyes and an impish grin that made him appear as if he had just kissed the Blarney Stone, would be sufficient to ensure a career as a professional entertainer.

However, Frawley's mother, Mary Ellen, a deeply religious woman who frowned on show business, wanted him to study bookkeeping and shorthand. "I can also vouch for the truth of Mother Frawley's distaste for theatrical careers for Bill and his brother, Paul," wrote Tom Green. Mary Ellen Frawley could be singularly manipulative in her effort to squelch her son's ever-burgeoning obsession with the stage. At her urging, young Bill eventually took a job in Chicago as a court reporter. Soon afterward, he settled in Omaha where he worked as a clerk for the Union Pacific Railroad.

But Frawley was ill-suited to a career as a nine-to-five clock-puncher. He certainly was not the type to meekly embrace a life of drudgery in Burlington, which to him was an obscure small town, or in what he perceived as the staid, boring Midwest.

In the early 1960s, when Frawley was appearing on the TV hit *My Three Sons*, Stanley Livingston, his young costar, asked Bill why he wanted to be an actor. "My recollection," Livingston says today, "is that he said he thought that would get him where he wanted to go in life. It was a ticket out from where he was."

The circumstances surrounding Frawley's entry into show business are masked in mystery. One account was that Frawley, just past—or maybe it was just before—his twentieth birthday in 1907, had gone to Chicago on railroad business. Another had it that he actually was relocated to Chicago. "I was the youngest tariff agent employed by the railroad when I was transferred to Chicago," Frawley told Bob Bruegger, editor of the *Burlington* (Iowa) *Hawk-Eye*, his hometown newspaper, near the end of his life.

On another occasion, Frawley described the circumstances upon which he entered show business. "One night I was with a bunch of fellows in a little cafe on the South Side [of Chicago]," he claimed, "and we started singing our repertory of old railroad favorites. Pretty soon, a stranger came up to me and said, with a voice like mine, he thought I should be in show business.

"I thought it was a gag at first, but he left me his card and I decided the next day it would do no harm to find him. Well, the upshot of the matter was that he got me into the chorus of a show running at the LaSalle Theater [in the Windy City], called *The Flirting Princess*. I was crazy about the theater from the first moment I set foot in it. It awed me, excited and thrilled me, beyond anything I'd ever done."

Other accounts had Frawley, wearied by the mundane life of a railroad employee, running off to Chicago with the specific intention of becoming an entertainer. One thing that is certain is that his mother quickly stifled his artistic aspirations.

After Bill landed in the chorus of *The Flirting Princess*, older brother Jay—who for a while had toiled as a clerk in Mike Frawley's insurance agency in Burlington—was dutifully dispatched to fetch him back home from Chicago. Along with Jay came a note, penned by Mrs. Frawley, in which she vowed that she would rather see him dead, and willingly would plant flowers on his grave, than watch him wreck his life as an actor. Frawley surrendered under such strong parental pressure. He quit *The Flirting Princess* and reluctantly returned to Burlington.

Indeed, Frawley's lifelong rancor toward women—which is exhibited in his troubled early marriage, his years of dedicated bachelorhood, and his disdain for Vivian Vance—might well be traced to his conflicted relationship with the domineering Mrs. Frawley.

Despite the determination of his mother to shape his young life, show business, as Bill once recalled, "was in my blood by this time and in spite of parental objections, I decided I must be backstage again in order to live at all."

After a year of dutifully working on the railroad, Frawley left home— this time for good. On this second effort to strike out on his own, he was joined by brother Paul, who also harbored dreams of being an entertainer. Yet here, too, the manner in which the brothers first organized their act is apocryphal. One account has William returning to Chicago with Paul and, as he once explained, "soon we had worked out a vaudeville [act] which we tried out in East St. Louis. It clicked and we took it on the road."

Another report had Frawley attending a vaudeville show and, as he discussed the merits of the program, insisting he could earn a week's wage as an actor. He and Paul then arranged an act in which Bill sang and Paul played the piano. With the help of Joe Erber, a friend who managed a vaudeville house in East St. Louis, the Frawleys appeared on a performance bill.

Afterward, Erber had some professional advice for Bill Frawley. The essence of his counsel, as recounted in a 1933 *New York American* newspaper feature on Frawley, was that young Bill should return to his day job. "Paul is a good-looking young man and he has no job, and the theater might be his mutton," Erber reportedly recommended. "As for you, you have a job, you are no beauty, and I suggest that you stick to your typewriter."

The story continues with the Frawley brothers returning to Iowa. A short time later, they repeated their East St. Louis act in a Burlington vaudeville house. Mama Frawley was in the audience. Afterward, she broke down and cried—not out of joy, but because she so heartily disapproved of a life in the theater for her sons. As a result, both Frawleys obediently agreed to abandon their theatrical dreams once and for all.

However, William soon penned a show entitled *Fun in a Vaudeville Agency*. He and Paul persuaded their cousin Tom Green, who during the summer months moonlighted as manager of Burlington's Garrick Theater, to let them produce the project using local talent. Green described the show as a "tuneful mélange" and, for his work, Frawley ended up pocketing $580—a very tidy sum for the times. From then on, there was no stopping William in his intense quest for a successful stage career. Mrs. Frawley eventually gave up hope of having her middle son settle in as a railroad man.

♥

No matter the circumstances surrounding their professional union, William and Paul did tour in vaudeville as the Frawley Brothers. The teaming was destined to be short-lived, as Paul dropped out on the insistence of their determined mother. However, instead of settling in at the railroad, Paul attended Creighton University in Omaha, where he sang in the college glee club and, as press agent Thoda Cocroft would later describe it, "frivoled in amateur theatricals."

Paul Frawley was a slimmer and more handsome and graceful version of his brother. He was sweet-looking, with a high forehead and soft features, sloping eyebrows, full lips, and a shock of wavy hair. Paul also was destined to predate William as a Broadway musical performer. After making his way to New York in the late 1910s, he came to prominence singing in the Ziegfeld production *Midnight Frolic*, an ongoing revue at the fabled New Amsterdam Roof Theater, a splashy showcase created by renowned stage designer Joseph Urban. At the time, Paul was referred to as a "singing juvenile." Through the early 1920s, Paul appeared as a musical-comedy and romantic juvenile in such Broadway shows as *Odds and Ends of 1917, Come Along, Three Showers, Kissing Time,* and *Helen of Troy, New York.*

In *Ned Wayburn's Demi Tasse Revue,* which played on Broadway in 1919, Paul was cast in various skits and performed musical duets. And his youthfulness and charm allowed him to be cast as "A Suitor," under warm romantic lighting, in a sketch titled "By the Firelight."

As the years passed, Paul Frawley grew in stature as a Broadway regular. In *The Music Box Revue* (1921–22), also known as *Irving Berlin's Music Box Revue,* he introduced Berlin's song "Say It with Music" in a duet with Wilda Bennett. In Jerome Kern's *Sunny,* which bowed in New York in 1925, he was the romantic lead opposite beautiful blonde Marilyn Miller. In *Treasure Girl,* which came three years later and was a rare failure for George and Ira Gershwin, Paul was billed right after Clifton Webb and was cast as the fiancé of the show's star, Gertrude Lawrence.

In a *New York World* photo whose caption announced that he "has been engaged for the new Gertrude Lawrence musical comedy," the good-looking Paul Frawley exudes the clean-cut Ivy League look of an Arrow shirt model. In mid-decade, a journalist described him as "one of the best juvenile leads in the country" as well as "handsomer, less aware of it, more graceful, democratic and musical as ever."

By the end of the 1920s, Paul still was being cast as romantic/comic leads—albeit older ones. In Guy Bolton, Bert Kalmar, and Harry Ruby's *Top Speed,* which opened on Christmas Day, 1929, he and Lester Allen played clerks—described as members "of the great army of workers"—who pose as millionaires to impress a pair of wealthy young ladies. One of the ladies was played by fast-rising Ginger Rogers, with whom Frawley performed the numbers "Keep Your Undershirt On" and "You Couldn't Blame Me for That."

Paul Frawley's popularity was at its peak in the late 1920s. A press release—written in conjunction with *Top Speed* when it played the Chestnut Street Opera House in Philadelphia—noted that he "is about five feet eight inches in height, and is of slight build. He has very fair hair and the bluest of eyes. On this account he has often been described by the susceptible matinee girl and her matron sister as 'heavenly. . . .'

"Firmly established, Paul Frawley's services are ever in demand," the press release concluded, "and he never has to worry about his next job."

Nonetheless, he clearly was aging. By the time Paul appeared in Peter Arno's *Here Goes the Bride* on Broadway in 1931, he was past forty—and was now deemed too mature to play the youthful sweetheart. Instead he took the part of a married man who has fallen out of love with his wife.

Paul Frawley's Broadway career petered out in the early 1930s. With the rare exception of a Dick Powell, male ingenues are unable to sustain their stardom as they age.

It was a good thing, then, for big brother Bill that he had an altogether different physical appearance, and that his career was destined to take a completely dissimilar show-business path.

Chapter Two

VAUDEVILLE ROOTS

By the time Paul Frawley arrived in New York in the late 1910s, brother Bill had already firmly established himself as a singer-comedian in vaudeville. After their act broke up over a decade earlier, Bill secured a yearlong solo gig in Denver, singing at the Rex Café, a popular nightspot. His salary was $23 per week. Then he joined up with Franz Rath, a piano player, in an act titled "A Man, a Piano and a Nut." The pair headed for San Francisco and spent four years touring in vaudeville.

While the silent cinema was then growing in popularity and attracting audiences of all economic brackets, traveling vaudevillians still were packing houses in cities across the country. There were jugglers, animal acts, ballet artists, singers, comedians, and dramatic artists, and it was in this busy and exciting show-business whirl that Frawley really cut his teeth on the stage. He and Rath toured along the Pacific Coast and across the western United States, playing big cities as well as wild, rural cow towns, from San Francisco all the way through Baker and Pendleton, Oregon, and Twin Falls and Blackfoot, Idaho. In some of the less populated areas, their act sometimes would compete for audiences with traveling rodeos and medicine shows.

Throughout his life, Frawley would remain in touch with his vaudeville roots. For example, in February 1947, he appeared on Bing Crosby's radio show that aired as part of *Philco Radio Time*. By then, he had lived in southern California for almost fifteen years and been cast in dozens of films. Yet at one point during the broadcast he proudly noted, "I spent most of my life in vaudeville."

It was his years trodding the boards that allowed Frawley to master his craft. By the time he was cast as TV's Fred Mertz in 1951, he had become an expert at reading an audience and reading a line, and had developed precision comic timing. He also was a brilliant ad-libber. During the early run of *I Love Lucy*, a bulletin board was posted backstage. On it were the names of the show's actors and crew members. A gold star would be placed next to each name when that individual spouted a funny offstage ad-lib.

The stars next to Frawley's name quickly outdistanced all others, and so the enterprise was discontinued because of the shortage of competition. This ability to spout fast quips and amusing one-liners and comebacks had been honed decades earlier, beginning in the early 1910s, as Frawley trod the vaudeville boards.

♥

Given Frawley's reputation as a drinker, it is apropos that one of his favorite late-career boasts was that he introduced the song "My Melancholy Baby" while performing in vaudeville with Franz Rath. Written by George A. Norton and Ernie Burnett and published in 1912, the song was popularized in vaudeville and eventually became the stereotypical moaning of the sentimental drunk in movies and later on television.

Actually, the song originally was titled "Melancholy." This version was published in 1911 and featured lyrics penned by Maybelle E. Watson, Burnett's wife. If Frawley did not actually introduce either rendition, he easily might have been one of its earliest performers.

He also claimed to have introduced Gus Kahn and Walter Donaldson's "Carolina in the Morning." This particular number, composed in 1922, was recorded that year by Ernie Hare and performed in New York by Al Jolson at his Winter Garden concerts and by the comedy team of Willie and Eugene Howard in the Broadway revue *The Passing Show of 1922*. Perhaps Frawley was one of the earliest to sing the song, while on the road. Years later, he and Vivian Vance performed it on *I Love Lucy* and also on *Dinner with the President*, a 1953 TV special. However, despite his claims, it would be erroneous to give Bill sole credit as the first entertainer to sing the song.

In 1958, as he was entering the homestretch of his tenure as sitcom's Fred Mertz, Frawley took advantage of his nationwide popularity and recorded an album, on the Dot label, titled *Bill Frawley Sings the Old Ones*. Here, you really get a full sense of his vaudeville roots and the Tin Pan Alley time period of American musical history, which he held so dear. On the disc, Frawley sings neither Gershwin nor Cole Porter, nor Rodgers and Hammerstein, nor Leiber and Stoller. He serenades listeners with "My Melancholy Baby" and "Carolina in the Morning" as well as other period ditties from his vaudeville years: "Pretty Baby," "Moonlight Bay," "Swanee River," "For Me and My Gal," "Dear Old Girl," "Meet Me Tonight in Dreamland," "June Night," "If You Were the Only Girl in the World," "Shine on Harvest Moon," "By the Light of the Silvery Moon," "I Wonder Who's Kissing Her Now," and "Cuddle Up a Little Closer."

You won't find any complex musical arrangements on *Bill Frawley Sings the Old Ones*. The accompaniment is basic: one or two instruments, including piano, drum, and banjo, per number. Rendering Frawley background vocal support is a barbershop quartet. His voice is relatively smooth and occasionally even sweet, and can be assumed to be a fair replica of what he sounded like four decades earlier on the vaudeville circuit. All of the numbers on *Bill Frawley Sings the Old Ones* are barbershop standards. Frawley was fabled to be an expert barbershop harmonizer—and barbershop-style singing was included in "Lucy's Show Biz Swan Song," an *I Love Lucy* episode in which the Ricardos and Mertzes harmonize on "Sweet Adeline."

Frawley became peeved during the show's rehearsal. He, after all, was an adroit barbershop singer, and here he was surrounded by rank incompetents, including "that goddamn Vivian Vance," Desi the "Cuban square," and Lucy, whose lone note during the number, according to Frawley, sounded like "a barrel of shit on a baked Alaska."

After splitting with Franz Rath, the twenty-something Frawley joined with a new vaudeville partner: Edna Louise Broedt, a young woman five years his junior, who hailed from San Diego, California. While Frawley eventually was to earn a well-developed reputation as a confirmed bachelor, he actually was married once upon a time. In 1914, he and Edna wed— and years later, Frawley recalled, "my wife Red—she had red hair—and I did a song-and-dance act in vaudeville. We called ourselves Frawley and Louise, and it was a pretty good act, but the marriage wasn't so good. How long can you tolerate women?"

Actually, Frawley did tolerate Edna for seven years—or perhaps she tolerated him—before they separated in 1921; they did not officially divorce for another six years (in December 1927). While they were together, Frawley and Edna toured the United States in an act consisting of singing, dancing, and George Burns–and–Gracie Allen–style comedy and patter, with Edna playing straight woman to Bill's clowning. Among their stage appearances, the team played at San Francisco's Hippodrome where their key turn was, "I'm going to hang around till I make you care for me." Frawley also performed with his wife at Al Levy's Spring Street Club in Los Angeles.

In his 1953 book, *Vaudeville: From the Honky-Tonks to the Palace*, vaudeville guru Joe Laurie Jr. cites the duo (whom he refers to as "Bill Frawley and Edna Louise") in a long list of "great comedy acts" in which "the woman did the 'straight.'" The Frawleys were in impressive company. Among the others Laurie listed were Billy (William) Gaxton and Ann Laughlin, Skeets Gallagher and Irene Martin, Jack Haley and Flo McFadden, Bert and Betty Wheeler, Bert Lahr and Mercedes, Joe E. Brown and Marion Sunshine, and Si Wills and Joan Davis.

The Frawleys played the prestigious Orpheum circuit, which billed itself as "Presenting the Leading Artists of the World in Vaudeville." Orpheum theaters were located in cities across the South, the Midwest, and the western United States, from San Francisco to St. Paul, Salt Lake City to Sioux City.

In 1915, the duo even achieved the ultimate for a vaudeville act: playing the famed Palace Theater in New York (which was affiliated with the Orpheum organization). However, first they won the number-four spot on a bill at the Majestic Theater in Chicago, which also was an Orpheum venue; they were hired to replace previously scheduled performers, who had to drop out because of illness. This directly led to the Palace booking. "You talked about the Palace before you played it," Frawley observed years later, "and you never stopped talking about it after you had."

It also was during this period that Frawley made his screen debut, appearing in *Lord Loveland Discovers America* (1916), a silent, five-reel Mutual comedy-drama directed by and starring Arthur Maude. *Lord Loveland Discovers America* chronicles the plight of a titled but poverty-stricken young Englishman (played by Maude) who comes to the United States with the intention of marrying an heiress. At one point, the penniless peer secures employment as a waiter. Frawley plays Tony Kidd, an industrious newspaper reporter who learns the identity of the waiter and pens a feature article for his paper about his discovery.

That same year, Frawley (billed as "Billy Frawley") and Edna were cast in *Persistent Percival*, a "Beauty" comedy—the brand name for a series of short, silent screen farces then being released weekly by the American Film Manufacturing Company. In the film, Frawley's character also is called Billy. The poor soul is robbed while entertaining a young woman (played by Edna) in a café. Billy's father—this may have been the lone time on stage or screen where Frawley's character actually had a visible papa—suggests that his disaster-prone son hire a guardian. After being rescued from a car accident by Percival, the title character (Orral Humphrey), Billy hires him as his protector. From then on, the pair are involved in a series of comic misadventures in which Percival attempts to prevent Billy from inappropriately romancing an attractive woman. Fiction and fact also blend in *Persistent Percival* when, at one point in the on-camera story, Frawley's character imbibes too much liquor.

Neither of these films was fated to establish Frawley as a motion-picture performer. In a review of *Lord Loveland Discovers America*, which appeared in *Moving Picture World*, critic Louis Reeves Harrison wrote, "The play gives Arthur Maude a role which suits him in every respect." Harrison went on to note, "In fact, the opportunity is so overwhelmingly his that there is almost nothing for the rest of the cast." William C. Esty II, reviewing the film in *Motion Picture News,* observed that "the support-ing cast is very strong, including in it Constance Crawley, William Carrol [*sic*], Charles Newton, and Neil Franzen." Tellingly, Frawley's name is omitted from the tributes. (Frawley would also work as an unbilled screen player at the Santa Barbara–based American "Flying A" company.)

Also in 1916, Edna Frawley appeared without her husband in two "Beauty" short screen comedies directed by Arthur MacMackin: *Billy Van Deusen's Wedding Eve* and *A Gay Blade's Last Scrape*. In *Billy Van Deusen's Wedding Eve*, Edna played Helen Galsworthy, the fiancée of the title char-acter. In *A Gay Blade's Last Scrape*, she was the wife of a character Frawley would be typecast as decades later in Hollywood: a police captain.

During these years, the Frawleys crisscrossed the country, playing the Orpheum circuit. In the program for the Orpheum venue in Memphis, dated February 16, 1920, it is announced that "Billy Frawley and Edna Louise" would be appearing the following week in a skit titled "Seven A.M.", authored by Jack Lait, a newspaperman and prolific vaudeville act writer. In "Seven A.M.", Frawley would be seen as "Dan, a night clerk" while Edna Louise's role would be "Mayme, a cigar girl."

Edna Frawley eventually tired of vaudeville *and* Frawley, and returned to her family in San Diego. For all intents and purposes, she disappeared from Frawley's life—except for one brief, near-disastrous later occasion.

Four months after the September 29, 1960, premiere of *My Three Sons*, Frawley's post–*I Love Lucy* TV sitcom, he was feted on *This Is Your Life* (1952–61), a popular weekly television series hosted by Ralph Edwards.

First, Edwards would surprise a celebrity. Then, family and friends—some of whom were long-lost—would appear and reminisce about the honoree's life. On *This Is Your Life*, Frawley's past was paraded before him—much to his consternation, particularly because one of the show's "surprise" guests was none other than Edna Frawley!

"He couldn't stand the woman, and had made a settlement with her," explains John Stephens, the production manager of *My Three Sons*, who got to know Frawley quite well during the last years of Bill's life and was involved in setting up the actor's appearance on *This Is Your Life*. The two had gone to what Frawley assumed would be a quiet dinner at Hollywood's Brown Derby restaurant. During their meal, Edwards popped in and informed Frawley that the evening would be like no other in his life.

"[Frawley] could have cared less," Stephens remembers of the tribute. "Then he was furious because they brought his ex-wife on. They put the kids on from *My Three Sons*, which was fine. But the next day he was yelling at me, 'Why'd they have my wife on?'"

Stephens adds, "If you ever wanted to get on his wrong side, ask him about his wife. He would have gone crazy."

After the *This Is Your Life* broadcast, Frawley was feted at the Roosevelt Hotel on Hollywood Boulevard. "I was playing with [kid brother] Barry and [*My Three Sons* costar] Don [Grady]," notes Stanley Livingston, who then was ten years old. "Don was probably just making the transition into being more of a mature teenager. But he was still young enough so that we could get him to go off from the party."

Livingston explains that "you can use the Roosevelt Hotel stairwell to climb all the way to the twelfth or thirteenth floor. It's one of those types of stairwells that goes around and around, and forms a hollow center.

"We wanted someone to go up there and see if they could spit all the way down, so we sent Don to the top. We yelled for him to go ahead, and the next thing you knew this thing hit me right in the eye! It was gross, but when you're ten you think, 'Wow, that was cool!'

"Had we told Frawley [what we had done], I'm sure he would have heartily approved, and said, 'Let me do it next.'"

Frawley, however, was in no condition to engage in boyish escapades that January night in 1961. Livingston recalls him as being "pretty soused . . . I remember him being very shaky that night." Tim Considine adds that, during the broadcast, "We were all terrified that he was going to say something awful. But he didn't."

Had Frawley uttered "something awful" on air, it more than likely would have been about ex-wife Edna.

Frawley's contempt for the institution of marriage is reflected in quite a few of his on-screen characters. In *Car 99* (1935), a long-forgotten B-movie Frawley made two years into his Paramount Pictures contract, he plays a sergeant in the Michigan State Police. "Are any of you fellas thinking of getting married?" he barks at his underlings at the film's outset. "Well, don't think of it." Next he offers a short diatribe in which he lists all the instances in which he almost got hitched, and concludes, "It was keepin' away from women that made me what I am today." Then, as he leads the patrolmen in physical exercise, he attempts to step up the pace by asking, "What'd ya do if ya mother-in-law was chasin' ya?"

In *Monsieur Verdoux* (1947), Charles Chaplin's classic black comedy, Frawley appears briefly in a wedding scene. "You know, it's a peculiar thing," his on-camera character observes. "At funerals, one's inclined to laugh. And at weddings, weep." Given Frawley's marital plight, he easily might have ad-libbed these lines of dialogue.

After his breakup with Edna, Frawley—who by now was billed as "Billy" or "William" but known as "Bill" to his friends and "Willie" to his closest intimates—would never, ever consider remarrying. (After leaving her husband and returning to her family, Edna Frawley never remarried. She lived to be one hundred, passing away in New Port Richey, Florida, on November 1, 1992.)

"He was gruff, and anything but a ladies' man," notes *My Three Sons* costar Don Grady. "There was a part of him that was a woman-hater. Something must have [happened] in his past. Maybe he didn't like his mom or something. He never talked to women, that I can remember. Anytime he mentioned a woman, it was usually with some kind of sarcasm. He had this shield up, I think." On the rare occasion that Frawley would mention his marriage, Grady reports that he would take on a tone of bitterness.

Sheila MacRae knew Frawley, but only casually. Her husband, Gordon MacRae, "used to drink and play cards with these rambunctious men. One was Bill Frawley. Another was [rotund character actor] Andy Devine."

MacRae describes Frawley as "tough. He was a tough man, a private kind of man. I have a feeling that he was a misogynist. I don't think he was crazy about women, in the business or out. Quite obviously, he was a lot like W. C. Fields. He really didn't like women."

When Bill Frawley separated from wife Edna in 1921, he was in his mid-thirties. By this time, all of his personality traits were solidly established and entrenched within him for life. When socializing, he preferred the camaraderie of like-minded men, whether they were athletes or fellow actors or old-time Tin Pan Alley songwriters. For Frawley, a grand time would be had at a ball game or the racetrack, or in a speakeasy with drink in hand, or beside a piano singing old-time songs.

"He was really a character out of the 1920s, you know," recalls *I Love Lucy* scribe Bob Schiller, "when men were men who would drink a lot and have very little to do with women outside of sex."

Frawley told actor Tim Considine that fellow Burlington native (and powerful Hollywood newspaper columnist) Louella Parsons once came up to him at his table in the Brown Derby restaurant. Parsons was said to have made a big fuss over Frawley, declaring, "Oh, Bill, I remember when I was just a little girl and you were a little boy and you used to throw rocks at me." Without missing a beat, Frawley responded, "If I had one right now I'd throw it at ya." "He thought that was great sport," reports Considine.

Don Grady adds, "He wasn't a sentimental kind of person. I remember him being warm, but he would never hug you. He might pat you on the back or something."

As one might expect, Frawley was anything but a clotheshorse. "He would throw a hat and sweater on when he left [the set], and didn't care what [*My Three Sons* costumers] gave him to wear," notes Grady. Yet despite this lack of concern with his appearance, Frawley insisted on polishing his nails—a throwback to his origins and the time in which he came of age. "He was really fussy about his hands," Grady continues. "He would [use] that real glossy nail polish. And he had these great big huge fingers—big, round-type fingers that are curved and not flat. I was always fascinated looking at his hands."

By the early 1920s, Frawley had lost all vestiges of any kind of youthful air. His hair was thinning, and he was balding—the curly locks his mother loved so much when he was a child now were all but memories— and he carried a bit of a middle-age spread. Now more than ever he resembled your uncle Willie, or the cop on the beat, or the guy who works next to you at the factory, with whom you might share a few after-hours beers in your corner saloon.

From his vaudeville years all the way to the end of his life, Frawley's appearance seemed to change little. Stanley Livingston recalls, "The thing that always struck me about Bill [was] that I'd see him in movies and my parents would say that this film was made back in the 30s or 40s. I'd say to Bill, 'How come you look the same back then as you do now?' This guy had to be, what, in his late sixties. [Actually, he was well into his seventies.] The movies were twenty-five years before that, yet he looked the same. He was one of those guys who looked old even when he was young. Probably when he was in fourth grade, he [already] had hair on his chest."

Frawley was the product of a time in which men were men, women were supposed to know their place, and blacks were expected to meekly accept their status as second-class Americans. Had he lived past the 1960s, Frawley more than likely would have been confounded by feminism and outraged by affirmative action. TV scriptwriter Bob Schiller, in fact, even goes so far as to dub the actor a "bigot."

Did Frawley really abhor minorities, or was he talking out of the side of his mouth when he casually referred to them in a less-than-enlightened manner? "I don't know whether he did or not," Schiller explains, "but he was not 'politically correct,' let's put it that way."

Bob Weiskopf, Schiller's fellow *I Love Lucy* writer, adds, "He was from that era, you know, where a Latino was a spic and all that kind of stuff. He used terrible language. Not on camera or anything, but in conversation. He had nicknames for all the races." Had he been a few years younger and lived a decade or two longer, Frawley would have been perfectly cast as lovable bigot Archie Bunker on *All in the Family*, the classic CBS sitcom that came to television in 1971.

More than likely, the truth of the matter was that Frawley, like Archie Bunker, was more of a loudmouth than a serious hatemonger who would don a Ku Klux Klan robe. He was irascible—and, according to Tim Considine, he was not to be taken seriously. "He liked to play grumpy," Considine recalls. "He would sometimes snap at people, but that was his sense of humor. If he spilled a little something on his shirt—and God forbid anyone who didn't know him said, 'Bill, you have a little something right here . . . ' —he'd grunt, 'I know it, goddamn it. I put it there.' That was him. That was his sense of humor. If you knew him, you'd laugh. If you didn't, you might be really taken aback."

By the mid-1910s, when he had established himself in vaudeville, Frawley was purposefully out of touch with his Burlington, Iowa, roots. His identity was no longer that of a Midwesterner. During his years in vaudeville, Frawley was a traveling actor. When he came to Broadway in the early 1920s, he became a New Yorker. After relocating to Hollywood in the early 1930s, he reinvented himself as a Californian—and remained so for the rest of his life. In fact, his last visit to Burlington came in 1921, when he attended his mother's funeral.

Those in his hometown certainly did not reject Frawley. "My brother, Jack, who's deceased, had some correspondence with Mr. Frawley with regard to maintaining an old, old Catholic cemetery [plot] up on what we call North Sixth Street here in Burlington," recalls Edward Dailey,

Frawley's cousin. "His mother and father are buried there. As I remember it, Mr. Frawley did not participate.

"Regretfully, he did not keep up much contact with Burlington."

A couple of decades later, in the mid-1950s, the Players Workshop, a Burlington community theater, thought to invite Frawley back to his hometown to appear in one of their productions. "He had been identified with this particular entertainment, whatever it was," explains Burlington resident Lloyd Maffitt, who recalls that possibly it was a production of *The Front Page*.

"And he sent word through his agent that, to get him back here, it would cost $750 for tickets for 'him and his chick.' He was then at least seventy years old. I assumed his 'chick' was at least half that age. Back then, of course, $750 meant a lot more money than it does today.

"The money was not forthcoming, and he did not come back," Maffitt adds.

Despite his aversion to returning to Iowa, Frawley was destined to make one last, memorable appearance in America's heartland. This came during his 1960s run on *My Three Sons*. Quaker Oats had become one of the TV show's sponsors, and he was invited to the company's national convention as the keynote speaker and guest of honor.

"I won't go unless John goes with me," Frawley proclaimed.

"John," of course, was John Stephens, the *My Three Sons* production manager. Don Fedderson, the show's executive producer, called Stephens and said, "Look, you gotta go with him."

Stephens reports that Frawley's way of handling the situation was by drinking . . . and drinking . . . and drinking. He would start off at breakfast with three or four gin fizzes. Then, at about eleven A.M., he would have a couple of Bloody Marys. Right before lunch would come a highball or two. Afterward he would savor some bourbon. Then, before dinner, he would down a couple of martinis. "I've never in my life—and I've seen a lot of drinkers—known anyone who could drink as much as he could in one day," Stephens says. "And that's not to mention the different types of drinks. The scare that I had was that . . . I would knock on his door and [find] that he'd be dead."

On the day of the convention dinner, Stephens attempted to warn the organizers of Frawley's condition. "Look, I want you to put this man on first, I want you to put him on right away," he told them. "'Cause if you don't do that, there's no way that I'm going to guarantee what he's going to say."

Frawley and Stephens arrived at the affair at around six P.M. Frawley already had imbibed five or six drinks, and the Quaker Oats people began offering him additional libations. One hour passed, and Frawley had not yet been called to the podium.

"By this time, he's almost totally smashed," Stephens recalls. "Finally, a guy gets on and introduces [Frawley]. You remember Bill Clinton's [1988] speech at the Democratic Convention, the one he got so teased about? This was almost the same length as that speech. He's going on and on about how [Frawley] is the greatest man, the most wonderful man.

"That sobered Frawley up a little bit. But he was getting madder and madder—and I'm getting more and more scared. 'Cause here you have all these Babbitt-type men, with their wonderful, proper wives. And I know this man, and I know what kind of language he uses."

The speaker finished his spiel by declaring, "And now, the greatest living American. I give you Bill Frawley."

As the audience stood up and applauded, Stephens slinked under the table. Frawley then staggered up to the microphone and announced, "All right, I gotta tell ya this. I've been introduced in a lot of places, by a lot of people, but never ever have I heard so much shit piled so high as this last guy who introduced me. I don't know who the fuck you are, but you are really full of shit. Thank you, and good night."

"The people were absolutely stunned," continues Stephens. "This was Bill Frawley, the guy from *I Love Lucy*. This was Bub from *My Three Sons*. All I could do was say, 'Look, I told you this was gonna happen.' So we get back [to the hotel] and Frawley says, 'Did I say something that somebody didn't like?' and I say, 'Nah, nah, Bill, don't worry about it.'"

When he was living in the Midwest, Frawley felt constricted, and this awkward return certainly did not evoke any "fond memories" of his young manhood.

Chapter Three

BROADWAY—1920s

When Bill Frawley's marriage ended in 1921, he chose to head east and settle in New York City. It is no surprise that he made this decision. Broadway was booming, with the 1921–22 season providing an outstanding moment in theater history. There were 196 new productions, forty more than the previous year. More than a dozen new theaters had opened, including a number of playhouses that could accommodate musical productions. Most prominent among them was the Shuberts' Jolson Theater on West Fifty-ninth Street. Broadway legend Al Jolson himself christened the venue, starring in the hit musical comedy *Bombo*.

If a performer could sing, dance, and play comedy, there were a wealth of stage revues and musical-comedy productions for which to audition. The 1921 edition of Florenz Ziegfeld's *Follies* was packing houses, partly because of the presence of a veteran vaudevillian named W. C. Fields. *George White's Scandals*, which offered more contemporary comic skits than the traditional *Follies*, featured a musical score by young George Gershwin. And the wide-mouthed grin of comic Joe E. Brown lit up the stage nightly at the Shubert Theater where *Greenwich Village Follies* was playing.

From 1916 to 1918, America had been enmeshed in the Great War, as World War I was then dubbed. Now that the bloodshed was over, the younger generation was craving distraction. Electric lights were no longer a treat for the wealthy; they were a means of turning big-city nights into playtime. If there had been no Great White Way before the 1920s, somebody surely would have invented it as the third decade of the century began.

Why trod the boards, traveling from one three-a-day vaudeville house to another, always searching for a new hotel and watering hole with an unfamiliar gathering of drinking mates, when the jobs and the action Frawley craved were available in Manhattan? With no one—no mother, and now, no wife—to hold him back professionally and socially, Bill packed his valise and headed east toward the lights of Broadway.

Broadway would be Frawley's base of operations from the early 1920s through 1933, during which period he appeared in a series of musical comedies and revues. It was with a sense of nostalgia and pride that Ed Sullivan, also a Broadway habitué during the Roaring Twenties, described Frawley to his *Toast of the Town* TV audience in 1954 by declaring, "This here was one of our great performers in New York."

At this time, however, Frawley did not work exclusively on Broadway. Between New York gigs, he could be found touring in shows and revues—and performing songs like "My Melancholy Baby" and "Carolina in the Morning" far from the Great White Way. At one point, he even returned to the West Coast to appear in *Be Careful Dearie*, a musical version of the 1918 stage farce *Nothing But Lies*.

Frawley's first show back East was a modest presentation, which opened at the Central Theater in April 1923 and enjoyed a limited run: *The Gingham Girl*, a musical comedy with songs by Albert Von Tilzer and Neville Fleeson, which was described by one critic as "a fresh, merry little show" with "a distinct flapper quality." The star was Eddie Buzzell, who subsequently would direct Frawley on-screen in Hollywood. Frawley's character is Jack Hayden, a worldly-wise big-city salesman who shakes up the lives of a few small-town folks when he provides the addresses of a few city girls to a young rube who already has an awfully sweet girlfriend back home. Originally Hayden was played by Russell Mack when *The Gingham Girl* made its official Broadway bow in August 1922 at the Earl Carroll; Frawley replaced Mack when the show was relocated to the Central.

Joseph P. Kennedy's fledgling film-production company, Film Booking Offices of America, eventually bought the motion-picture rights to *The Gingham Girl*, and it was produced as a silent comedy-drama in 1927. In the film version, the part of Hayden was played by character actor Jed Prouty.

Given his background, Frawley was ideally cast in his next New York production: *Keep Kool*, a revue authored by Paul Gerard Smith, a veteran vaudeville skit writer. *Keep Kool* was advertised as "a musical revelation in 24 scenes" featuring "a smart cast and a smart chorus." Its title was a clever reworking of "Keep Cool with Coolidge!" President Calvin Coolidge's campaign slogan.

When the show played Wilmington, Delaware, in mid-April 1924, Frawley could be found cavorting in a skit, set in a taxi, playing "A Man about Town" opposite Hazel Dawn's "A Girl in a Hurry." He also did a duet with Dawn in "Out Where the Pavement Ends," and vocalized "The Coming of Dawn" as a solo. Even though she was considered to be a star on the descent, what a feather in Frawley's cap to be sharing the stage with still-beautiful Hazel Dawn! (Back in 1916, she had delighted Broadway theatergoers in the coveted title role of *The Century Girl*, a Charles Dillingham–Florenz Ziegfeld extravaganza with songs by Victor Herbert and Irving Berlin.)

Frawley was especially well suited for his role in another skit in *Keep Kool*: "With Apologies To (A Cosy Corner in the Friars Club)," a spoof in which he impersonated George M. Cohan, the legendary entertainer-songwriter-playwright and "Yankee Doodle Boy." Yet as the *Keep Kool* company neared New York and its Broadway bow, Frawley's onstage responsibilities were reduced. When the show played the Montauk Theater in Brooklyn during the week beginning May 12, Frawley still could be found in Act One, Scene Five, as "A Man about Town" opposite Hazel

Dawn. However, Charles King now was playing Cohan onstage. For more than a decade, dapper singer-dancer King had had successful spots in New York revues. He was a bigger name than Frawley, and the hope was that his presence in *Keep Kool* would ensure a healthier box office. King was soon to ride the crest of Broadway stardom in his role in the Herbert Fields–Vincent Youmans musical, *Hit the Deck*. And he soon would be one of the first musical stars of the American sound-film era.

Then, ten days after the Montauk Theater booking, *Keep Kool* opened in Manhattan at the Morosco Theater. By then, King also had replaced Frawley in the taxi skit and Bill was no longer in the cast. Though it boasted a first-rate troupe, *Keep Kool* was fated to be a minor revue of the 1923–24 season. Parts of the show actually were more successfully presented the following season when the best numbers were interwoven with the highlights of the Ziegfeld *Follies* for a Chicago run.

In retrospect, *Keep Kool* is of note for one of the young women in that "smart chorus," who also played a few minor roles and was one of the "Keep Kool Cuties": superstar-to-be Ruby Stevens, who eventually would change her name to Barbara Stanwyck.

Frawley's first success in a New York musical comedy was *Merry Merry*, which opened at the Vanderbilt Theater in September 1925 and had a five-month run. The show's music was by Harry Archer, who began his career as Harry Auracher, a writer of songs that were crowd pleasers but not enduring standards. Archer's biggest hit had come at the start of the 1923–24 season with *Little Jessie James*, which proved to be the season's most popular musical. With fresh remembrances of that show in mind, audiences had high hopes for *Merry Merry*.

In a way, the plot of this musical comedy is a skewed precursor to *I Love Lucy*. In *Merry Merry*, naive Eve Walters (played by Broadway newcomer Marie Saxon) travels to New York with aspirations of being in show business. After recognizing that her roommate and fellow member of the chorus is a crook, she relinquishes her aspirations for a career onstage to marry a regular Joe. One can imagine Eve ten years down the road hankering for her lost career in the theater, and her husband blocking her every opportunity to reenter show business.

Frawley was ideally cast in *Merry Merry* in a prime featured role: a vaudevillian named J. Horatio Diggs. He performed two duets: "We Were a Wow," with Virginia Smith, and "Oh, Wasn't It Lovely," opposite Perqueta Courtney.

Bide Dudley, critiquing *Merry Merry* in the *New York Evening World*, judged the show "a bright, more or less non-sensical [*sic*], tuneful fast-stepping musical cocktail" and reported that "the bulk of the comedy falls to William Frawley." Fabled columnist Walter Winchell, in reviewing the show, referred to Frawley as a "seasoned two-a-dayer" and added, "Frawley's conception of a small-time actor was genuine." Don Carle Gillette, writing in *The Billboard*, noted, "William Frawley and Virginia Smith are the mediums thru [*sic*] which most of the comedy—the rather commonplace comedy, remember—is dispensed." He added, "And be it said to their credit that they dispense it with pretty good results under the circumstances."

Merry Merry eventually went on the road. When the musical played in Boston in April 1926, the *Boston Transcript*'s theater critic wrote that Frawley and Smith "act a pair of vaudevillian troopers. They are anything but guileless, though that fact does not make them less comical. Their musical narrative of the tank-towns in which their turn proved a wow is engaging. Their imitation of a ventriloquial skit approaches the hilarious."

The original program for *Merry Merry* displays a photograph of Frawley, in a fitted suit and tie, seated with one hand on his left knee. Smith, wearing a short, full-skirted dress, is perched bowlegged on his right knee. She wears a goofy, open-mouthed grin, and Frawley's face is turned toward her, seriously concentrating on her demeanor, apparently pulling a string behind her back to make her mouth open and close.

♥

"On the street level, Broadway was brash and cosmopolitan," *New York Times* theater critic Brooks Atkinson once noted of the Great White Way during the 1920s, adding, "Night was its natural hour."

Frawley, now approaching his fortieth birthday, fit right into this heady flow of life in the mid-1920s. When not rehearsing or performing or on the road, he could be found schmoozing with his pals or filling space in one of several Broadway speakeasies. He also was a longtime member of the Friars Club, a fraternal organization of entertainers. One of the Friars' amenities was a dining room, located in its former clubhouse on West Forty-eighth Street, which served delicious food at ridiculously low prices. In fact, the Manhattan-based facility kept in business even though it lost $50,000 a year. Its main customers were vaudevillians past and present—and one easily can picture Frawley in this setting, chomping away on corned beef and cabbage with a wee bit of Irish soda bread on the side.

By now, he had become celebrated among his fellow actors as a great teller of tales, tall and otherwise. With a touch of satire, it was announced in the program of a Friars testimonial to fellow member Joe Laurie Jr.— held in October 1926, and attended by such confreres as Bobby Clark, William Collier, Louis Silvers, and James J. Walker, then the mayor of New York City—that the "running and announcing of the unique stage entertainment will be under the personal supervision and direction of FRIAR WILLIAM FRAWLEY (the Friars' briefest speech-maker)."

Years later, during Frawley's 1954 appearance on the *Toast of the Town* tribute to *I Love Lucy*, Bill chatted amiably with Ed Sullivan. This time it was Sullivan who made the speeches.

"Of course, Bill and I go back a long way in New York," he noted.

"Yes, we do," Frawley said.

Sullivan recalled that "the first time I ever met him was in [Mama] Leone's restaurant. . . . First time I ever met you, Bill, I don't know if you remember, Jimmy Walker introduced us. . . ."

"That is correct," Frawley responded.

And Sullivan concluded, "So I've gotten the most tremendous kick out of your success with *I Love Lucy*. But I knew it was a cinch all the time."

Later on in the show, the host affectionately referred to his guest as "the handsome Frawley."

Then as now, New York was a mecca for professional athletics and this delighted Frawley, the sports fan's sports fan. Of course, the city then sported three major-league ball clubs: the Brooklyn Dodgers, New York Giants, and New York Yankees. Of the trio, Bill's favorite was the Yanks, and he had much to roar about as the team (as well as the city) dominated during the decade. For three seasons beginning in 1921, the Yanks battled the Giants in the World Series. The first two contests, all games were played in the Polo Grounds; the last was split between the Giants' home field and the newly minted Yankee Stadium in the Bronx. The "Jints" (as Frawley called them) played the Washington Senators in 1924, while the Yanks and their legendary Murderers' Row returned to the Fall Classic in 1926, 1927, and 1928.

Frawley also was a great fight fan, and often could be found ringside at venues across the city cheering on assorted boxers as they pummeled their opponents. This avocation stretched through the rest of his life. *I Love Lucy* scripter Bob Schiller recalls, "I'll always remember one of his sayings: 'He hit him right in the grapes.' Such a 1920s expression!"

Given his status as a Broadway actor, Frawley also was able to cultivate relationships with big-time sports figures. One easily can envision the Irishman hoisting a few in a Manhattan speakeasy and savoring the company of such icons of the era as baseball's Babe Ruth and John McGraw, or boxing's Jack Dempsey. "I knew all the top ballplayers when I lived in New York," Frawley explained, with a touch of melancholy, in 1961.

For his entire life, Frawley was to remain a proud product of the rip-roaring 1920s. At the same time, back when he was trodding the Broadway boards in mid-decade, he captured the prevailing mood of pre-Depression urban America as he gave a reporter a lengthy diagnosis of a disease then afflicting his fellow countrymen, which he dubbed "Americanitis." He ended his discourse by declaring, "Now you can readily understand why this is an age of speed and youth. Everything is done in a hurry and completed before you have come to determine whether it is right or wrong.

"It is an age where you've got to keep going at a fast pace to be up with the forerunners and know what it is all about. There is no place in America today for gray hairs and old age. Today, youth doesn't live that long. Remember—Americanitis!"

On another occasion, the actor authored a brief but funny and revealing newspaper article, which appeared in the daily *New York World*. In it, Frawley's cantankerous personality shines like a beacon through a fog as he touches on everything from his rationale for his lifestyle to his unyielding view of women.

In the piece, which was published on November 5, 1927, Frawley wrote, "The only reason I hope to live to be one hundred is that I want to be interviewed just once by a reporter who will ask the cause of my longevity. I have always wanted to tabulate my vices. Thus far I've been so busy I haven't got by the first fifty."

Frawley then revealed that he was a believer in "drinking, smoking, profanity, golf and pyorrhea, just for the sake of being different. I would be a poor sort . . . if I had nothing to think about but my own goodness." Despite these imperfections, he added that his "health manages to stand up under the strain and I can dance and sing as well at twenty-nine as I could at twenty-eight. All the success I have attained is undoubtedly due to the fact that I have always yielded to temptation, no matter what its form."

He then noted that, long before he came to New York—in fact, way back when he "was but a cunning child"—he "used to like to talk a good deal. This passion never quit me, although all my friends did. Finally, to be revenged on these friends, I decided to become an actor. No power on earth can make an actor stop talking but a stage director."

Frawley concluded with a jab at one of his favorite targets: marriage. "A director of stage productions," he observed, "is a man who can make everybody stop talking but his wife."

♥

Bide Dudley, with Louis Simon, were co-authors of the book for *Bye Bye Bonnie*, another of the 1920s Broadway musical comedies in which Frawley was featured. The show, euphoniously billed as a "musical bonbon," opened at the Ritz Theater during the second week of January 1927.

The score was written by Albert Von Tilzer and Neville Fleeson, the composers of the songs for Frawley's first New York show, *The Gingham Girl*. Although Von Tilzer had written a number of classic songs—he had composed "Take Me Out to the Ballgame" with lyricist Jack Norworth in 1908—there were no outstanding numbers in these two Frawley productions.

By the time *Bye Bye Bonnie* debuted in New York, there had been major problems with its leading ladies. Both female stars—the middle-aged, operatic-voiced Fritzi Scheff (who had begun her New York stage career in 1901) and baby-talker Frances White (who was vaudeville headliner Frank Fay's first wife before he married Barbara Stanwyck)—left the show during its out-of-town tryouts. Now *Bye Bye Bonnie* would be coming to Broadway with no star names above the title. This was a sure sign to in-the-know Broadwayites that the inbound vehicle was in trouble.

By this point, Frawley had well established himself as a dependable Broadway hand, so much so that a role in a show might be written specifically for him. Such was the case in *Bye Bye Bonnie*, which one critic described as being about "the clean, lovely and exquisitely legitimate crime of bootlegging." With Frawley in mind, Dudley and Simon created the part of a comical hooligan named "Butch" Hogan.

Frawley's two musical numbers were "I Like to Make It Cozy," which he performed with Cecil Owen (playing a warden) and several "gentlemen of the ensemble" (cast as convicts); and "Tampico Tap," which highlighted an up-and-coming tap dancer named Ruby Keeler.

While *Bye Bye Bonnie* earned decidedly mixed reviews, Frawley's contribution was in no way faulted. Frank Vreeland, writing in the *New York Telegram*, observed that Frawley "[was] an amusing thug who should have been allowed to bulge entertainingly into the first act." Percy Hammond, the *New York Herald Tribune* critic, noted, "A rough though cautious clown named Frawley impersonated a burlesque yeggman [burglar] with humorous and convincing detail."

"For years a vaudeville favorite," was how Frawley was described in the *Bye Bye Bonnie* playbill. It also was noted that "Paul Frawley, singing juvenile, is his brother."

Despite its behind-the-scenes problems and mixed press, *Bye Bye Bonnie* enjoyed a four-month Broadway run. Still, in no way could it match *The Desert Song, Rio Rita,* and *Hit the Deck,* three smash hit musicals of the 1926–27 season.

Frawley's next New York outing was *Talk About Girls,* an Irving Caesar–Harold Orlob–Stephen Jones musical which opened at the Waldorf Theater in June, at the tail end of the Broadway season, before the summer doldrums set in. The actor was cast as Henry Quill, the "subnormal constable" of the small town of Lower Falls, Massachusetts. While the offering was something less than a smash—it closed after only thirteen performances—Bill emerged unscathed. "William Frawley, as the village constable, helped along the fun," wrote Stephen Rathbun in the *New York Sun.*

At this point in his career, Frawley knew all too well that he was a solid and dependable character performer and established Broadway hand. The question was, would he ever win a breakthrough role in a breakout stage musical? He kept working, to be sure, but he could not seem to connect with a job in a really prestigious hit show.

Kid brother Paul, meanwhile, was headlining in such big-league productions as the long-running *Sunny* (1925). And less than two months prior to *Talk About Girls, Hit the Deck* had opened and become a hit, with top-notch songs such as "Sometimes I'm Happy." Featured cast member Charles King, who had replaced Bill Frawley in 1924's *Keep Kool,* now was wowing audiences in this lively musical with a naval theme, while Frawley was working in a lesser show that had little chance of succeeding. *Hit the Deck* boasted a Broadway run of 352 performances, and later became a motion picture in 1930, and again in 1955.

Frawley must have been discouraged as he pondered the handsome King's steady rise to Broadway fame while his own career stayed rock-steady in limbo. The actor hoped that his next show would give him the acclaim he sought. In *She's My Baby,* which debuted at the Globe Theater on the third day of January, 1928, he appeared with a stellar cast: Beatrice Lillie, Jack Whiting, Clifton Webb—who, later in the year, would play with Paul Frawley in *Treasure Girl*—and a pert ingenue named Irene

Dunne. The show boasted a book by Bert Kalmar and Harry Ruby (who had taken a break from songwriting) along with Guy Bolton, and featured a score by Richard Rodgers and Lorenz Hart.

Despite his thirst for a smash hit show, Frawley's gruff demeanor would cost him his job in *She's My Baby*. Indeed, the macho actor's casting with the effete, delicate, and very acerbic Clifton Webb was to disprove the adage that opposites attract. "I was thrown out of that one for punching Clifton Webb in the nose," Frawley remembered. "He spoke nasty to me a couple of times and I told him that if he did that again I'd sock him in the nose. He did and I did, and I got kicked out."

With or without Frawley, *She's My Baby* was a disappointment in spite of its talented cast and creators. It ran for nine weeks and then was quickly forgotten—unlike *Show Boat,* with music by Jerome Kern and book and lyrics by Oscar Hammerstein II, which opened just one week before *She's My Baby. Show Boat* was to be the musical hit of the season, and decades later continues to be admired and revived with great success.

Could Frawley have been cast in the classic *Show Boat?* One certainly can imagine him as the comic featured character Frank Schultz, one-half of the dancing vaudeville team of Ellie and Frank, played onstage by Sammy White, who danced with his real-life wife and partner, Eva Puck. Frawley was even perfectly capable of playing one of the show's leads: Captain Andy, the colorful head of a Mississippi River entertainment vessel.

Twenty-six years later, on an *I Love Lucy* episode entitled "Mertz and Kurtz," the part of Fred Mertz's vaudeville partner Barney Kurtz would be played by Charles Winninger, who was the original Captain Andy in *Show Boat.* As Frawley rehearsed with Winninger, was he thinking back to Winninger's outstanding success in *Show Boat?* Was he pondering what his plight might have been had he been cast as Frank Schultz, or as Captain Andy?

After his dismissal from *She's My Baby,* Frawley did not remain unemployed for long. His follow-up show was *Here's Howe!*, billed as "the new

Spring Musical Comedy." The production opened in May 1928 at the Broadhurst Theater, but was fated to close by summer after playing only seventy-one performances.

In *Here's Howe!*, Frawley played "Sweeny" Toplis, a hard-boiled but comical killer, and again his performance transcended his material. Katharine Zimmermann reported in the *New York Telegram*, "Frawley has a few moments and makes the most of them. His account of blowing up [an] old lady's home and his generally carnal attitude ring up practically all the laughs in the show." Brooks Atkinson, in the *New York Times*, was particularly amused by "the obtuse, domineering William Frawley," and added, "As the leader of a jack-in-the-box parcel of cut throats he fare[s] better in *Here's Howe!* than he has for the past two seasons. He is tough and awkwardly perpendicular." Frawley, though, was not a part of the show's high point: the joyful, foot-tapping, jazz number "Crazy Rhythm," written by Roger Wolf Kahn, Joseph Meyer, and Irving Caesar and performed by Peggy Chamberlain, June O'Dea, and orchestra leader Ben Bernie.

During this period, Frawley did not confine his career to the stage. Because of his vaudeville and Broadway credits, the common assumption about the actor is that his screen debut came with the signing of his Paramount Pictures contract in 1933. Yet in addition to the silent films he made in 1916, he also appeared in *Fancy That* and *Turkey for Two*, a pair of Pathé two-reel musical shorts filmed in New York and released in 1929.

Both films are unmemorable. According to *Exhibitors Herald-World*, a motion-picture trade publication, *Fancy That* depicted "what a party would look like if two hobos suddenly became millionaires." In the film, Frawley sings "Dearest One," a forgettable ditty that was guaranteed not to allow him to challenge the popularity of Rudy Vallee, then America's most popular crooner.

The quaint plot of *Turkey for Two* is also described in *Exhibitors Herald-World*: "Two escaped convicts with a fondness for turkey come to a Westchester [New York] inn at Thanksgiving. Jack LeMaire's Golden Rooster Orchestra features 'I'll Say She's Pretty.'" The film was directed by George LeMaire, who at the time was being publicized for producing and directing "Manhattan Comedies—All Music-Sound-Dialogue Comedies for the 'Big Time'" featuring such "Big Time Broadway funsters as Louis Simon, Lew Hearn, and Harry Holman." It is revealing that Frawley, despite his status as a veteran entertainer, was not included in the puffery.

For as Brooks Atkinson so pointedly noted in his review of *Here's Howe!*, Frawley "was still awaiting his perfect part."

Chapter Four

BREAKTHROUGH

While not quite providing him with a "perfect part," William Frawley's next Broadway outing did offer one of his best non-dramatic stage roles. In *Sons O' Guns*, which opened at the Imperial Theater in November 1929, he played Hobson, "personal valet" to a playboy (Jack Donahue), who becomes his former boss's harsh-voiced top sergeant. The show was a solid hit, lasting 295 performances. *Sons O' Guns* also kept Frawley steadily employed. Exactly a year after its Great White Way bow, he was playing in the show on the road (with Al Jolson protégé Harry Richman replacing Donahue).

In October 1929, a month before *Sons O' Guns* opened on Broadway, the Wall Street stock-market crash dramatically altered the lifestyles of millions of Americans, including Manhattan's urbane, theatergoing crowd. No longer would the well-to-dos pass their evenings recklessly spending money in stylish eateries or at adventuresome illegal speakeasies. Nor would they be paying to see lushly produced musical extravaganzas by Florenz Ziegfeld and Charles Dillingham. The appeal of musicals now would be focused on escapism, rather than on costly productions. And less opulent straight plays became more common than the endless revues that had been staged throughout the 1920s.

As a result of this trend, the number of jobs for musical-comedy performers dwindled as shows cut back budgets and included smaller casts. Frawley was fortunate to have regular employment in *Sons O' Guns* at a time when so many of his once-hired fellow actors were pounding the Broadway pavement for jobs.

While the stock-market crash and subsequent economic Depression (not to mention the popularity of the new all-singing, all-dancing, all-talking movies) slowed the pace of Broadway, there still was life on the Great White Way. Musical comedies such as *Sons O' Guns* and Cole Porter's *Fifty Million Frenchmen*, which opened at the same time, could attract a steady flow of theatergoers seeking diversion from the newly minted hard times. Meanwhile, George and Ira Gershwin were creating a new kind of musical genre that melded clever story lines with innovative songs. For the 1929–30 season, they offered *Strike Up the Band*; their hit during the 1930–31 season was *Girl Crazy*, featuring a young, golden-voiced Vinton Freedley discovery named Ethel Merman.

Frawley followed his lengthy run in *Sons O' Guns* with a role in an undistinguished farce titled *She Lived Next to the Firehouse*, employing what one critic described as "his hard-boiled musical show technique" in his role as the city-slicker mate of the title "She." No more notable was *Tell Her the Truth*, a musical version of the 1916 farce *Nothing But the Truth* (which in 1927 was produced as *Yes, Yes, Yvette*, a follow-up of sorts to 1925's *No, No, Nanette*).

Tell Her the Truth unfolded the story of Bobbie Bennett, a chap who bets $10,000 that he can utter only the unblemished truth for a twenty-four-hour period. More than two decades later, the same plot line was used for the *I Love Lucy* episode entitled "Lucy Tells the Truth." Here, Ricky, Fred, and Ethel bet Lucy $100 that she cannot tell the complete truth for twenty-four hours. (A similar plot would form the basis of such movies as Bob Hope's *Nothing But the Truth*, 1941, and Jim Carrey's *Liar Liar*, 1997.)

In *Tell Her the Truth,* Frawley played Mr. Parkin, a shady character who gathers funds for charity, some of which he invests in his company's bad real estate. Yet again, Frawley found himself winning solid reviews in a show that was destined to flop. Typical was columnist Walter Winchell, who noted that Frawley "registers best" in the production. Critics in particular singled out his rousing performance of a number titled "Sing, Brothers," which was the show's principal song.

Cast with Frawley in *Tell Her the Truth* was Margaret Dumont, the buxom character actress who was in the process of becoming one of the cinema's most beloved comic foils, playing the laughably stiff, dim dowager in several Marx Brothers vehicles. Legend has it that Dumont was as dense as the characters she portrayed. One can imagine Frawley chortling backstage, using her as the butt of his anti-female humor just as Groucho Marx did so wickedly on stage and screen.

♥

Frawley's most prominent (not to mention his all-time favorite) Broadway role was destined to come in a non-musical show. He was featured in *Twentieth Century*, a lunatic farce that was aptly billed as "The Laughing Riot" when it opened at the Broadhurst Theater during the final week of 1932.

Twentieth Century was one of the most anticipated Broadway shows of the 1932–33 season. For one thing, it was written by Ben Hecht and Charles MacArthur, former newspapermen who had become popular, eccentric Great White Way characters—back in 1928, they had turned their journalistic expertise into a highly successful stage comedy called *The Front Page*. For another, the producers of *Twentieth Century*, Philip Dunning and George Abbott (who also staged the production), had an enviable track record in the theater. They were well remembered for a play they had written called *Broadway*, which had been one of the major hits of the 1926–27 season.

The plot of *Twentieth Century* centers on the antics of zany, money-hungry theatrical producer Oscar Jaffe, who must get the signature of movie star/ex-lover Lily Garland on a contract, in order to satisfy several angry bankers. The two tussle in a raging battle of the sexes on board the *Twentieth Century Limited* deluxe train, as Oscar promises Lily that he will produce *The Passion Play* with her as The Magdalene. Frawley was cast as

Owen O'Malley, an irrepressible Broadway press agent—and yet another part the actor was born to play.

Frawley was suggested for *Twentieth Century* by Philip Dunning. The pair had crossed paths several years earlier during the run of *Sunny*, in which Bill's brother Paul was the lead and Dunning the stage manager. When *Twentieth Century* was being cast, Frawley was appearing in the ill-fated *Tell Her the Truth*. Dunning and Abbott took in his performance. Abbott felt that Frawley was not all that good in the show. Dunning, sensing that the actor was a victim of poor material—and remembering his performance as the top sergeant three years earlier in *Sons O' Guns*—was convinced that Frawley was right for Owen O'Malley. Abbott went along, but with reservations, and the results were fortuitous for all concerned. In fact, in his autobiography, Abbott even singled out the actor, noting, "Bill Frawley was funny in the supporting part." Richard Maney, himself a real-life publicist, chimed in, "As the disillusioned press agent, Bill Frawley was superb."

Percy Hammond, reviewing *Twentieth Century* in the *New York Herald Tribune*, was quite taken by Frawley's character *and* his performance. In his piece, he devoted considerable space to them both, characterizing Owen O'Malley as "a profane and humorous two-bottle chap who, when assisted by a couple of drinks, thumbs his nose wittily at Art and the universe." Hammond described the press agent as "no ordinary Broadway yes-man, dispensing mimeographed and insignificant information to the newspapers, but a ruthless Field Marshall, telling one and all, including the N.Y. *Central*, the N.Y. *Herald Tribune* and the N.Y. *Times* where to get off."

The critic incorporated O'Malley's over-the-top personality and Frawley's deft performance as he added, "[O'Malley's] speech, when invigorated with alcohol, is arrogant and satirical. He calls his employer 'Sire' and, though loyal to the phony cause, he sneers earnestly and quizzically at grotesque weaknesses. When a masculine lady-physician enters breezily and shouts, 'I am Doctor Johnson!' Mr. Frawley looks her over coldly and inquires, 'Which Doctor Johnson—Sam or Ben?' That line may give you an idea of the author's urbane and literate humor."

After that description, one only can imagine Frawley relishing playing Owen O'Malley—and delighting theatergoers as this rich stage character. To a certain degree, he was to keep playing O'Malley, both on and off camera, for the rest of his life.

"If William Frawley is remembered for nothing else along Broadway," wrote the *Brooklyn Daily Eagle* six years after he left for Hollywood, "it will be for his inimitable portrayal of the fabulous press agent, drawn by Ben Hecht and Charlie MacArthur, in their play, *Twentieth Century.* . . ."

Considering what a funny play it is and how timely the humor was, it was unfortunate that the comedy remained on Broadway for only 154 performances: a fairly successful but not outstanding run for a show of its caliber. But alas, it became a victim of the Depression. "*Twentieth Century* was an immediate hit," recalled Richard Maney. "But business wilted when banks started to explode like Chinese firecrackers. During Franklin Roosevelt's Bank Holiday, the Broadhurst accepted checks from strangers from Bismarck to Terre Haute.

"Fortunately, Dunning, Frawley and I could sign tabs at Frankie and Johnny's, a speakeasy half a block from the stage door."

Eventually there were many productions of *Twentieth Century* besides the one on Broadway, including a national tour with several of the original cast (but not Frawley). Through the decades, the play often has been revived. In 1949, it was adapted for television's *Ford Theater* in a production starring Fredric March and Lilli Palmer and helmed by *I Love Lucy*'s first director, Marc Daniels. It also was the basis of a 1978 Broadway musical called *On the Twentieth Century,* with book and lyrics by Betty Comden and Adolph Green and music by Cy Coleman.

Frawley, of course, certainly would have shone in the screen version of *Twentieth Century* (1934), but he did not get to replay Owen O'Malley in the screwball-comedy classic, which was produced by Columbia Pictures and starred John Barrymore and Carole Lombard.

Back in 1915, Harry Cohn, the studio's future president, had been toiling as a Tin Pan Alley song plugger. One evening, as Jess Oppenheimer recalled in his posthumously published memoirs, an overly aggressive

Cohn knocked on Frawley's dressing-room door at the Palace Theater and attempted to sell him a song. Frawley "politely explained to Cohn that he considered his dressing room to be like his home," and added, "If you'll just wait outside with the other song pluggers, I'll be happy to discuss the tune with you." A miffed Cohn stormed away—and neither forgot nor forgave Frawley for what he considered an insult.

Two decades later, Cohn—now the head honcho at Columbia—was on hand for a Frawley performance in *Twentieth Century*. "Everyone expected Hollywood to make it into a major motion picture," Oppenheimer noted. "Suddenly there was a knock on Frawley's dressing-room door. Frawley opened the door. It was Harry Cohn."

The studio boss asked the actor if he knew who he was. Frawley answered in the affirmative. Cohn inquired if the actor recalled that long-ago night at the Palace. Frawley responded that he did.

"Well," Cohn declared, "I've just bought this show for Columbia, and I just came backstage to tell you you're not going to be in the picture!" Ultimately, veteran character actor Roscoe Karns was cast in the key screen role.

♥

Frawley was to appear in one last Broadway production before heading to Hollywood. It was *The Ghost Writer*, a drama also written by a former newspaperman: Martin Mooney, a retired crime reporter who had won a bit of notoriety by facing a prison sentence for refusing to reveal his news sources. Unlike *Twentieth Century*, *The Ghost Writer* was not a standout. The show opened at the Masque Theater in June 1933 and closed after twenty-four performances.

Frawley became involved in the production even though his character, Joe Gordon, was a rip-off of *Twentieth Century*'s Owen O'Malley; Gordon was described by Arthur Ruhl in the *New York Herald Tribune* as "a promoter out to promote anything that gives him a suitable rake-off." Once again, Frawley's performance outshone his material. "It was very mixed up and queer," added Ruhl, "with bits of comedy here and there and occasionally amusing lines, mostly from Mr. Frawley's Joe Gordon. Mr. Frawley, indeed, was about the only person present who seemed fairly at ease, and his role was easily the best written and most plausible."

Despite the negative reviews and brief run, Frawley shared the stage with a sensational, now forgotten actor named Hal Skelly. Back in 1927, Skelly had made a hit with Broadway audiences as Skid, the inebriated husband in the comedy-melodrama *Burlesque*, playing opposite Barbara Stanwyck. While Stanwyck's role proved the springboard to her stellar Hollywood career, Skelly starred in only a few early sound films. He died in 1934 in a freak accident, when the car in which he was a passenger was hit by a train at a crossing near West Cornwall, Connecticut.

♥

If Frawley's success in *Twentieth Century* did not make him a Broadway headliner, it at least secured him a Hollywood contract. As it turned out, *The Ghost Writer* was a brief interlude between his hit in *Twentieth Century* and his permanent sojourn to the West Coast—when the actor would get to ride the real Twentieth Century Limited as he journeyed from New York to Chicago en route to Hollywood.

The legitimate theater now was a part of his past. "Sometimes, when I talk over the old stage days with [fellow character actors] Walter Connolly, Minor Watson, or other old-timers," he declared in 1939, "I feel the urge to go back to Broadway again for another play. But they have kept me so busy in Hollywood I don't have a chance to brood about it very long."

At the time, he added, almost wishfully, "Just the same, someday I'll pack a bag and go back to New York for at least one more play." This was not meant to be. As he aged, Frawley became less and less interested in even attending the theater.

"There's nothing much to see on Broadway anymore," he declared in 1961. In what by then was the lovably terse and inimitable style he had developed over the course of a lifetime, he was quick to add, "*South Pacific* was lousy and *Guys and Dolls* stinks."

Chapter Five

HOLLYWOOD

When sound came to movies in the late 1920s, Hollywood promptly raided Broadway for the best young actors and writers willing to head west. Frawley's turn came in mid-1933 when, at age forty-six, he signed a standard seven-year contract with Paramount Pictures.

When Frawley came to Paramount, the studio was among the most prestigious of the Golden Era movie factories. Exactly a decade earlier, it had released two of Hollywood's biggest box-office hits: James Cruze's influential Western, *The Covered Wagon,* and Cecil B. DeMille's biblical epic, *The Ten Commandments.* In 1933 alone, Paramount produced a smorgasbord of features, including *Design for Living*, a chic adaptation of the Noël Coward play, featuring Fredric March, Gary Cooper, and Miriam Hopkins; *The Eagle and the Hawk,* a potent anti-war drama with March, Cary Grant, Jack Oakie, and Carole Lombard; and *The Story of Temple Drake*, a sizzling and controversial adaptation of William Faulkner's *Sanctuary,* starring Hopkins, William Gargan, and Jack La Rue. Music and comedy were well served by the Marx Brothers frolicking in *Duck Soup*; W. C. Fields and George Burns and Gracie Allen cavorting in *International House*; Fields and Alison Skipworth eliciting chuckles in *Tillie and Gus*; Bing Crosby, Richard Arlen, Oakie, and Burns and Allen cheering on the coeds in *College Humor*; and Mae West strutting her stuff in *I'm No Angel* and *She Done Him Wrong*. West was Paramount's biggest box-office draw. She earned $220,000 per year, making her the highest-salaried woman in the United States and helping the studio stay profitable during the Great Depression.

Other talent working on the Paramount lot included Marlene Dietrich, Claudette Colbert, Maurice Chevalier, George Raft, and directors Josef von Sternberg, Ernst Lubitsch, and Rouben Mamoulian—screen legends all. Among the supporting and character performers appearing in Paramount releases in 1933 were Edward Everett Horton, Sir Guy Standing, Franklin Pangborn, Jane Darwell, Louise Beavers, Sterling Holloway, and Edgar Kennedy.

So when Frawley signed on with the studio, he found himself in heady company. However, MGM almost beat Paramount in the Frawley sweepstakes. "He had been a well-known Broadway actor when Metro-Goldwyn-Mayer brought him out to California to play in a picture to be produced by Harry Rapf," recalled Oscar-winning movie star Ray Milland in his 1974 autobiography. "Upon his arrival he was immediately ushered into Rapf's offices, where several of the studio executives were gathered discussing the imminent production, which was to be quite a big project. He was seated facing all six of them, and then Rapf started.

"'Mr. Frawley, you're new out here. We'd like to know something of your background, what experience you've had. Also give us a rundown on the parts you've played.' The rather sparse hair on Frawley's neck began to rise like a grouse's ruff, but he calmed himself and began reeling off his credits, which were considerable. When he finished there was a silence and then one of the executives, I think it was Eddie Mannix, said, 'We were figuring on somebody with more hair.'

"At that, Frawley's cork went, and he stood up and roared with quite some choler, 'If it's hair you want, hire a fucking lion!' And then he stalked out in high dudgeon."

So from the very beginning of his active movie career, brash, outspoken Frawley mixed with important studio executives like oil with water. A decade and a half later, when his screen roles were disappearing and just before he was hired to play Fred Mertz, Frawley was especially vindictive toward the very studio executives who once hired him but now refused to look his way.

Upon inking with Paramount, Frawley quickly became quite active on the studio lot in Hollywood. The studio publicity machine immediately began feeding Frawley-related tidbits to the media. On July 24, 1933, the *Los Angeles Times* reported, "William Frawley is definitely under contract to Paramount and comes [w]est soon." The following day, the paper noted, "William Frawley, just signed up by Paramount, will play his first lead in *Search for Beauty*, which has already had various experts seeking 'most beautiful' girls, who are to appear in the feature." Four days later, the publication added, "William Frawley will arrive in town today to prepare for *Captain Jericho*, with Richard Arlen. Baby LeRoy is in the picture." And six weeks later, the *Times* reported, "William Frawley is to appear in *Come On, Marines*, with Cary Grant, and *All of Me*, with George Raft and Carole Lombard, and then later in *Search for Beauty*. He is now working in *Capt.* [sic] *Jericho*."

Frawley never did play the lead in *Search for Beauty*, which Paramount made in 1934 with Larry "Buster" Crabbe, Ida Lupino, Robert Armstrong, and James Gleason (Frawley's pal, who later became a prime candidate for the role of Fred Mertz). Nevertheless, he would have been perfectly cast as either of the rascally scam-artist characters played by Armstrong and Gleason.

The fact was that, throughout his screen career, Frawley hardly ever had starring roles. His largest parts came in such B-films as *Stop Look and Love* (1939), a domestic comedy in which he is the top-billed male (after Jean Rogers, playing his daughter). Frawley is cast in what for him was a most unusual role: a family man. Yet even here, he was at home in the part if only because his wife (played by Minna Gombell) is meddlesome and domineering.

Neither Frawley nor Cary Grant proved to be cast in *Come On, Marines*, a 1934 military comedy-drama that eventually starred Richard Arlen, Ida Lupino, and Roscoe Karns. Here, he also would have been perfect for the role played by Karns: Terence V. "Spud" McGurke, a cab driver and marine deserter. Neither Frawley nor Lombard was seen in *All of Me,* a 1934 drama that did star Raft (along with Fredric March and Miriam Hopkins), but the trio of Frawley, Lombard, and Raft was featured in *Bolero* (1934), a musical drama in which Frawley was cast as the brother/manager of coal miner–turned–dancer Raft.

The *Los Angeles Times* was partially correct on one Frawley project. He was in the cast of the *Captain Jericho* vehicle, which starred Arlen and was released in 1933 as *Hell and High Water*. On paper at least, Frawley might have been ideally cast as Jericho, the lead character, if only because he starts out as a miserly confirmed bachelor. However, Jericho's anti-female view is destined to change when a dancehall dancer (Judith Allen) falls in love with him. Frawley's part instead is a supporting one: Milton J. Bunsey, a disingenuous civic leader.

Baby LeRoy, however, was not in *Hell and High Water*. Frawley instead appeared with the tyke performer (who was an especially adept foil for W. C. Fields, and who retired from movies at age four in 1936) in three features: *Miss Fane's Baby Is Stolen* (1933), in which Baby LeRoy plays the title toddler and Frawley appears as a cop; the 1934 version of *The Lemon Drop Kid*, a Damon Runyon yarn featuring Frawley as a con man; and *It's a Great Life!* (1936), a musical comedy/drama with Frawley seen as the head honcho of a Civilian Conservation Corps camp. Frawley was born to croon one of the songs in the latter: "When Irish Eyes Are Smiling."

During this period, Frawley was linked with individuals from his past and future. For example, in 1936, he appeared in *Three Married Men*, a domestic comedy directed by Eddie Buzzell, with whom Frawley had shared the stage thirteen years earlier in *The Gingham Girl*. In this screen entry he and Lynne Overman play married brothers who set out to wreck their sister's upcoming nuptials. And Frawley's first Hollywood feature, a Depression-era backstage musical titled *Moonlight and Pretzels* (1933), was co-directed by Karl Freund, who was to be the staff cinematographer of *I Love Lucy*. *Moonlight and Pretzels* actually was released by Universal; during the length of his Paramount contract, Frawley frequently was lent out to work at other Hollywood studios.

♥

When Frawley's Paramount contract ended in 1940, his option for renewal was exercised for an additional year. From then on he freelanced, working at just about all the major (and many of the lesser) studios. During his time at Paramount, he averaged over six films a year, par for the course for a contract film player of the time.

Through the 1930s and 1940s, Frawley appeared in every kind of film: Westerns, comedies, musicals, dramas, adventures, biographies, romances. While he had developed a reputation for being ornery on and off the set, he also won respect for his professionalism. Dale Evans, who appeared with him in *Hitchhike to Happiness* (1945), recalls that Frawley was "a joy to work with and well-thought-of by both cast and crew."

Others who worked with Frawley during his movie period have wry recollections of him. After completing *Bolero* (1934), star-to-be Ray Milland, who had a supporting role in the film, was called back to the studio to reshoot a sequence. The reason: In the scene, Frawley—who was cast as George Raft's talent agent—could be seen in the bedroom slippers he usually wore between takes. "He said his mother had given them to him twenty years before, and you could well believe it. They were pretty scruffy," Milland reminisced.

"Quite a character, Frawley," he continued.

Others remember Frawley more fondly, if at times less clearly. Actor Marc Lawrence has no specific recollection of the "three or four films" in which they appeared, but he does add, "I do recall with affection a face and a voice of a lovable bully—easily the equal of Wallace Beery." Robert Douglas, who acted with Frawley in *The Lady Takes a Sailor* (1949), describes his friendship with Frawley as "quite casual" and adds, "I just remember a charming personality, and an excellent actor." Gloria Henry, who was in "my early twenties—or mid-twenties—who's counting?" when she appeared with Frawley in *Kill the Umpire* (1950) and *Rancho Notorious* (1952), recalls, "He was an absolute delight—funny and crusty and kind, and I felt so fortunate to be able to work with and learn from such pros as him and Bill Bendix." However, Henry adds, "All I can tell you [is] his sense of humor was wonderfully naughty."

But the fact remained that few of William Frawley's many films were memorable—which, unfortunately, mirrors his experience on Broadway. While he was cast often enough to have become a familiar presence to moviegoers, Frawley's career never developed into something extra-special: a character performer of the stature of a Claude Rains, Thomas Mitchell, Charles Coburn, Edward Everett Horton, or Edmund Gwenn.

Still, while he did not consistently appear in high-quality films, Frawley was a pro, through and through. He was, within the boundaries of the screen roles in which he was cast, incapable of giving a lackluster performance.

Perhaps Frawley's best early film part was Brighton, a tipsy American gunrunner in 1930s Shanghai, in *The General Died at Dawn* (1936), a war drama directed by Lewis Milestone. While the *Variety* reviewer aptly referred to Frawley as "another cast standout," the assignment ultimately was a subsidiary one: the crux of the picture involved soldier-of-fortune Gary Cooper tussling with Chinese warlord Akim Tamiroff and romancing pretty Madeleine Carroll.

Throughout his screen career, Frawley did appear in a few celluloid classics and Oscar winners, including the blarney-soaked Bing Crosby–Barry Fitzgerald *Going My Way* (1944), in which he was cast as a music publisher; Chaplin's *Monsieur Verdoux* (1947), playing a police inspector; and the Christmas favorite *Miracle on 34th Street* (1947), in which he is seen as a politician.

Yet even in these films, he was shortchanged on-screen. His characters never are fully fleshed out. Rather, Frawley appears only briefly, and his roles are two-dimensional. He merely is a plot device, with his purpose being to keep the story pushing onward.

The tone of his screen career was set early on, upon the release of *Moonlight and Pretzels.* While the *Variety* scribe declared that the film "moves along at a sprightly pace and has sufficient pop to hold interest," he also observed, with some admiration for Frawley, "Bill Frawley oke [*sic*] with the scant opportunities allotted him; he could have been given more."

And even then, for every two or three A-list films in which he was cast, Frawley found himself languishing in a dozen B-level programmers with seventy-minute running times. Some were entertaining: *Variety* termed *F-Man* (1936), which starred Jack Haley, a "good, zippy comedy, judiciously salted with burlesque." Notwithstanding, one too many were of the quality of *Welcome Home* (1935), which starred James Dunn as a con artist and was criticized by *Variety* for its "indifferent story and adaptation, wandering direction and overplaying"; and *It's a Great Life!* (1936), described in a throwaway review as "slightly ornamented" and "unentrancing."

And just as on Broadway, whenever he was cited by reviewers, Frawley earned consistently good notices. Of his work in *F-Man*, the *Variety* critic wrote, "William Frawley, as the G-man, is uniformly good." Despite the "overplaying" complaint, the *Welcome Home* reviewer did note that "William Frawley is tops as one of Dunn's aides." And despite the indifferent notice, the *It's a Great Life!* critic added that "William Frawley as the camp boss and army officer is the most natural character in the film."

Frawley acknowledged this lack of quality in his screen career when he recalled, "The money was great and you had a ball. I played in ninety-six pictures—maybe one or two good ones."

♥

One of Frawley's better movie roles came as fight manager-trainer Billy Delaney in Raoul Walsh's *Gentleman Jim* (1942), starring Errol Flynn as James J. Corbett, who was Frawley's old crony. Walsh cited Frawley— along with Edward G. Robinson, Thomas Mitchell, Robert Ryan, Peter Lorre, James Whitmore, and Walter Brennan (Brennan the three-time

Oscar-winning character actor, not the self-caricature he became years later on television's *The Real McCoys*)—as one of the "staunch heroes of the movies—the 'character men' whose great talents helped me over many a rough spot through the years."

Because of his gruff exterior, Frawley mainly was cast in "tough mug" character roles on camera. Because he did not have the looks to be a screen crooner, little effort was made to exploit his musical/vaudeville background.

One newspaper reportedly described his voice as having "that soft, confidential tone similar to those of Bing Crosby and Rudy Vallee." Bill's cousin, Tom Green, labeled Frawley a "fine tenor" whose voice was "more inclined to the baritone side of the larynx." Nonetheless, when he was cast as a gangster in the Samuel Goldwyn–produced Eddie Cantor/Ethel Merman musical *Strike Me Pink* (1936), he pleaded in vain with the higher-ups to allow him to sing.

Once in a while, Frawley did get to croon on-screen. And on rare occasion—for example, in *Harmony Lane* (1935), a biography of Stephen Foster, in which he was cast as real-life minstrel-show producer E. P. Christy—he was allowed to utilize the sweet, almost lilting voice he had employed onstage. More than any other film, *Harmony Lane* serves as a celluloid reflection of Frawley's vaudeville and stage musical roots.

Bill's screen part as E. P. Christy parallels his assignment, years later, in *My Wild Irish Rose* (1947), in which he is Billy Scanlon, a famous Irish actor-tenor who is losing his voice. Frawley played the character with a froggy voice and a toupee, looking in some scenes like the later Zero Mostel.

Another intriguing vaudeville-related Frawley credit is *Rose of Washington Square* (1939), based on "I Love That Man," an unpublished story inspired by the life of Fanny Brice. The film stars Al Jolson as a vaudevillian named Ted Cotter, along with Alice Faye as the Brice-like character and Tyrone Power as the gambler (and Nicky Arnstein clone) with whom she falls in love.

Brice was so incensed by *Rose of Washington Square* that she filed a claim for damages against Twentieth Century-Fox, which produced the film, along with Faye, Power, and Jolson—but not Frawley, who had fourth billing in the picture as Harry Long, a talent agent. The suit was for $100,000, but was settled out of court for $40,000; Arnstein, who also brought suit, received $25,000.

According to John Stephens, the *My Three Sons* TV production manager, Frawley had no love for the legendary Jolson. In fact, he may have detested Jolson even more than Vivian Vance. "He'd go on and on about Jolson," Stephens says. "He couldn't stand him. He just despised him." Surely, Frawley was miffed when the *New York Herald Tribune* reported, in a puff piece printed in conjunction with the *Rose of Washington Square* release in 1939, that "Jolson is probably the only important member of the cast with vaudeville experience—Tyrone Power and Alice Faye are too young to have been much more than spectators. . . ."

Given his looks and demeanor, Frawley often was called upon to play Irishmen on-screen. In addition to E. P. Christy, Billy Delaney, and Billy Scanlon, his characters' surnames included Mullins, Sharkey, Donlan, Hogan, McNulty, O'Malley, and O'Brien.

On occasion, these film jobs would be as stereotypically silly Irish lushes. For example, in *Professor Beware* (1938), a Harold Lloyd comedy, Frawley plays Snoop Donlan, a perpetually inebriated talent scout who utters the line, "Why don'cha lemme take care of the situation like a man who knows what he's doing?" This, even though he is so stewed that he has stripped down to his underwear while seated in the back of a car. "I'll dress you," Lloyd, playing the title character, tells him. "Okay, okay okay—and I'll buy ya a drink," Frawley's Snoop responds.

Even on the radio, where he was heard but not seen, Frawley was cast accordingly. In November 1937, he appeared with pal Bing Crosby on a *Lux Radio Theater* presentation of *She Loves Me Not*, based on a popular Howard Lindsay play. Supporting Crosby were Joan Blondell, Nan Gray, Sterling Holloway, and Barbara Weeks, and the show was hosted by Cecil B. DeMille; three years earlier, Crosby had starred in the property on-screen with a different cast. In the radio version, Frawley played Gus

McNeal, the fast-talking publicity director of Supersound Pictures, and growled such lines as "Well, I'll be a ring-tailed baboon"; "Be quiet, when I want an answer I'll ask for it"; and "Nix, Curley, nix."

Keeping to an Irish theme, he was to become Michael Francis "Bub" O'Casey on TV's *My Three Sons*. And, of course, quite a few of Frawley's celluloid Irishmen were cops: Captain Murphy, Sergeant Christie, Sheriff McGee, Police Chief O'Hara, Chief of Police Magoun, Private Detective O'Bleery. He also played countless non-ethnic cops including sergeants, lieutenants, captains, detectives, inspectors, and chiefs of police, with characters called Inspector Weber, Sergeant Barrel, Detective Ramsey, Detective Roberts, Inspector Harry B. Manning, Jean La Salle the Police Inspector, or simply Police Lieutenant or Police Captain.

Frawley quite frequently was seen in movies as characters with nicknames. In addition to Snoop Donlan, he was Smooth "Wolf" Wylie, Knobby Walsh, Baldy Gunder, Chancy Beheegan, Briney O'Brien, Bruiser Brown, "Bang" Carson, Honey Wiggen, Mushy Harrington, Soapy Moreland, Scoop Trimble, and Sunshine Joe. A few had only a single moniker: Painless, Hotfoot, Bright Eyes, Cap, and "The Duke." In the 1934 version of *The Lemon Drop Kid*, he was The Professor. In the 1951 remake of the Damon Runyon–based comedy, he was Gloomy Willie.

Chapter Six

TWO-STRIKE COUNT

William Frawley's casting in both versions of *The Lemon Drop Kid* was more than fitting, being that a fair percentage of his Hollywood films also were set in the world of athletics.

In these two features he went to the races, playing racetrack con men. However, in most of his sports movies, Frawley was cast as managers, coaches, and trainers. He found himself in the fight world in *Gentleman Jim* (1942), *Ex-Champ* (1939), *Golden Gloves* (1940), and *Joe Palooka in Winner Take All* (1948). He appeared in such gridiron epics as *Hold 'Em Yale* (1935), *Rose Bowl* (1936), *Touchdown Army* (1938), and *The Quarterback* (1940); and the baseball tales *Alibi Ike* (1935), *It Happened in Flatbush* (1942), *The Babe Ruth Story* (1948), *Kill the Umpire* (1950), *Rhubarb* (1951), and *Safe at Home!* (1962).

Just as the 1937 baseball season was getting under way, Frawley made one of his many appearances on *Lux Radio Theater* in an adaptation of *Alibi Ike*, based on the Ring Lardner story. His co-players were Joe E. Brown (who had starred in the Warner Bros. film), Helen Chandler, and Roscoe

Karns. Bill repeated the role he played on-screen: Cap, the manager of the Chicago Cubs, who contends with the antics of the title character, a talented but eccentric rookie hurler. Well over a decade later, Frawley taped a half-hour radio version of *The Babe Ruth Story*, which starred Ward Bond and was produced by the United States Information Agency and aired on the Voice of America.

Given the actor's obsession with athletics, it must have been particularly rewarding for him to be able to spout sports-related dialogue on-screen. He was particularly well suited for his role as Billy Delaney in *Gentleman Jim* if only because not only did he claim that, as a boy, he used to see the boxer play minor-league baseball, but also that he and "Gentleman Jim" Corbett (who died in 1933) had been close pals.

Corbett did travel in theatrical circles. Back in the late nineteenth century, he capitalized on his fame in the ring by starring in various plays (including one titled, appropriately, *Gentleman Jack*) and then going into vaudeville, and he counted among his pals the likes of matinee idol Maurice Barrymore and Irish tenor John McCormack.

My Three Sons' John Stephens confirms that Frawley occasionally would talk about his friendship with Corbett, but also adds, "Of course, naturally, he really loved John L. Sullivan. And he used to say, 'Ah, Corbett was a sissy.' Whether he knew John L. Sullivan or not, who knows? But he loved Sullivan. He also liked this fighter from San Diego named Irish Bob Murphy, who fought Joey Maxim and Harry Matthews and people like that."

Frawley was extremely knowledgeable about athletics. Team rosters, batting averages, and win-loss records were emblazoned in his memory. "He was like a sports encyclopedia," explains actor Don Grady. "If you had a question about sports, you went and talked to Bill."

"The funny thing about Frawley is, around showbiz people, he really didn't care that much," notes John Stephens. "He wasn't awed by them. He was awed by sports people. I think he always had a secret dream, as a lot of kids, [to] have been shortstop for the Yankees or something." Frawley himself even admitted, "Mostly, my friends are in baseball or they're golfers. I just don't go to dinner at people's houses. I don't even know the names of the people next door at the Knickerbocker Hotel [on Hollywood Boulevard] where I live. I don't mix easily, and mostly I mind my own business."

One can easily imagine Frawley fitting in perfectly in the locker-room/barroom world of athletes. In his day, this was a domain that, like Frawley, was awash in political incorrectness. While on a panel at the 1998 Society for American Baseball Research (SABR) national convention in San Francisco, sixty-eight-year-old ex–major leaguer Gino Cimoli matter-of-factly stated that his fellow ballplayers, managers, and coaches called him Dago; nor was Cimoli at all bothered by this. Meanwhile, Pacific Coast League veteran Bud Watkins, sharing the podium with Cimoli, casually referred to legendary minor-league home-run hitter Steve Bilko as "that big Polack."

Frawley surely would be unable to relate to the contemporary, college-educated pro ballplayer who is more likely to be found studying the New York Stock Exchange's highs and lows on the Internet or in a newspaper's business section than checking out batting or pitching statistics on ESPN. As crusty, eighty-one-year-old former big-leaguer Hank Sauer noted, while on another SABR convention panel, "We carried cases of beer. Today, they carry attaché cases full of money."

It was not that Bill Frawley lacked friends in the entertainment industry. He did in fact enjoy the company of like-minded performers, mostly Irishmen and/or those who savored the spirits. John Stephens reports that, among actors, Frawley loved Spencer Tracy, James Gleason, Frank McHugh, and Pat O'Brien. The latter, who had his own short-lived sitcom, *Harrigan and Son* (1960–61), was an occasional visitor to the *My Three Sons* set. Among Frawley's other pals were John Gallaudet and Minor Watson, two lesser-known character types who, like Frawley, were on the Broadway stage during the 1920s and went on to appear in a good number of feature films without ever laying claim to star parts.

Bing Crosby was another Frawley pal—and offstage singing partner. Frawley in fact was cast in four movies with the actor-crooner: *Here Is My*

Heart (1934), *Double or Nothing* (1937), *Rhythm on the River* (1940), and *Going My Way* (1944). During his 1947 appearance on Crosby's radio show, the two shared easy conversation.

Bing observed that he and Bill hadn't sung together in "quite a spell."

"The fault is yours," responded Frawley, adding that "the same old guys" are still hanging around the Brown Derby restaurant and that "you never come around and harmonize with us anymore."

Bing noted that he has been "pretty tired lately," what with shooting *The Road to Rio* (1947) with Bob Hope.

"Why don't you and I have a go with one of our old favorites right now," Bing declared, and soon he and Frawley were tickling the audience's funny bone as they comically clowned while singing "Ida, Sweet as Apple Cider," written by Eddie Leonard. The song, which dates from 1903, was popularized by Eddie Cantor (whose wife was named Ida).

After he and Crosby finished performing, fellow guest Judy Garland commented, "That was great, fellas. I wonder why girls don't get together and sing like men do." Crosby responded, "Well, that's mainly, Judy, because they don't hang around the barbershop."

Frawley then asked Bing, "Why don't you drop over to the barbershop some afternoon? Our quartet needs a fifth." And Bing quipped, "Bring it with you when you come."

"[Frawley] was a great joke-teller," notes Chuck Stevens, a major-league first-baseman during the 1940s and Frawley's friend for a quarter century. "You get [Frawley] and Pat O'Brien and two or three of those guys together, and they'd have you rolling in the aisles."

When asked if he could recall any of Frawley's movie-star friends, Stevens cites O'Brien and notes that the actor "spent a little time with Spencer Tracy." Then he changes course and begins listing ballplayers from the long-forgotten to the Hall of Famer. "He liked [Casey] Stengel," Stevens declares, "and he loved [Lefty] O'Doul." Francis Joseph O'Doul played in the major leagues between 1919 and 1934 and was a longtime minor-league manager. Even though he passed away in 1969, the San Francisco restaurant that bears his name still is in existence. It is located on Geary

Street, right off Union Square. Hanging over the bar, directly to the left of the entrance and amid the dozens of baseball photos that give the saloon its flavor, is a large head shot of Frawley, circa *I Love Lucy*. It is inscribed, "Best on earth to my pal Frank [O'Doul] from his pal Bill Frawley."

"I think he and DiMag [Joe DiMaggio] became good friends," Stevens adds. "Whenever DiMag was in town, he'd call [Frawley]. There also was a fellow named "Sloppy" Thurston—Hollis Thurston, who was a pitcher with the Chicago White Sox in the late 1920s and early 1930s. They were good friends. There was a fellow named Bert Niehoff, who was a good big-league ballplayer way back. I know they were good friends. Another ballplayer he really liked was Bill Sweeney, who managed out in the Pacific Coast League."

Dom DiMaggio, Joe D's kid brother, who played in the Pacific Coast League during the 1930s and in Boston during the 1940s and early 1950s, offers a typical ballplayer comment about Frawley when he notes, "I liked Bill very, very much. To me, he was very pleasant. He was a very rabid baseball fan, and knowledgeable about the game."

When Frawley came to Hollywood in 1933, he insisted on a clause being inserted in his studio contract that permitted him time off each fall to attend the World Series. "Once I used it," he recalled, "[and] in fact I even wound up getting a ticket for the producer of the film on which I'd stopped work temporarily."

The Detroit Tigers won the American League pennant in 1934 and 1935, and went on to face the St. Louis Cardinals and Chicago Cubs in the World Series. One of the stars of the Tigers pitching staff was Elden Auker. "Bill Frawley and his friend, George Raft, attended both World Series together," Auker recalls. "They were both friends of our manager, Mickey Cochrane. On opening day of each series, they visited our clubhouse and personally shook hands with each Tiger player.

"Mr. Frawley was a very gregarious person and the players were happy to talk to him. We were a little more reluctant to talk to Raft, because we knew of his public image as a gambler. . . . [But] we had no hesitation to talk to Mr. Frawley, because we trusted him and enjoyed talking to him. He was just a funny man and very entertaining.

"I feel fortunate to this day that I had the good fortune to have known him personally, long before he became a TV star," Auker adds. In fact, even ballplayers who were not personally acquainted with Frawley admired him and his work, especially as Fred Mertz. When asked, Ted Williams did not recall meeting Frawley, but he did express his admiration for *I Love Lucy*.

While Frawley certainly was in his element in the company of athletes, some of the ballplayers did pick up on his gruff side. "On the one hand, I thought he kind of stood aloof," recalls Dom DiMaggio. "I met him a few times, at the Brown Derby with Bob Cobb [of Cobb salad fame, who was the restaurant's owner]. I used to go in there [in the 1930s] when I played for the San Francisco ballclub and went through Hollywood."

At the same time, DiMaggio is quick to add that once you got beyond Frawley's facade he invariably "was very, very friendly. We always sat down for a few minutes and talked. We'd always have a very pleasant chat."

If he had not become an entertainer, Frawley surely would have relished being professionally connected to the National Pastime—if only because it would have allowed him to savor the company of ballplayers on a full-time basis.

"If he had the millions [he] might have competed with Budweiser for the purchase of the St. Louis Cardinals," wrote Frawley's cousin, Tom Green, in 1953. Yet Frawley did become a baseball-team owner of sorts. In 1938, the cash-strapped San Francisco Missions, of the minor-league Pacific Coast League, were moved to Hollywood and renamed the Stars. Herbert Fleishacker, the club's principal owner, had sold the team to a group led by Los Angeles businessmen Don Francisco and George Young.

Of all the team's new owners, the one most in the public spotlight was Bob Cobb, who at the time was married to actress (and Frawley's fellow Paramount contract player) Gail Patrick—and who, according to sportswriter Al Stump, was "reported to sneeze into $100 bills."

Cobb became the team's president, and Frawley was one of an array of movieland names who purchased nominal amounts of stock in the Stars, joining Cecil B. DeMille, Robert Taylor, George Raft, Bing Crosby, Gary Cooper, Barbara Stanwyck, Gene Autry, William Powell, and George Burns and Gracie Allen.

The Stars played one season at Wrigley Field, home of the Los Angeles Angels, the team's Pacific Coast League rivals. They then moved into Gilmore Field, a small but colorful wooden park in the Hollywood area (where Farmers Market is now), which seated 11,500. When it opened, on May 2, 1939, Gail Patrick threw out the first pitch to Joe E. Brown, with young Jane Withers at bat. More than likely, Frawley was in attendance; across the years, he was to be a regular at Stars games. John Stephens describes him as "a big, big fan" of the team. "I have fond memories of Bill Frawley," notes Tony Lupien, former major-leaguer and Hollywood Stars player. "Like many other showpeople of that era, we saw them each night at the ballpark. . . ." According to Cliff Dapper, another ex-Star, Frawley had a box right behind the home team dugout, and "even attended Sunday doubleheaders." Adds Chuck Stevens, who also played with the Stars, "It would be very common to begin a ballgame, and there would be everybody imaginable at the ballpark. Robert Taylor. Frank Lovejoy. Cyd Charisse and Tony Martin. Groucho [Marx]. Phil Silvers. All of the comedians. . . . A frequent visitor was Mickey Cohen, the little hood. Sat behind third base, with a couple of gunsels."

Stevens recalls first meeting Frawley before World War II, at Wrigley Field. The actor was hanging out in the clubhouse with B-western star Bob Steele. "It probably was in October, during an exhibition game," he notes. "Bob Feller pitched against Satchel Paige. It was the whites against the black players." Stevens additionally reports that Frawley often could be found in the Stars' clubhouse. "You didn't allow a lot of people in," he explains, "but he pretty much had free rein there because he and [Stars, manager] Fred Haney were pretty good friends." Another Frawley hangout was the Gilmore Field pressroom. Stevens frequently would find him there, savoring a drink or a soda. "We'd shoot the bull," he recalls, "and go over the day's ball game or whatever.

"It would not be at all unheard of for him to come up to San Francisco if we had a key series going on up there or in Oakland," he adds. "During the war, I was in the Air Force. We played some exhibition games in this area and Frawley was there, too."

Irv Noren, an ex–Hollywood Star who was to enjoy an eleven-year major-league career, met Frawley in 1949. "He got a few of us [roles] in a couple baseball movies," notes Noren. "He knew we weren't making much money playing ball in those days, so he wanted to help us." Frawley appeared in one of the two films cited by Noren, *Kill the Umpire* (1950). The other was *The Winning Team* (1952), which featured Ronald Reagan and Doris Day as Grover Cleveland and Aimee Alexander. Like so many of his baseball pals, Noren describes Frawley as "a great fan and a great guy" who had "a great sense of humor and [was] a sincere man."

Chuck Stevens reports that Frawley attended "probably ten or fifteen or twenty" annual dinners sponsored by his organization, the Association of Professional Baseball Players, which offers assistance to ailing and financially troubled ballplayers. "He would sit at the head table, and he would entertain. Five hundred baseball people would be there."

At these affairs, Frawley would be seated right beside the likes of his pals Joe DiMaggio and Lefty O'Doul or some other big-name ballplayer, and would amuse those on hand with picturesque, sports-related anecdotes.

Frawley attended a number of these dinners in the late 1940s and early 1950s. While he was a much-in-demand star of the dinner program, his screen career then was perilously on the ropes.

The actor was now in his early sixties, and nearing what many would consider retirement age. His Paramount affiliation had ended almost a decade earlier. Since then, he had been freelancing, hopping from project to project at studio after studio.

Meanwhile, it now was the post–World War II era, and the face of American society was changing rapidly. When Frawley had first signed his Paramount contract, the Hollywood studio system was firmly in place. Actors, directors, screenwriters, and other movie-industry workers toiled for individual film lots, and earned weekly paychecks. Now, television was in the process of replacing radio and the movies as the opiate of the entertainment-seeking masses. Why should the multitude of war veterans and their wives, who were beginning to raise families, hire babysitters and hop into their Chevrolets and drive to movie theaters only to spend further dollars with ticket sellers? Now they could purchase a TV, stay home, and be entertained for free, seven nights of the week. Even more specifically, why should fight fans—including Frawley—trek to some arena to witness a boxing card? Now, all they need do is stroll a couple of blocks to their corner saloon, where they could share drinks with their pals and cheer their favorite fighters on TV, which then was airing boxing matches most every night of the week.

In any case, the suburban communities then sprouting up across the country were miles away from the urban entertainment centers. From the 1920s through mid-1940s, movie palaces often were filled to capacity. In 1946, the initial postwar year, an average of 82.4 million movie tickets were sold each week. Yet by 1953, that number had been sliced almost in half.

As a result, the economics of the movie industry were quickly changing. In 1948, the *Wall Street Journal* published a report on the state of Hollywood moviemaking headlined, "Hollywood's Wallet: Film Economy Splurge Is Succeeding; More Movies for Less Money . . . $2 Million Picture Made for $850,000; Shooting Time Is Cut; Sets, Scripts Cheaper—Unemployment Is Increasing."

All of this translated into the dismantling of the studio system of the Golden Age of Hollywood. Actors no longer were being signed to long-term contracts, but instead were working freelance. This was true for the top star as well as the fringe player. Even at Metro-Goldwyn-Mayer, the crown jewel of Hollywood studios, the layoffs were massive. Such expensive screen legends as Judy Garland, Clark Gable, Spencer Tracy, Katharine Hepburn, Fred Astaire, and Betty Hutton were among the many who sooner or later found their studio affiliations severed.

Hundreds of movie actors began guest-starring on dozens of dramatic anthology series and comedy and variety shows. Early TV converts ranged from Bing Crosby to Claudette Colbert, Paul Muni to Margaret Sullavan and Loretta Young. They were followed by everyone from Bogie to Harpo to the Duke—with quite a few (including William Holden, Richard Widmark, Orson Welles, Rock Hudson, Cornel Wilde, Van Johnson—and Harpo and the Duke) eventually appearing on *I Love Lucy*.

Gradually but most assuredly, Frawley was finding it increasingly difficult to secure screen roles. It was dawning on him that he no longer was solidly ensconced in Hollywood.

Bill may have been ideally cast as celluloid baseball managers, press agents, and policemen. However, at this juncture, he was assigned a role that seemed to portend his future: the aptly named Bill the Bartender in *East Side, West Side* (1949), a sophisticated drama of infidelity starring Barbara Stanwyck, James Mason, Van Heflin, and Ava Gardner, and based on Marcia Davenport's best-selling novel.

During the final stages of his life, performing for Frawley was to become nothing more than a way to make a living. He often stated that, if acting roles dried out, he would be just as happy becoming a real-life Bill the Bartender, mixing drinks in a neighborhood pub—and, more than likely, imbibing the profits.

William Frawley might easily have ended up mired in obscurity, serving up scotch on the rocks and boilermakers from behind a bar and yammering on and on about his days on the vaudeville and Broadway boards.

This easily might have been his fate in the early 1950s and 1960s—if not for *I Love Lucy*.

Part Two

VIVIAN VANCE
BEFORE ETHEL

Broadway showgirl Vance. (PHOTO COURTESY OF THE SHUBERT ARCHIVE)

Inset: Young Vance in her riding gear, circa 1930. (PHOTO COURTESY OF ALBUQUERQUE LITTLE THEATER)

Chapter Seven

VIVIAN ROBERTA JONES

In 1909, twenty-two-year-old William Frawley was beginning his career in vaudeville. On July 26 of that year, a blue-eyed baby girl named Vivian Roberta Jones entered the world. She would grow up to become Vivian Vance, Frawley's costar on the TV classic, *I Love Lucy*.

Vivian was of Welsh-Irish-English stock. She was born in Cherryvale, Kansas, a comfortable small town in Montgomery County, in the southeastern part of the state, right along the Missouri border. On its Web site, Cherryvale describes itself as "the Friendly Little City since 1871" and "a wonderful community to raise your children and a friendly hometown for those who are searching for a peaceful community to spend their retirement."

During her decades as an actress, Vance would have you believe that her birth year was 1912. This is the year listed in scores of Vance-related references. The headline of her *New York Times* obituary, dated August 18, 1979, informed the world that "Vivian Vance, Actress, Dies at 66 . . ." Even that would have been incorrect had Vance been born in 1912; she would have been three weeks past her sixty-seventh birthday.

The fact was that she was three years older. This may be verified by examining the United States Government Social Security Death Index. Here, it is noted that Vivian Vance—Social Security Number: 110-09-0642—was born "26 Jul 1909."

There were six children in the Jones family. The eldest was a daughter, Venus. Next came Vivian. She was followed by Dorothy, Maxine (who was nicknamed Mickey), Robert Jr., and the youngest, Lou Ann.

Vivian's parents, Robert Andrew Jones and Euphemia Mae Ragan Jones, were wed in 1903 in Oswego, Kansas. Initially, they lived in Cherokee, Kansas. Venus was born there in 1905, the year in which they moved to 311 East Fifth Street in Cherryvale. At this time, Bob Jones was attempting to find a professional niche, one that would allow him to support his young family. First, he was the proprietor of the Bob Jones Café on West Main Street. Prior to Vivian's birth, he sold that business and hired on as a switch-man with the Frisco Railroad. Then the Joneses resettled in the large, two-story white house, at 309 West Sixth Street, in which Vivian was born; eventually they moved yet again, to 322 West Second Street.

Today, the house in which Vivian was born remains a part of the Jones-Ragan family. For decades, Imogene Littell, whose father was Vivian's first cousin, has lived there. "We didn't know that [Vivian was born there] at the time we bought the house," Littell explains. "Her mother, Aunt Mae, and Uncle Bob told us when we stopped one year in Albuquerque [where they eventually settled] and visited them while on our way to California for a vacation. This was sometime in the early 1950s.

"A couple years ago," Littell continues, "a lady from Parsons, a neighboring town, called me. She had heard that Vivian was born in this house. She wanted to come over and bring her niece, who was around seven or eight, because [the child] was such a great fan of the *I Love Lucy* show. I invited them over and [the child] was delighted that she got to see the home, and the room where Vivian was born. She just loved Vivian, she loved Lucy, she loved the show, this little kid."

One of Venus's and Vivian's playmates while they were growing up was the legendary cult silent star Louise Brooks, who was born in Cherryvale in 1906. In his biography of Brooks, Barry Paris quotes Venus as saying, "Vivian was born funny. Viv was comical when she was just two and three years old. We lived across the street from the Brookses for about a year, and I remember Viv and Louise as children playing together."

The sibling born directly after Viv was Dorothy, who was six years her junior. "She and I were really close, and great friends," explains Dorothy Jones O'Neal. "We did many, many things together. We had the same sense of humor, and she was loads of fun.

"The main thing was how wonderful she was," O'Neal adds. "There was never anything mean about her. She was very kind and generous. She loved everybody, and everybody loved her." Imogene Littell concurs with O'Neal when she declares, "[Vivian] loved people. She loved being with people. She was vivacious, a gregarious type of person. Just being with her, you could tell that she loved life."

♥

When Vivian was six, the Jones clan moved to Independence, another Montgomery County town located fifteen miles from Cherryvale. With his brother Ralph, Bob Jones opened the Jones Brothers Grocery at Sixteenth and Myrtle Streets, and the family settled into a modest house on West Maple Street.

"[Bob Jones] loved all his kids," recalls Imogene Littell, "but would talk about Vivian because she was in television." She also notes, "[Vivian's] mother was such a nice person. She was always, well, kind of like Vivian. [She was] vivacious, and loved people."

Notwithstanding, while Mae was outgoing, she also was devoutly and dogmatically religious, in a hellfire-and-brimstone manner. As a "religious fundamentalist," she was determined to lasso in her free-spirited daughter and raise her within the confines of her own conservative lifestyle. Whatever acceptance Vivian ever was to win from her mother was destined to come after much and great anguish.

Vivian, additionally, was coming to maturity during the Jazz Age, a time when the younger generation was breaking ties with the

Victorian/Edwardian ways of their elders. One of her fellow Independence residents was the anonymous author of a 1952 profile of Vivian that appeared in the *Kansas City Star*. "Vivian's parents were strict," the writer recalled. "They did not permit her to have dates for the high school dances, which was too much to bear for this lively youngster."

Yet Vivian was not one to passively accept these constraints. "We remember," the writer continued, "that she occasionally overcame the barrier by climbing out of a window of her home to join a party of her classmates who were waiting nearby. Later one of the girls in the group would have to spend the night at the Jones home to help forestall parental wrath."

Vivian's mother in particular would criticize her daughter for her vanity and interest in boys and parties. Mae Jones would incessantly harp on her belief that the world in which her "wayward child" sought to live would result in her quite literally burning in hell.

From an early age, Vivian savored dancing and singing—and expressed an interest in a career as an actress. And her mother attempted to thwart that attraction. Mrs. Jones was convinced that show business was an evil and immoral profession. "Back then, actors and actresses were thought to be wild," admits Imogene Littell. "[Viv's parents'] lifestyle was so much different. They thought [the acting] life involved drinking and that sort of thing. They thought it would corrupt her morals, I suppose."

And so their disapproval of their daughter's burgeoning obsession with the stage helped to foster within Vivian a deep insecurity, which ultimately was fated to play wicked tricks on her psyche.

Even as a youngster, Vivian needed to be at the center of every activity. She simply had to succeed—and to succeed smashingly—at all her endeavors. Yet when she did, she rarely felt happy. Instead, she more often than not experienced chronic fatigue. And when she failed, even in the smallest way, she was devastated.

♥

Despite her parents' displeasure with Vivian's love of acting, she remained determined to pursue a stage career. And it was in Independence that she really came in touch with her talent for performing. "Vivian was quite a talker then, too, having won a state declamation contest," recalled the anonymous *Kansas City Star* reporter.

Even more tellingly, she became fiercely involved in school dramatics. Whatever encouragement Viv lacked at home was counterbalanced by Anna Ingleman, her drama teacher at Independence High School, who proved a key influence at this stage of Vivian's life. Ingleman considered the youngster the most multifaceted of her students, one of whom was playwright-to-be William Inge, who was born in Independence and was four years Viv's junior.

"That Vivian Jones would make good, I always knew," Ingleman declared in 1956. "She had a real talent and I believe she was the most versatile student I ever had."

On one occasion, Ingleman was staging a production of Samuel Shipman and John B. Hymer's Broadway hit, *East Is West.* One of its characters is an aged Chinese man, and the teacher felt she had no male student capable of playing the role. "I suggested to Vivian that she should try out for the part," Ingleman recalled. "She did and got it.

"The night of the play she was disguised so well and gave such an outstanding portrayal her own father did not recognize her. I remember at the end of the first act he said to Vivian's mother, 'I thought Vivian was to be in this play.' I always felt that was the grandest compliment Vivian would ever receive."

Vivian was a natural blonde whose hair turned ash-blonde when she was about sixteen. Those who can perceive of her only as dowdy Ethel Mertz would be surprised to learn that Vivian Jones was a high school cheerleader. And around this time, a bathing suit–clad Viv represented the city of Independence in a statewide beauty contest.

Her favorite colors were red and blue. Her favorite meal was meat, mashed potatoes with gravy, pie, and coffee. She liked to chew gum. She had developed a love for cars, which she began cultivating as a preteen. Even after moving to New York she still owned an automobile, and had one car to which she was particularly attached. While visiting Vivian's parents in Albuquerque during the 1950s, Imogene Littell recalls that her father "showed us a car, a convertible. It may have been a Cadillac. It was from the 1930s. Vivian wanted to save it, so it was [kept] there at their home in Albuquerque. But he had to show us that, one of Vivian's early cars."

♥

In 1928, the Joneses headed west and settled in the sleepy, sunlit city of Albuquerque, New Mexico, residing on La Vega Road SW. Their second daughter did not accompany them. A year earlier, Vivian had left Independence in order to seek her own independence. She went on the road, with the intention of breaking into show business by picking up singing and dancing gigs.

Before departing Independence, she selected a stage name: Vivian Vance. She borrowed the moniker from Vance Randolph, a member of the local theater crowd.

However, Vivian's attempt to establish her identity was short-lived. She soon met Joseph Shearer Danneck Jr. and, according to Karol Kennedy of the Dubuque County Recorder's office, Danneck and Vivian—who legally still was known as Vivian Roberta Jones—were wed in Dubuque, Iowa, on October 6, 1928.

Very little is known about Danneck and his marriage to Vivian. On their marriage license, filled out the day before their nuptials, Danneck's occupation is vaguely listed as "theater work." He notes that he is twenty-three years old and a native of Van Buren, Indiana. His mother's maiden name is Katherine Lytle. Danneck gives his place of residence as Paola, Kansas, located twenty-two miles southwest of Kansas City, while Vivian lists her place of residence as Albuquerque and her age as nineteen—which offers further proof that her true birth year is 1909.

One thing is certain, though; the union of Mr. and Mrs. Danneck Jr. was made in haste (as opposed to heaven), and was fated to soon crumble. The pair ended up in Albuquerque, which was really an unlikely destination, given that Viv was so anxious to be liberated from her parents. It was not long before she and Danneck realized how unhappy they were with their lives and their marriage. Eventually Danneck left town and Vivian took the opportunity to file for divorce, citing abandonment. Their marriage lasted but a year and a half.

Upon her divorce, Vivian remained in New Mexico and moved in with her parents. Despite the fact that she did not come to Albuquerque until she was an adult, this became her "official" hometown. While appearing on *Toast of the Town*'s 1954 *I Love Lucy* TV tribute, Ed Sullivan asked her where she was from "originally." "Albuquerque," Vivian responded. Later on in the show, host Sullivan endearingly referred to Vance as "the Indian squaw from Albuquerque."

It wasn't that Vivian was ashamed of her Kansas roots. The occasion simply called for a one-word answer, and not a detailed explanation of her childhood geography.

Vivian first met her cousin from Kansas, Imogene Littell, in 1959, when Littell and her husband John made one of their trips to California— and Viv was at the tail end of her tenure as Ethel Mertz. "We stopped by to see her," Littell recalls. "She invited us to come to the studio the next day, and we watched the [show's] filming. We met Lucy and Desi. Milton Berle was on this particular episode.

"Viv was very up. She was excited to see us. She took us to dinner that evening, to a little German restaurant. She was just excited to see someone from Cherryvale."

♥

In 1930, Vance, a newly minted twenty-one-year-old divorcée, was for the time being destined to remain in the Southwest. If her parents disapproved of her desire for a theater career, she felt no such objection from Albuquerque's budding theatrical community. Vivian became the protégée of Kathryn Kennedy, a New York actress who had been the understudy for Jeanne Eagels in *Rain* (1922) and who for health reasons had settled in Albuquerque.

Kennedy and her husband, James O'Connor, then were in the process of establishing the Albuquerque Little Theater, which was the brainchild of Irene Fisher, society editor of the *Albuquerque Tribune*, who raised

$1,000 to start the enterprise. The theater commenced operation in 1930 and exists to this day. In 1998, it was described by the Albuquerque Convention and Visitors Bureau as being in its "sixty-eighth season on Historic Route 66."

By the late 1970s, the theater, according to Lynn Buckingham Villella, writing in *Albuquerque* magazine, had "settled rather grandly into facilities on San Pasquale NW valued at several hundred thousands of dollars. With holdings of at least a half million dollars, Albuquerque Little Theater has a paid staff of eleven, six hundred to seven hundred all-volunteer local performers, tech crews, ushers and supporters plus a rather impressive list of paid guest stars."

Back when Vivian was appearing with the theater, there was no permanent facility. Plays were performed between film screenings at the KiMo Theater, a "pueblo deco" movie palace in downtown Albuquerque. Rehearsals often were held in barns. The Albuquerque Little Theater's original venue, called the Community Playhouse, was dedicated in 1936— long after Viv had left town for New York. According to Villella, it was "built in a community endeavor reminiscent of a pioneer barn-raising."

Kennedy, who guided the theatrical enterprise until 1961, cast Viv in the very first Albuquerque Little Theater production: the Edwin Burke romantic comedy *This Thing Called Love,* in which she portrayed a vamp. She went on to play a variety of challenging roles, running the gamut from Lil, the chorus-girl sweetie of a two-bit hoofer who becomes enmeshed in murder, in *Broadway*—to the gypsy girl in Tolstoy's *Redemption.*

In her autobiography, Kennedy recalled Vivian as "a young girl [with a] superlative talent [who] showed up at one of our tryouts. The audience fell in love with Vivian here, just as they did the world over in *I Love Lucy.*"

Kennedy continued, "Vivian played many types of roles while a young girl here, some glamorous, some comical, some sentimental, but one I remember in particular because it convinced me of her ability to make an audience respond as she wanted them to. It was the role of a pinched, frustrated character in which Vivian savored words and gave flavor and meaning to the character and completely obscured her own earthy personality."

On one occasion, Viv fell off a horse and sustained a black eye. She then was playing Thérèse of the Cross in an adaptation of Gregorio and Maria Martinez Sierra's *The Cradle Song,* and Kennedy observed, "That night, painful or not, she 'went on with the show.' And when at the climax of the play she cried and the tears washed away the makeup covering the black eye, the women in the audience never noticed because they were blinded by their own tears."

Vivian really had an ally in Kathryn Kennedy, who also recalled an occasion in which Viv was "appearing happily and hilariously in one of our comedies, wearing a dress which had been provided for her by our costume mistress. The dress, a little blue silk number costing about $15.95, was pretty and set off Vivian's blonde good looks."

Kennedy then reported that a rival cast member, who happened to be the proprietress of a dress shop, chose to garb herself in a "'splendid original' of the cheap little blue copy that Vivian was wearing onstage." The director added, "[I] yanked the dress shop femme fatale toward me and whispered menacingly, 'You've one minute before you go on. You go back to your dressing room and change into the pink dress, or so help me, I'll slap you so hard, you won't be able to go on at all.'"

Viv's rival complied, and quickly switched garments. Kennedy concluded the anecdote by observing, "Vivian never knew how near she came to the cold and condescending pity of every woman in the audience."

Kennedy felt that Albuquerque was too small a town for this blossoming Katharine Cornell. Certainly, Vivian had all the necessary talent to become a Broadway star. First, though, she would need seasoning. Perhaps she could study with Eva Le Gallienne, the legendary stage actress who then was operating her own small—albeit much-heralded—Manhattan art-theater company, the Civic Repertory Theater. Le Gallienne had founded the troupe in 1926, and since then had mounted productions of plays by Shakespeare, Molnar, Molière, Ibsen, Chekhov, and Barrie. Most assuredly, Kennedy felt that her protégée would thrive in such a stimulating environment.

At the same time, Viv longed to relocate to New York. The only trouble was, she could not afford the rail fare let alone have any sort of nest egg that would allow her to rent a room and feed herself while studying with Le Gallienne. So the theatergoing citizens of Albuquerque organized a benefit in her honor. She would entertain them with a special performance of *The Trial of Mary Dugan*, Bayard Veiller's popular courtroom melodrama. Her role would be the lead: a showgirl on trial for murdering her paramour. They in turn would purchase enough tickets so that the profits would allow her to head for Broadway.

"They were so wonderful about it," Vance would recall of her Albuquerque supporters. "What did a few thousand miles or a few thousand dollars matter! Train fares? Expenses? They were problems to be disposed of quickly. Everybody said, 'Arrange a benefit. We'll come.'"

Years later, Viv was to pay homage to Albuquerque and its Little Theater on *I Love Lucy*. Before marrying Fred Mertz, Ethel Mertz (whose maiden name was Potter but whose middle name was alternately Louise, Roberta, and Mae) had been a stage performer who hailed from Albuquerque. In an episode titled "Ethel's Home Town," first broadcast in 1955, the Ricardos and Mertzes visit the community on their trip to Hollywood. Only the townspeople think Ethel, rather than Ricky (who is heading west to break into motion pictures), is the movie star in their midst. At one point in the story, Ethel performs at Albuquerque's "Little Theater" (where the marquee reads "Ethel Mae Potter—We Never Forgot Her").

Chapter Eight

BROADWAY—1930s

The benefit for *The Trial of Mary Dugan* took place in July 1932. Two months later, twenty-three-year-old Vivian Vance arrived in Manhattan, full of hope that momentarily she would be mingling with theatrical heavyweights and lighting up Broadway. She took up residence at the MacDougal Street Girls' Club in Greenwich Village.

Those who have seen Vivian Vance solely on *I Love Lucy* know her only as an overweight, middle-aged lady who is an appropriate mate for an old coot like Fred Mertz. In sequence after sequence on the show, Ethel's pudginess cannot help but be contrasted to Lucy's somewhat slimmer forty-something figure.

Yet when Vance—like thousands of other young hopefuls from the hinterlands before and after her—came to New York to try to break into the theater, she was an attractive young woman. In fact, in March 1938— three months after first seeing her name up in lights on a Broadway marquee as a star of *Hooray for What!*—a newspaper feature writer described her as "a tall, young, blond, good-looking girl." In the Playbill for *Out from*

Under, which opened and closed in May 1940, Vance was labeled "the little Albuquerque bombshell."

While Vance may have been a star back home, she quickly learned that landing a job—any job—in the New York theater would be something else altogether. For openers, she arrived at the Civic Repertory's Fourteenth Street Theater with a letter to Eva Le Gallienne from Kathryn Kennedy and two test scenes that she had meticulously prepared with her mentor. Vance was granted an audition, but Le Gallienne did not hire her. In fact, it would have been surprising if the great actress-producer signed on anyone new for that season. This was a difficult time for the Civic Repertory, as its founder was struggling to keep it operating in this lean Depression year. In 1933, Le Gallienne was forced to suspend the group's operations for lack of sufficient financial backing.

So the newcomer had two choices: to admit failure and take the next train back to Albuquerque, or remain in New York and join the legions of other would-be actors in endless rounds of auditions . . . and endless rounds of casting-call rejections.

Vance was in turmoil over her inability to join Le Gallienne's company. Because she was unaware of the theater's financial crisis, she took the setback personally. "When I got to New York," she remembered years later, "I found I wasn't as good as my friends thought I was. But of course I couldn't go back." On one occasion, as her list of credits was growing, she did return to Albuquerque for a respite only to be met at the train station by a brass band. She was summarily paraded about like a returning hero. The folks in her New Mexico town may have loved her, but she believed she had done nothing to merit their approval.

"That did something to me," Vance later recalled. "I had to turn right around and go back to New York and really make good. I had to go through all the dismal business of plying managers with requests and being auditioned and never getting a job."

Eventually, her persistence paid dividends. Before her first year in New York was out, she heard of an upcoming audition at the Alvin Theater for *Music in the Air*, a new Jerome Kern–Oscar Hammerstein II musical. While

Vance had come to New York to be a dramatic actress, she knew she had a pleasant singing voice—one that can be heard on plenty of episodes of *I Love Lucy*—and was not averse to auditioning for a musical comedy. So she decided to try out for the show.

Vance waited backstage with the other chorus member wanna-bes. Each had been requested to display a voice trained in operetta. Vance's turn came late in the round of auditions. Garbed in a tweed suit and matching hat, she informed the piano-playing accompanist to feed her an E-flat. Differing reports have her rousing her judges with one of two numbers: a spicy rendition of "After You've Gone," a song that is more Sophie Tucker than Sigmund Romberg; and "The Japanese Sandman," which was popularized in vaudeville by Nora Bayes. One thing that is certain is that Vance concluded to cries of, "Take down her name. We want her," and she was hired for the chorus by Vinton Freedley, then one of the Great White Way's reigning producers.

In *Music in the Air*, as a member of the "Edendorf Choral Society" and "Edendorf Walking Club," Vance sang "Melodies of May" along with thirty-nine other anonymous chorus members. When the show played Philadelphia's Garrick Theater a month before its November 1932 Broadway opening, Vance was listed as one of the altos in the "Society," right between June Elkins and Rose Collins, and an alto in the "Club," between Tamara Zoya and Frances Marion. *Music in the Air* opened at the Alvin Theater and went on to enjoy a seven-month Broadway run.

At least Vance now had steady employment—even if the truth of the matter was that she was cast as much for her curves as her talent. Continental Walter Slezak, then thirty years old and in his pre-rotund years, appeared in the show. According to the actor: ". . . and the GIRLS, never before or after have I seen so many gorgeous females on one stage. . . . [There were] sixteen singers. Not only did they possess first-class voices, but they too were lookers."

Meanwhile, Vance supplemented her $35-a-week salary by singing in such Manhattan nightspots as the Biltmore Roof, Mon Paree, House of

Lords, and Club Simplon. Two of her favored numbers were "The Japanese Sandman" and "Danny Boy."

One contemporary newspaper item, from the *New York Morning Telegraph*, begins, "Vivian Vance, modernistic dancer, joins the Fall Frolics at Jimmy Kelly's, the Montmartre of New York, next Wednesday night. Miss Vance's new offering will be the 'Powder Puff Ballet.'"

♥

It is highly conceivable that, during this period, Vivian Vance and William Frawley may have crossed paths—if only on the street, going to and from their respective Broadway jobs. Just as *Music in the Air* was opening, *Tell Her the Truth*—Frawley's last Broadway musical—was having its final curtain at the Cort Theater after a disappointing one-and-a-half-week run. As she was cavorting in the *Music in the Air* chorus, he was making a hit in *Twentieth Century*. Just as *Music in the Air* was closing, he made his last, albeit brief, appearance in New York in *The Ghost Writer* before forever abandoning the Great White Way.

While Frawley and Vance both were a part of the Broadway community in the early 1930s, they represented two uniquely different aspects of the New York stage world. Frawley was an entertainer of the old guard. He played vaudevillians who sang and danced in revue-style musicals. His roles were stock characters: fast-talking city-slicker con men who were subtle, and sometimes not-so-subtle, updates of the sorts of roles found in plays written in the nineteenth century.

From the start, Vance found herself mingling with the more innovative, educated, creative artists who then were transforming Broadway into a mecca for sophisticated entertainment. In the early 1930s, the twentieth century's all-time great Broadway legends were then establishing themselves in New York theater. Reading through Vance's stageography is like browsing an honor roll of Broadway elite. As the decade progressed and segued into the 1940s, she would work in productions featuring the talents of Jerome Kern, Cole Porter, Antoinette Perry, George Abbott, Howard Lindsay, Russel Crouse, Gertrude Lawrence, Ethel Merman, Bob Hope, and Danny Kaye.

While even the more successful productions in which Frawley appeared have dated badly—with the notable exception of *Twentieth Century*—the majority of the shows in which Vance would be cast had a modern feel, a sophistication, and a freewheeling good humor.

What was it that allowed Vance an entree to the better Broadway shows? While attractive, she certainly was not a Miss America candidate. Her voice, after all, was pleasing but not outstanding.

What she did have was class. Viv carried herself straight and tall. She already had developed a refined way of talking and moving. She was solid and tough on the inside, but with a debutante's exterior.

All of these attributes would permit her to excel in any sort of well-written role. She could be a foil to the top comics. She could play a well-meaning Goldilocks, or a nasty little bitch—and without class, a nasty bitch is just a plain whore and, as such, has no place in chic plays. If Vance had lacked a sense of refinement, she could not have been effective in comedy. In essence, she was a bit like Margaret Dumont but with youth, looks, and a lot of innate savvy.

Finally, if Vance was lacking this inborn class, Lucille Ball would not have wanted to play off her in *I Love Lucy*, because Ethel Mertz without class is just an aging landlord's wife rather than the essentially delightful human being created by Vivian Vance.

During this period, Vance's life did not only consist of attempting to establish herself on Broadway. She was a young woman in the Big City. And she finally was permanently out from under the watchful gazes of her parents. It was around this time that Vance met George Koch, a dance-band violinist. They were married on January 6, 1933.

Compared to Joe Danneck, who shared with Viv a Midwestern Christian background, Koch was downright exotic. He was born and raised in the Flatbush section of Brooklyn and was a Jew. Imagine the response of Vivian's conservative mother to such a union! Furthermore, Koch was not physically attractive. He was stout, and when Vance wore high heels he was no taller than she. And their personalities did not mesh. Viv was gregarious, while Koch was quiet and reserved.

So what prompted Vivian to marry Koch? She certainly did not love him, just as she had not loved Joe Danneck, her first spouse. One speculates that she craved more economic security than her theater jobs provided. She had quickly tired of going home to a small, sparsely decorated room. As so many other chorus girls, she was using the money she earned to purchase evening dresses, shoes, beaded handbags, and other frills—items that would make her look the part of a glamorous New York doll. She did not want to rely on occasional dates in order to be assured of a square meal. And so essentially Koch was for Vivian little more than a meal ticket.

In 1934, Vinton Freedley gave Vance another chorus job, this time in *Anything Goes*, a fun-filled new Cole Porter musical that opened in November at the Alvin Theater. *Anything Goes* was an instant hit, and down through the years has been filmed twice (both times with Bing Crosby, in 1936 and 1956), and revived onstage with great success.

Because *Anything Goes* was a prestige show, being in the chorus was not a bad situation for any young performer intent on building a resumé. Vance's chorus work segued into a small role, and a job as understudy to the show's bombastic star, Ethel Merman. At the time, Merman was just past the beginning of a notable career in theater and film. She may have been approximately the same age as Vivian, but while Viv was struggling to keep employed, Merman already had established herself as an outstanding musical talent. In 1929, she had played the Palace Theater with Clayton, Jackson, and (Jimmy) Durante, a top vaudeville act. A year later, she won acclaim in the George and Ira Gershwin hit musical, *Girl Crazy*. From then on, theatergoers clamored to hear the buxom young woman with the booming voice.

As *Anything Goes* settled into its run, Merman was forced to miss two performances because of laryngitis. So Vance—unlike many understudies who lament that they never, ever play the role that they so carefully rehearsed—went on as Merman's character, Reno Sweeney. As Reno, Vance belted out the Cole Porter classics "You're the Top" and "Blow, Gabriel, Blow," and vocalized "I Get a Kick Out of You" plus the title number.

Vance now was making a dent in the Broadway musical scene. And she won two important allies in Howard Lindsay and Russel Crouse, who had revised P. G. Wodehouse and Guy Bolton's book for *Anything Goes*. While working on the show, according to Crouse, they were compelled to throw several dialogue lines to chorus girls. "This we are always reluctant to do," recalled Crouse, "because while chorus girls, as chorus girls, are perhaps the most efficient and hardest-working and even the most charming element in the theater, they rarely know how to read lines." Vance proved an exception. "We found immediately that whenever Miss Vance had anything to say, she said it as though she meant it," Crouse continued. "And so she got four lines in *Anything Goes*. I can still hear her saying all of them—because she meant them."

Still, Vance's aspirations were to be a "legitimate" actress. "It may not be a dramatic role," she said of Reno Sweeney, "but if I sing at the top of my lungs often enough maybe I'll get a dramatic role." After leaving the show, Vance was hired to star as Reno Sweeney in a road-company production and also continued with her nightclub gigs. In retrospect, however, she thought little of her experience in *Anything Goes*. "But believe you me," Vance remarked years later, "I did not feel I had won stardom through that short experience."

She was correct. No immediate offers to star in a Broadway musical were forthcoming. Vivian simply was a substitute, proving she could adequately replace an ailing star. On the other hand, the experience demonstrated that she could effectively head a show's cast. All the leads she had played at the Albuquerque Little Theater had allowed her to acquire a confidence in performing that made her a dependable stand-in to a Broadway leading lady.

And yet, despite her elevation from the chorus, being a shadow to Ethel Merman was hurtful in the long run to Vance's stage career. Merman was, after all, the belle of Broadway musicals. The critics adored her, and audiences loved her vivacious personality and distinctive, loud, full-blown voice. How could Vance compete for such attention? To be sure, she lacked Merman's special stage presence. As Merman's understudy, Vivian was subjected to comparisons with the unique star. Once she got out from under that kind of analysis, she was in a stronger position to develop her own stage persona.

While working in *Anything Goes*, Vance earned the respect of Merman, who liked her and appreciated her talent. Summarily, the two became life-long friends. Vance, along with Lucille Ball, held a bridal shower in Merman's honor in 1964, when Ethel wed actor Ernest Borgnine.

Merman was one of the headliners of the next Broadway show in which Vance appeared, *Red, Hot and Blue!*—another high-profile Cole Porter musical that premiered in October 1936, also at the Alvin Theater. Merman's costars were a pair of comedy legends: Jimmy Durante, who recently had been the star of Billy Rose's *Jumbo* (and with whom Ethel had appeared at the Palace seven years earlier); and Bob Hope, who had enjoyed much success in Jerome Kern's *Roberta* in 1933 and Florenz Ziegfeld's *Follies of 1936.*

Howard Lindsay and Russel Crouse proclaimed that they would create a role with Vance in mind for their next show, which turned out to be *Red, Hot and Blue!* Unfortunately, the character—whose name was Vivian—was pared down during rewrites, in rehearsal, and during tryouts, to the point where Vivian ended up with what amounted to a mere walk-on. In it, she had but one line, which consisted of a single word: "Who?" She also came on at the very beginning of the show, as one of a group of reporters.

Of her one-word part, Vance joked to Crouse, "At least you can't cut it."

"Just for that," Crouse responded, "after this you say, 'Wh—?'"

Chapter Nine

STARDOM

The following season (1937–38), Vance won her first major Broadway role: Stephanie Stephanovich, also known as Stefania Stevanova, an international spy, in *Hooray for What!*—which starred the great stage and radio comedian Ed Wynn and opened at the Winter Garden on the first day of December, 1937.

Actually, Vance was hired for the chorus and to understudy Kay Thompson, who originally was cast as the spy. "We didn't think of [Vance] for Stefania Stevanova," said Crouse, who also authored the show's book with Howard Lindsay, "because we knew a 'name' was wanted. We were a little ashamed to talk to her because we felt we had let her down. But she wasn't afraid to talk to us. 'All right,' she said, when she heard the bad news, 'I'll go into the chorus again.'"

What followed was a scenario right from the pages of *42nd Street.* (1933). Thompson, the future creator of the children's-book character Eloise, abruptly bowed out of *Hooray for What!* on the second night of the Boston tryout. On seven hours' notice Vance was asked to replace her, and did so after only one quick, far-from-perfect rehearsal.

"It was a matinee," recalled Crouse, "and in view of what had happened, I thought it best to pop into the dressing room and steady a girl who had every right to be completely shaken. I did. I thought I'd done a pretty good job, too. I just talked generalities to her—not mentioning the show at all. You know, just light conversation to quiet the nerves. I rose to go. The curtain was about to go up, and she was about to go on. It was probably the most important moment in her theatrical life. Suddenly she reached over and patted me on the shoulder. 'Now, Russel,' she said, 'don't you be nervous.'

"There, ladies and gentlemen, is a trouper!"

Vance was to have the role until a bigger name could be found to take over the key assignment. She would be expected to smile brightly, entertain the out-of-town audiences, and then step aside for the crucial New York opening.

Yet she did so well that she was not replaced. An original copy of a press release for the show has Thompson's name crossed out and "Vivian Vance" scrawled in script directly to its right. At the top of a list titled "HOORAY FOR WHAT COSTUMES," right under "FEMALE PRINCIPALS," it is typewritten "Made for KAY THOMPSON—Now Worn by VIVIAN VANCE." The image of shapely Vivian trying to slip into the clothing designed for a slim, hipless Thompson is near comical. One imagines that, in refitting the costumes, the seamstress quite literally had her work cut out for her!

The title page of the show's program reads, "Messrs. Shubert present ED WYNN [The Perfect Fool] returning to the stage in his biggest laugh musical HOORAY FOR WHAT! with Paul Haakon, June Clyde, Vivian Vance and Jack Whiting and 125 others including Broadway's Most Stunning Beauties." Now—finally—Vivian Vance had risen from the show-business crowd. She was no longer an anonymous chorus girl, one of the "125 others," nor was she an unheralded stand-in. What's more, for the first time, she had her name in lights on a Broadway marquee.

Reported Crouse, "At almost every performance she played in the remaining weeks of the tryout, there sat out front a [nameless] star eager to take over the role. Miss Vance knew of the presence of this star. And yet her performance on each of these occasions was such that the star went back to New York and Miss Vance continued in the part." She learned that she had won the role only two days prior to the New York opening. "I suppose I should cry," Crouse had her exclaiming, "but I'm not going to."

Unfortunately, the critics did not proclaim her an instant star. Brooks Atkinson, in the all-powerful *New York Times*, observed, "June Clyde and Vivian Vance sing as well as they can, which is nothing remarkable. . . ." Burns Mantle, in the *New York Daily News*, cattily noted, "Vivian Vance is the torch lady, hailing, I suspect, from the nightclub circuits. Her voice is a nightclub voice, at any rate. You get used to it after a while. About four in the morning I have an idea it is quite effective."

Nonetheless, Vance was described as "positively giggling with excitement" just after opening night. And she had plenty for which to be grateful. She was in a show that was destined to enjoy a healthy six-month run. Several motion-picture companies were inquiring as to her future status. (However, nothing came of this.) Vance proclaimed that Lindsay and Crouse "gave me that chance and I'll always be grateful to them."

♥

The one disappointment for Vance was that she still was appearing solely in musical comedies. So a pivotal credit for her was her first non-musical role: Myra Stanhope, a Hollywood siren otherwise known as the "Brooklyn bombshell," in *Kiss the Boys Goodbye*, Clare Boothe's satire of David O. Selznick's highly publicized search for an actress to play Scarlett O'Hara in *Gone with the Wind*. Vance joined the Chicago company in January 1939— Benay Venuta, who coincidentally had replaced Ethel Merman in *Anything Goes*, had played the role on Broadway—and soon afterward Vance and Loring Smith were added to the road company. In May, the show played Detroit. Vance's colorfully worded *Playgoer* biography reported that, after "banging around the Broadway nightclubs as a hot cha 'single,' the blonde Vivian scored last season with Ed Wynn. . . . Asked how she was selected for the present role, the blonde Vivian said she simply walked into the office [of the play's producer, Brock Pemberton] and vamped everyone in sight."

Two months later, *Kiss the Boys Goodbye* made the summer theater rounds, with Vance reprising Myra Stanhope. One of her fellow cast members was a thirty-seven-year-old actor who had created his role on Broadway. The part was Horace Rand, editor of the *Manhattan Man*. The actor in question was the tall and well-built, handsome and erudite Philip Ober.

Philip Nott Ober, whose father, Frank, was the secretary of the international committee of the Young Men's Christian Association, grew up in White Plains, New York. He went to a preparatory school and Princeton University, and then worked in advertising before breaking into the theater. By the early 1930s, he was appearing on Broadway and setting the groundwork for his stage career. Ober made his screen debut in *Chloe: Love Is Calling You* (1934), a lurid, ultra-low-budget melodrama filmed in St. Petersburg, Florida, in which he played a role most Caucasian actors would spurn—a light-skinned black who wishes to wed the title character, a half-caste.

Ober and Vance appeared in *Kiss the Boys Goodbye* for the week beginning July 10 at the Deertrees Theater in Harrison, Maine. The following week, the show moved to the Spa Theater in Saratoga Springs, New York. Also in the Saratoga cast were two television stars-to-be: William Talman, destined to win his greatest fame as Hamilton Burger on *Perry Mason* (1957–66); and a teenaged Marjorie Lord, eighteen years away from replacing Jean Hagen and playing Kathy "Clancey" Williams opposite Danny Thomas on *The Danny Thomas Show* from 1957 to 1964.

According to the Spa Theater program, Vance had "turned down the Rainbow Room at Rockefeller Center to come here for the Saratoga Players." If this is true, it was a fortuitous decision because, upon meeting Ober, she fell instantly and wholeheartedly in love.

Marjorie Lord recalls those days: "We first met when I was in summer stock in Saratoga, New York. We were both in *Kiss the Boys Goodbye* there together. I was the ingenue and she was the second leading woman. We were living in the same boardinghouse together. That was about the time she fell in love with Phil, Phil Ober.

"She was married before Phil, and not happy at all. Then she met Phil, and it was love at first sight for both of them."

It was at this time that Lord met Vance's second husband (to whom she was still married at the time)—George Koch. "He was kind of short and stocky, not at all attractive like Phil," she explains. "I don't know, he just didn't have the class that Phil had. Phil was a very attractive man at that time. [Koch] wasn't up to Viv. There was no way that he was. I saw that when I met him.

"I was kind of 'Miss Goody Two-shoes' in those days, and I thought [regarding Vance's feelings for Ober], 'Oh, this is terrible.' But when I met [Koch] I thought, 'Oh, no, you're not for Vivian.' I hate to say that, because I only met him one night."

Meanwhile, Vance's career continued evolving. She was to win one of her steadiest jobs when playwright Samson Raphaelson saw her performance in *Kiss the Boys Goodbye* at the Cape Playhouse in Dennis, Massachusetts. Raphaelson was in the process of developing *Skylark*, a drawing-room comedy based on *The Streamlined Heart*, a story he had sold to the *Saturday Evening Post*. The first version of *Skylark* already had played in Boston to middling success. The playwright-director was in Dennis to stage an updated interpretation when he caught Vivian's performance and immediately cast her as Myrtle Valentine, the shrewish, social-climbing wife of a millionaire. Prior to Vance's signing-on, her character had been called "Paulette Valentine," and was played by Lee Patrick.

Headlining *Skylark* was chic British stage star Gertrude Lawrence playing Lydia Kenyon, the disillusioned wife of an advertising executive, and the show opened in October 1939 at the Morosco Theater. The exact date was October 11—three days before Vivian's future employer, Desi Arnaz, came to Broadway's Imperial Theater with his breakthrough stage performance in the Richard Rodgers–Lorenz Hart musical, *Too Many Girls*.

From the pros with whom she worked, Vance now was endlessly learning tricks of the theatrical trade. Gertrude Lawrence gave her fashion tips: to gain attention, wear a lightly but attractively colored chiffon scarf; if you wish to appear as if you weigh less, wear a size larger than your actual one. From Antoinette Perry (the director of *Kiss the Boys Goodbye* and *Out from Under*), she learned that wrinkling her forehead would mar her appearance. From Paul Muni (with whom she would tour in *Counsellor-at-Law*), she learned how to use her hands. From George Abbott (who was to direct her in *It Takes Two*), she came to comprehend the essence of comedy.

"He once had me do a scene forty-seven times," Vance recalled years later. "Then he finally said, 'Viv, you're being funny in a funny part.' At last I knew what he meant: If the writer has done his job, all you have to do is read it. It was a flop show, but that didn't matter. Think of what I'd learned."

Skylark, meanwhile, was a milestone for Vance as a non-musical performer. Winsor French, reviewing the play in Cleveland during its pre-Broadway run, observed, "Vivian Vance is outstanding as the plotting wench Miss Lawrence uses another and somewhat more graphic word to describe." Added fellow Cleveland scribe William F. McDermott, "There are good performances by everybody else in the cast, including a vivid and acid portrayal of a hussy by Vivian Vance. . . ."

The New York critics echoed those in Cleveland. Brooks Atkinson noted in the *New York Times* that "Vivian Vance plays the unpleasant part of a blonde harpy with sleek venom." Burns Mantle, in the *Daily News*, wrote, "Vivian Vance serves the hell-cat admirably. . . ." Added John Mason Brown in the *New York Post*, "Vivian Vance is worthy of at least a red ribbon as a female candidate for the Dog Show."

Primarily, though, *Skylark* was conceived and written by Raphaelson as a star vehicle for Gertrude Lawrence. Sidney Whipple, reviewing the play in the *New York World-Telegram*, captured this in his write-up—while at the same time singling out Vance. Under the headline "Gertrude Lawrence Liked in Skylark, a New Comedy," Whipple noted, "Horace Sinclair, Walter Gilbert, William David, Gertrude Bryan, Robert Burton, and, in particular, Miss Vivian Vance gave excellent support."

Finally, Viv, at age thirty, was beginning to achieve her show-business dreams. She had a splashy role in a successful Broadway show that was *not* a musical, and she was being noticed by the critics.

Plus, for the first time in her life, she was truly, passionately, in love.

Chapter Ten

SCANDAL

With *Skylark*, Vivian Vance was assured of a long run in a solid Broadway hit. Nevertheless, six months after its October 1939 opening, Vivian was replaced by Florence Sundstrom and loaned out for a new show: *Out from Under*. This comedy, which was produced by Brock Pemberton and authored by John Walter Kelly, opened at the Biltmore Theater in May 1940. In retrospect, it is easy to understand why Vance was anxious to take a role in this production. One of her fellow players would be Phil Ober.

In *Out from Under*, Vance interpreted yet another un/Ethel Mertz/like role: a sultry, sexy character described by reviewers as a "hussy" and "blonde menace." It might be said that, just as Vivian became stereotyped as Ethel Mertz later on, she was pigeonholed at this point of her career as alluring vixens and "other women." In his *New York Daily Mirror* review, Robert Coleman wrote, "Philip Ober is as caddish and Vivian Vance as vampish as their roles demand." Otherwise, the play received indifferent reviews and closed after only nine performances.

Fortunately for Vance, after the failure of *Out from Under* she was able to immediately rejoin the *Skylark* cast. While *Out from Under* had quickly folded, what was destined to last was her relationship, which by now was quite romantic in nature, with Phil Ober. In July 1940, she returned to Albuquerque and obtained a divorce from George Koch on grounds of incompatibility.

After their divorce, Koch—like Danneck—was heard from no more. He moved around quite a bit and changed addresses almost yearly. According to directories maintained by New York City Local 802 of the American Federation of Musicians of the United States and Canada, he resided on different streets in Brooklyn through the 1940s. In 1950, he moved to Floral Park, Long Island, and then frequently switched residences in Queens and on Long Island. Over the next two decades he resided in Floral Park, Bayside, Fresh Meadows (where he lived the longest, at 67-55 B 193rd Lane, between 1955 and 1961), Forest Hills, Bayside again, and Flushing—and, in the early 1970s, settled in Miami Beach.

For all intents and purposes Vance's first two husbands ceased to exist in her life. These marriages would be viewed as little secrets, youthful follies. She eventually would wed Phil Ober and, to the world, he was known as her first husband.

While Vance was Mrs. George Koch when she became enamored with Ober, he, too, was officially unavailable. His wife was the former Phyllis Roper—from a socially prominent Westchester, New York, family—whom he had married in 1923. What's more, he was the father of a daughter, Emily.

From the very beginning of their friendship, according to Marjorie Lord, Vance "made no secret of her attraction to [Ober]. I know she went through a lot, [because] Phil, too, was married. His wife was kind of wild, I guess, and crazy. She was very hard on Vivian. But they had decided that they were for each other."

After one too many late nights out with Vivian, Ober was suspected by his wife of dallying in an extramarital affair. So she hired three private detectives to spy on him. Coincidentally, at the time, Ober was appearing on Broadway as a detective in the Owen Davis mystery-comedy *Mr. and Mrs. North.*

At the divorce hearing that followed, detective Michael J. Karmaly testified before Justice Philip J. McCook that on the night of February 6, 1941, he observed Vance meet Ober by the stage door of the Belasco Theater, the venue that housed *Mr. and Mrs. North.* The sleuth followed them to Vance's apartment, number 7B, at 1 University Place, a stylish building in Greenwich Village. Before arriving there, they stopped to purchase sandwiches. Ober remained in Vance's apartment even after the lights were extinguished at two A.M.

The scenario was repeated the following evening. On that occasion, Karmaly and his cronies remained by the apartment in a parked car until eight A.M. One newspaper report had the detectives then calling Mrs. Ober, who in the company of her brother paid a visit to 1 University Place. Another report had Phyllis Roper Ober joining the gumshoes during their vigil—and Karmaly placing one of her hairpins in Vance's door in such a way that it would fall if the door were to be opened.

In any event, Karmaly, Mrs. Ober, and the others eventually "walked boldly up to the door" (as one newspaper described it). "I rang the doorbell," Mrs. Ober alleged in her complaint, "and was answered by a woman's voice demanding to know who I was. I told her I wanted my husband. She replied, 'Mr. Ober is not here.' I just kept ringing the bell for twenty-five minutes. Then the door suddenly opened and my husband stepped out."

Another tabloid account reported the facts a bit differently. Here, Mrs. Ober and company actually entered Vance's apartment, where they found Ober in pajamas. In a third, it was alleged that "Miss Vance, said Karmaly, could be seen through the door—and it was no stage costume she had on."

The press had a field day with the story, printing articles with such headlines as "Wife of Actor Tells of Raid" and "Linked to Blonde—Pin Didn't Drop." One blurb, titled "Actor's Wife Sues; Names Blonde Star," spotlighted a picture of Vivian which emphasized her shapely gams. Another, headlined, "Linked to Blonde by Drop of a Pin," included a head shot of Vance in which she looked like a tough and world-weary dame in a Warner Bros. melodrama. A third, titled "Vivian Denies Everything," featured a photo of a sultry, pouting Vance that made her appear to be a cross between Mata Hari and Cleopatra. It reported that, subsequent to the divorce hearing, Vance had filed an affidavit in which she denied that she shared her apartment with Ober or that the actor had bought her a car. She also labeled Mrs. Ober's charges "ridiculous," and described her friendship with Ober as "platonic."

One of the newspaper reports—which certainly would have turned Fred and Ethel Mertz purple—described her as "blonde, lissome Vivian Vance, once of the *Red, Hot and Blue!* cast." Others labeled her "comely Vivian Vance" and "the beautiful Vivian Vance."

In her divorce suit, Mrs. Ober also charged that her husband had not supported her for ten months. Earlier, she had been awarded $75 a week temporary alimony by Justice Aaron J. Levy, pending a hearing on the matter. Then she was granted her divorce by Justice McCook, along with custody of their daughter and 35 percent of Ober's future income.

Ober did not contest the decision.

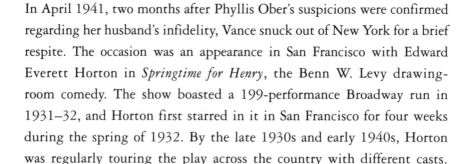

In April 1941, two months after Phyllis Ober's suspicions were confirmed regarding her husband's infidelity, Vance snuck out of New York for a brief respite. The occasion was an appearance in San Francisco with Edward Everett Horton in *Springtime for Henry*, the Benn W. Levy drawing-room comedy. The show boasted a 199-performance Broadway run in 1931–32, and Horton first starred in it in San Francisco for four weeks during the spring of 1932. By the late 1930s and early 1940s, Horton was regularly touring the play across the country with different casts. One of the many venues in which he performed it was the Albuquerque Little Theater.

Marjorie Lord occasionally appeared opposite Horton; she previously had been in the show when it played at, among other venues, the Ridgeway Theater in White Plains, the Brighton Theater in Brooklyn, and the Bass Rocks Theater in Gloucester, Massachusetts. Vance joined Horton and Lord at San Francisco's Alcazar Theater. Her role was Julia Jelliwell, a married woman involved in an affair with her husband's best friend.

"She and I lived together for about two months," remembers Lord. "First we stayed in Edward's guest house [in Los Angeles] for a few weeks, and would work at his house rehearsing, and then up in San Francisco we had an apartment together.

"We came out on the train together with Edward. He would have loved to have had her stay and do the show in Los Angeles, but she didn't because of Phil. She wouldn't come back to Los Angeles with us because she was so in love with Phil. She wanted to get back to New York."

By that time, Lord and Vance had become fast friends, a relationship they maintained for the rest of Viv's life. "I was crazy about Vivian," Lord notes. "She was very straightforward, so funny. She was naturally funny. She would come out with remarks that were very amusing."

Lord cites an incident that dates to the time when she and Vance were appearing in *Springtime for Henry*. "I was raised in San Francisco, and it's rather a dressy city," she explains. "One day I was going out and had gotten a little careless.

"Vivian said, '*Where* are your gloves? You *can't* go out in San Francisco without your gloves. You ought to know that!' Then later in Los Angeles one day I ran into her and we were talking and I said, 'I remember how tough you were on me when I didn't wear my gloves.' She said, 'Oh God, I'm *all* over that now. I'm in Los Angeles, so who cares!'"

♥

By late spring, when Vance returned to New York, Ober's divorce was final. The lovers were married on August 12, 1941 in Marblehead, Massachusetts, where he was playing in a summer theater production of *Mr. and Mrs. North*. The two set up housekeeping in an apartment on West Ninth Street in Greenwich Village.

It was around this time that Sheila MacRae—who was then known as Sheila Stephens—met Viv and Phil. "I was fifteen and Gordy [her future husband, Gordon MacRae] was in a play that Vivian Vance's husband was in. He was charming and gorgeous.

"She was a very sweet person. She wasn't at all acerbic, like the character she played [on *I Love Lucy*]. But he [Ober] was the breadwinner then. He was the guy. He was very good onstage."

Vance also then became acquainted with performer Elliott Reid, who years later would appear on both *I Love Lucy* and *The Lucy Show*. "I liked her, and got along well with her," recalls Reid. "I first met Vivian back in 1941 at a summer theater in White Plains, New York. She was married then to an actor named Philip Ober, an amiable man and a good actor, and Vivian came up from New York to see the show he and I were in and I recall our standing around a large convertible, in a big lot behind the theater, and listening [for the first time, in my case] to Henry Morgan, whose irreverent disdain for his sponsors had burst upon the radio scene and was something truly new and funny. We all laughed a lot and Vivian was very pretty and—obviously—had an excellent sense of humor."

During this period, Vance returned to the Albuquerque Little Theater to star as *Anna Christie,* Eugene O'Neill's Swedish prostitute heroine. She always would think warmly and highly of the theater, and the citizens of what now was her official hometown. Upon the success of her next Broadway musical, Cole Porter's *Let's Face It*, she smiled, "Now, won't Albuquerque be pleased!" Proudly, she billed herself in the show's program as "Albuquerque's gift to the theater."

The story goes that Broadway producer Vinton Freedley, who previously had viewed Vance only as a lady of the chorus or understudy, saw Viv in *Springtime for Henry* in San Francisco. He was impressed and eventually signed her for a featured role in *Let's Face It*, which primarily served as a showcase for a young Brooklyn-born comedian named Danny Kaye.

The show was an adaptation of *The Cradle Snatchers,* a hit 1925 farce about a trio of capricious, middle-aged wives who hire three inexperienced youths (one of whom was played by twenty-five-year-old Humphrey Bogart) to romance them because they think their own husbands are unfaithful. In the musical update, the gigolos became young draftees.

Let's Face It opened in October 1941 at the Imperial Theater. By this time, war had been raging in Europe for two years. Would America enter the fray, and go into battle against Adolf Hitler's Third Reich? Or would the United States remain on the sidelines, and continue embracing an iso-lationist foreign policy?

Despite the chaos abroad, Broadway then was home to a host of mem-orable shows, including Lillian Hellman's dramatic *Watch on the Rhine,* Noël Coward's amusing *Blithe Spirit,* and Joseph Kesselring's hilarious *Arsenic and Old Lace.* Concluding its lengthy New York run at the time was *Lady in the Dark,* with a sophisticated libretto about psychoanalysis writ-ten by Moss Hart, with music and lyrics by Kurt Weill and Ira Gershwin. In the lead was Gertrude Lawrence, the star of *Skylark.* Giving a star-mak-ing turn in support was Danny Kaye, who would leave that show to head-line in *Let's Face It.*

Vance, Eve Arden, and Edith Meiser appeared in the new production as the married women. While Kaye (playing one of the GIs) received the bulk of the critical kudos, Vance and her fellow performers were not ignored. Wrote John Anderson in the *New York Journal-American,* "As the three frustrated matrons, Miss Arden, Edith Meiser, and Vivian Vance are immensely amusing." Added John Mason Brown in the *New York World-Telegram,* "As the erring wives Vivian Vance, Edith Meiser, and Eve Arden are highly entertaining. Miss Vance has an agreeable blond insouciance."

As *Let's Face It* settled in at the Imperial, Ober, too, found a role in a hit play: *Junior Miss,* the Jerome Chodorov–Joseph Fields comedy, charting the antics of the thirteen-year-old title character, which debuted at the Lyceum. "His stage door and mine are only a block away," Vance commented at the time. "We're just about the luckiest and happiest couple in New York. Think of each of us being in a Broadway hit with a long run ahead."

Still, the underlying tension and competitiveness that was to charac-terize their relationship—a union of two actors with fragile egos—was apparent as Vance added, "But it wasn't quite so simple when we were both rehearsing." On the day after *Let's Face It* opened and was certified a hit, there was a special preview performance of *Junior Miss* before it began its out-of-town tryout. "Phil came to the first night of our show," Vance continued, "and it did look like a hit. We were delighted, but there wasn't a wink of sleep in our apartment that night. By the time I calmed down from the excitement of my opening he began to worry and shudder over his preview. I couldn't sleep because I was happy and he couldn't sleep because he was miserable."

By now, the manner in which Vance and Ober's adultery and Ober's subsequent divorce had been publicized was long-forgotten by the ever-fickle media. Prior to its Broadway bow, *Let's Face It* previewed in Boston—and, in his *Boston American* column, journalist George Holland depicted the duo as lovebirds. Holland wrote, "The ROMANTIC STATUS OF VIVIAN VANCE [the caps are Holland's], the beautiful Mrs. Bewildered of 'Let's Face It,' and Phil Ober, the fine actor, was confirmed at [Boston's] Latin Quarter . . . Phil is rehearsing in the most important role [in] 'Junior Miss,' the Max Gordon show soon to be in our midst . . . But Phil flew to Boston yesterday . . . Not only did he and Miss Vance sit in adjacent seats at the Latin Quarter's ringside, they insisted on holding hands . . . The censor, however, could have no solid grounds for objection . . . Miss Vance is Mrs. Phil Ober. . . . "

Another report, published in the *New York Herald Tribune* a year into the Broadway runs of *Let's Face It* and *Junior Miss*, portrayed Vance and Ober as an amiable if slightly competitive theatrical couple. They had friendly wagers on whose show would outlast the other, and would accompany each other to radio interviews. "Invite Ober to do a broadcast on behalf of 'Junior Miss,'" wrote the anonymous scribe, "and invariably Miss Vance trots along to say something about 'Let's Face It,' and vice versa. They have probably done more radio work as a husband and wife team for their respective productions than any pair this season."

At this point in time, the Obers each were theatrical nomads who had not set down roots. Now they were newlyweds, with what they had every reason to believe would be a happy marriage in front of them, and so they felt compelled to add some degree of permanency to their lives. Viv had remained especially fond of the Southwest, and so she contacted her kid brother, Robert, in Albuquerque with a request: "Find us a piece of New Mexico." She and Phil sent him a movie camera to shoot available acreage.

Viv's obliging sibling shot footage of four acres in Cubero, west of Albuquerque, near Mount Taylor and just off what then was known as Highway 66. The Obers purchased the property, on which they built a modest adobe house. They had their own electricity and a well from which they fetched their water. Over the course of their marriage, this house would serve as their getaway, their haven from the professional rat race in New York and Los Angeles.

♥

In the early 1940s, in between her theatrical gigs, Vance became involved in the activities of the American Theater Wing, which today is best known as the sponsor of Broadway's Tony Awards. The organization's roots date back to 1917, also marking the United States' entry into World War I. At that time, seven women of the stage—Rachel Crothers, Louise Closser Hale, Dorothy Donnelly, Josephine Hull, Minnie Dupree, Bessie Tyree, and Louise Drew—came together and instigated the formation of Stage Women's War Relief. This committee coordinated the collection of clothing and food for war refugees, spearheaded Liberty Bond drives, established a Broadway "canteen" as a spot in which soldiers could socialize, and organized groups of performers who went off to entertain the troops.

In 1939, upon Hitler's invasion of Poland and the official outset of World War II, the committee was reinitiated and soon renamed the American Theater Wing. For a brief while, it became a branch of the British War Relief Society. Minutes from a workroom committee, headed by actress Lucile Watson and dated June 9, 1940, indicate that Vance (along with Ruth Gordon, Uta Hagen, and Peggy Conklin) was in attendance.

Five weeks after *Let's Face It* made its Broadway bow in the fall of 1941, and Viv settled in for what would be a 547-performance run, the Japanese bombed Pearl Harbor and the United States was thrust into World War II. With box-office profits earned from the film *Stage Door Canteen* (1943), which dramatized the activities of the fabled haven for troops, the Wing handed $75,000 over to the USO to initiate performances of dramatic plays to be mounted for GIs stationed overseas.

In 1944, after her tenure in *Let's Face It*, Vance and Ober traveled to North Africa and Italy as part of the initial USO dramatic unit to be sent abroad. Viv appeared as an offbeat writer à la Dorothy Parker, whose middle-aged husband suffers through the severity of life in officers' candidate school, in a mounting of Ruth Gordon's wartime comedy *Over 21*. This production had the distinction of being the initial full-length play presented by American actors in a theater of war.

"I am sure we had lots more fun than the companies that came later after the rules were set up," Vance once noted. "We performed everywhere. We played the Opera House in Algiers one week. We played a whitewashed barn on the edge of nowhere the next. It went on like that for months."

However, this chaotic wartime experience was only a prelude to Vivian's abrupt awareness of a battle she unknowingly had been fighting within herself for her entire life.

Chapter Eleven

BREAKDOWN

Of her early years in New York, Vance recalled midway through her 1950s tenure on *I Love Lucy*, "I just kept working at everything in every spot I could find. I got plenty of experience and you know it all comes in handy now. It seems there isn't much I can't do when it comes to working out routines on this TV show. There's nothing like a lot of experience when the big break comes."

This last statement is particularly revealing. Despite her years on the stage, earning the respect of noted playwright Russel Crouse and being featured with the likes of such talent as Danny Kaye and Ed Wynn and Gertrude Lawrence and seeing her name shining in lights on a Broadway marquee, Vance did not think much of her pre–*I Love Lucy* show-business career.

As she won fame playing Ethel Mertz, she perceived all of her theater work not as an end in itself, let alone the fulfillment of a childhood dream, but solely as preparation for *I Love Lucy*. She never really could savor the fact that, while no Broadway legend, she had become a respected and regularly employed working actress.

Those who would meet Vance during this period would be impressed by her extroverted personality, her effervescence and gregariousness and generosity. Yet there was a dark and disturbing side to her, an aspect of her character that came to overwhelm her to the point where, almost immediately upon her return home after her *Over 21* USO tour, she had a nervous breakdown. Vivian would readily admit to her illness over the course of the decades—even when she was at her peak as Ethel Mertz.

Vance first revealed the details of her trouble in 1955, when her byline appeared on an article in *McCall's* magazine headlined, "I Don't Run Away Any More." In it, she described the breakdown in no uncertain terms as "plain hell." "I have never told this story before," Vance wrote. "I have not wished to. The reasons aren't difficult to understand. They have nothing to do with vanity, or endangering my career, or even the possibility of relapse should I open an old wound. There simply seemed no reason to tell the story. My case, I felt, was as special as a clinical history of beri-beri, as isolated from common problems as dengue fever, and therefore of no conceivable general interest, let alone therapeutic value or assistance."

Vance then declared that she had chosen to make known her plight because she had since learned that there were millions like her living "in the gray-night world from which I have been led. . . . I know them and they are my friends. Not because we have met, but because of the sympathetic bond between us. I know that their hands perspire in strange, unidentified fears, that their stomachs contract in nausea if their boss fails to smile at them, that they walk alone in queer, numbing depression wherever they may be, and that always they are afraid."

These were somber and disturbing words coming from one of America's most celebrated television clowns.

Vance then went on to declare that the emotional help she had received came through psychiatry, which enabled her to realize that her primary enemy was "ignorance" and that "you cannot conquer fear until you have learned what it is you're afraid of." Then she added, "I had passed thirty-five before I realized that one can no more neglect chronic unhappiness than one can neglect an infected tooth. If misery, like a tooth, is left too long to fester the infection spreads and deepens. This is what happened to me."

♥

Vivian's predicament had been apparent for years before it actually manifested itself. For example, back in 1937–38 when she was appearing in the musical *Hooray for What!*, she should have been jubilant because she finally had won a starring role on Broadway. Yet beyond her surface glee, she really was anything but happy. During the 200-performance run of the show, Vance recalled, "I was the tiredest person you have ever heard of. I rested every moment I was not on my feet, but I was never refreshed."

Vance slept for ten hours each night. During the day, she was constantly sneaking catnaps. Yet she still was endlessly fatigued. She was feeling pain in her left arm, and for long periods of time was unable to digest her food. One of her fellow actors told her that her problems were "psychosomatic." "I had never heard the word until then," Vance remembered. "I looked it up. Strangely enough, this amateur Dr. Freud was, in all likelihood, correct."

In 1945, upon her return home from playing *Over 21* abroad for the troops, Vance joined the Chicago company of *The Voice of the Turtle,* John Van Druten's smash-hit romantic comedy. The venue was the Selwyn Theater and her costars were Hugh Marlowe and K. T. Stevens, who were real-life husband and wife. She replaced Betty Lawford in the "other woman" role of Olive Lashbrooke, a wisecracking actress played in the 1947 screen version by Eve Arden, who had been Vance's co-conspirator in *Let's Face It.*

In a publicity still for the tour of *The Voice of the Turtle,* taken with Marlowe and Stevens, Vance is garbed fashionably in a Chanel-style suit and ankle-strapped pumps. Her hair is carefully coifed in tight curls, and she appears to be cool, composed, and in control. Yet Vivian was, after all, no more than an actress playing a role and posing for a photograph. Inside, she was akin to a time bomb ticking down, perilous seconds away from exploding.

"One day I was up and around, no more or less unhappy than usual, not conscious that for years I had been building up to what happened," Vance later wrote. "The next I was lying in bed in my hotel room, my hands shaking helplessly, in violent nausea, weeping hysterically from causes I did not know, unable for a long while to move."

Several days earlier, all of this was foreshadowed when Vance was onstage at the Windy City's Selwyn Theater. In one scene, she was supposed to lift an ashtray. "I began to do it, and could not move," she remembered. "The brain ordered, but the arm declined. It was one of the most sickening moments I have ever gone through."

Eventually, Vance was able to reach a telephone. Because she knew no physicians in Chicago, she phoned one from out of town who recommended two local doctors. Vance eventually visited both, neither of whom recognized that she was in the throes of mental distress. The first bluntly explained that she was perfectly fine. The second suggested she take vitamin B1.

So Vance continued to outwardly function in her world. She was unable to perform on the night of her hotel-room episode. As she had no understudy at the time, the show was canceled, but she quickly pulled herself together and continued playing acerbic Olive Lashbrooke.

All the while, she was having difficulty keeping her equilibrium. "Every normal function of my body—heart, blood, pulse—roared in my ears," Vance revealed. "I do not mean that I *thought* they roared. They roared. I wept ceaselessly over nothing. I was exhausted, but I could not sleep. I was afraid to leave my room and afraid to stay in it. The walls grew closer. Long after midnight, time after time, I had to leave the hotel and take endless, aimless walks through Chicago streets. . . ."

Nor did Vance choose to inform her husband, Phil Ober, of the experience. At the time, Ober was appearing in a San Francisco production of the Norman Krasna comedy *Dear Ruth*. "I could not, you see, bring myself to be a burden to him or to anyone else," Vance explained. "In some people that is a noble reflex. In me it was just another neurotic symptom."

Eventually, after a second episode that rivaled the first in intensity—this one on the final day of 1945—Ober was called to the scene. He and Vance returned to San Francisco for some rest, and she even recuperated to the point where she was able to rejoin the Chicago cast of *The Voice of the Turtle*. After yet another breakdown, she finally left the show and joined Ober in New York and then on the road.

During this time, Vance did little more than ponder her plight in solitary confinement. She was barely able to leave her living quarters under her own power. "Once in a while I would make it, but not often," she recalled. "But even then I could not, without Phil, walk farther than the nearest corner, hurrying back again in terror to this psychological blanket I had pulled over myself."

The hastiness of Vance's exit from *The Voice of the Turtle* is reflected in the show's *Stagebill*. In the program, issued for the week beginning Sunday, January 6, 1946, it is noted that *The Voice of the Turtle* is a three-character play. However, on page 5 are the credits "Alfred de Liagre, Jr. presents John Van Druten's Comedy THE VOICE OF THE TURTLE with K. T. Stevens and Hugh Marlowe." On pages 7 and 8 are the biographies of Stevens and Marlowe. On page 11 is the cast list: Sally Middleton . . . K. T. Stevens; Olive Lashbrooke . . . Patricia Neal; and Bill Page . . . Hugh Marlowe.

There is no bio of relative newcomer Patricia Neal. This is her first mention in the *Stagebill*. Yet on page 15, there is a photo of four smiling faces with the following caption: "Hugh Marlowe, K. T. Stevens, producer Alfred de Liagre, Jr., and Vivian Vance sang 'Happy Birthday To Us' at a party recently held to celebrate the first anniversary of the Chicago engagement of *The Voice of the Turtle*."

Patricia Neal recalls that she recently had come to Chicago to understudy the two women's roles in the play. "I was much too young—only nineteen at the time," she explains, "but the darling producer, Alfred de Liagre, seemed to like me. I understudied first in New York and then was sent to Chicago where Vivian and K. T. Stevens played the parts. I am not sure how many weeks I was there, maybe two months, when Vivian had a terrible nervous breakdown on New Year's Eve. I played the part from then for about three weeks until they found a replacement.

"Vivian had left Chicago with her husband. I really didn't know her well, but she was very kind to me."

In retrospect, some of Vance's friends could see her full breakdown coming. Hugh Marlowe eventually told her that he and K. T. Stevens had observed disturbing behavior on her part at the time. For one thing, she was putting forth an overly impassioned display of affection toward her dog, to the point where she was using baby talk in public to communicate with the pet. For another, she had let her dressing room deteriorate into a mess, even though she was known for being systematically tidy.

In February 1947, over a full year after that final, calamitous emotional collapse in Chicago, Vance had recovered to the point where she was able to accept work in a new, George Abbott–directed production. She appeared with her good friends Martha Scott and Hugh Marlowe in *It Takes Two*, a poorly reviewed "comedy of marital manners" that closed after eight performances. By now, Vance—like Bill Frawley—would receive critical accolades even when the vehicle she was in was beneath her talents. A typical example was the *Variety* review. While the play was panned, the critic observed that "Vivian Vance, with some of the sharper lines in the show, does fine." Under the headline, *"It Takes Two* Is Just a Thin and Shaky Comedy about Our Housing Shortage," *New York Sun* reviewer Ward Morehouse noted, "Vivian Vance, pride of Albuquerque, N.M., gets touches of comedy into the role of a well-meaning and sharp-cracking friend."

Clearly, though, Vance still was deeply troubled. "When we worked together," Scott would recall decades later, "Viv was as effervescent offstage as on. She often had me screaming with laughter. She has always been so generous that people hesitate to admire anything she owns for fear she'll insist on giving it to them. But in those days . . . she was also very much wrapped up in herself. When we roomed together during a Boston tryout, I began to realize what an awful time she was having inside herself."

Vance remembered that George Abbott, the director of *It Takes Two*, aided her immensely "by handling me with a sort of brisk nonsympathy— that is, with neither more nor less sympathy than he would have shown a stable person. And my dear friend [Broadway and radio star] Shirley Booth, who had had more than a spot of upset herself, would sit and try to cheer me over an endless succession of lunches at Sardi's, driving in again and again with the affirmation that this, too, would pass."

Yet Vance was far from over her frightening, consuming malaise. During this time, whenever she would venture from her living quarters out into the world, she would write her name and address on a piece of paper and place it in her handbag. She did so purely as a precaution, just so she would have proper identification if she "went crazy, which I firmly thought I was going to do."

During the hot months of 1947, Vance appeared in summer stock in *Counsellor-at-Law*, Elmer Rice's biting drama about a fabled Jewish lawyer threatened with disbarment because of a prior violation of ethics. The star was the great Paul Muni. Helming the production was Marc Daniels, who would go on to become *I Love Lucy*'s first director in 1951.

The tour was mercifully brief, with the play being presented only in a high school auditorium in Marblehead, Massachusetts, and at the McCarter Theater in Princeton, New Jersey. Yet it was not fleeting enough for Vance to avoid developing a sexual interest in fifty-one-year-old Muni. While romance and sexual coupling among actors who work closely together for brief periods of time is not unheard of, this infatuation was like playing with fire for all concerned, given Vance's highly fragile emotional state.

In December 1947, Vance returned to Broadway in a prestigious— albeit brief—tenth-anniversary revival of *The Cradle Will Rock*, Marc Blitzstein's controversial, incendiary Depression-era musical. Its scenario pits Mr. Mister, an avaricious town patriarch, against Larry Foreman, a socially committed activist who organizes the workers in Mr. Mister's steel factory into a union.

Vance was second-billed after star Alfred Drake, who was cast as Foreman. She played Mrs. Mister opposite Will Geer's Mr. Mister; Geer, who was to become known to a generation of television viewers as Grandpa on *The Waltons* (1972–78), was the lone member of the cast who had appeared in the show's original production. Howard da Silva, the director of the revival, had played Foreman in the earlier version.

Vance's "Who's Who in the Cast" biography breathlessly and merrily spun off her credits: "Vinton Freedley's *Anything Goes* . . . an assignment in his *Red, Hot and Blue!* . . . a musical fling in Ed Wynn's *Hooray for What!* . . ." and so on through *It Takes Two*, which came "on the heels of a long engagement in the Chicago variation of *The Voice of the Turtle*." And Ward Morehouse, reviewing the show in the *New York Sun*, observed, "Vivian Vance, always a good trouper, brings exuberance to her playing as Mrs. Mister."

To the outside world, Vance was a solid and busy stage actress. There was, of course, still no public hint of her psychological turmoil.

The light at the end of Vance's tunnel of hell initially appeared when she and Ober were attending a party in Philadelphia. She found herself fascinated by a fellow guest, a woman whom she learned was a psychiatrist. Vance inquired if she could see the doctor the next time she "went overboard." Thus initiated her journey to understanding—and truly recovering from—her illness.

"The beginnings of most psychiatric difficulties go back to childhood, and mine were no different," Vance explained. "I was beset [this was not to be revealed until my cure, and was never up to then a part of my conscious knowledge] by a sense of wrongdoing, actually of sin."

On one hand, Vance had been possessed by "a compulsive, an irresistible, urge to act. I could no more have fought it than I could have willed myself not to breathe." Yet at the same time, she had to contend with "the deep-set, unshakable conviction on the part of my mother and father, splendid folk but tempered in inflexible religious and moral dogma, that the stage was a sinful business."

And so, Vance concluded, "The conflict thus set up within me started a neurosis. . . ."

From an early age, her interest in (not to mention talent for) dramatics was evident. Young Vivian had given such an effective performance as an elderly Chinaman in her high school production of *East Is West* that she had fooled her father. At the same time, she did not receive the support and encouragement for her endeavors that every child deserves from every parent. As a result, she was overwhelmed by conflict and guilt.

It took decades for Vance to reconcile herself with her parents. "When he died [in 1958]," she said of her father decades later, "there was a great void in my life, because he was always the one I wanted to show. . . . He was the one I called up first and said, 'Daddy, I just won an Emmy.'" This was in 1954, for playing Ethel Mertz. "It's only recently, since television, that I've made my peace with my mother," Viv added. "Now she can sit in the living room and say, 'That's my girl there on the TV.'"

Despite her early professional encouragement from Kathryn Kennedy and the others at the Albuquerque Little Theater, Vance had won neither immediate nor smashing success on the New York stage. Many starry-eyed hopefuls would come to New York or Hollywood only to meet with constant rejection and end up quietly returning in defeat to Des Moines or Dubuque or Albuquerque. This may not have been Vance's career fate, but she initially lived the insecure lifestyle of a struggling actress: a member of the chorus and an understudy and featured performer who did not know how long or short her next run would be. Yet Vance was driven by an unquenchable thirst for fame. This is emphasized in the headlines of two newspaper features on her as she won her initial Broadway laurels: "She Wouldn't Quit Trying" and "An Author's Heart-Rending Tale of a Girl's Fight to Make Good."

While she did not earn high-level stardom, Vance eventually did achieve the respect of her peers and a certain modicum of success on the stage. Her list of credits steadily grew, and she won over a host of influential allies. Yet she was miserable and insecure. "Nothing but flamboyant triumph could overcome my sense of inadequacy," Vance observed, "and even that, as I was to learn, did not overcome it—it merely anesthetized."

So this "sense of inadequacy" only compounded her neuroses. As her stage career progressed, Vance received her share of positive and complimentary press. For instance, a *New York World-Telegram* profile of Vance, published way back in December 1937, when she was appearing in *Hooray for What!*, was headlined: "Albuquerque Gave Benefit to Send Her Here, and Now Vivian Vance's Name Is Up in Lights." Despite this accomplishment, she still felt she had yet to prove herself as a performer by embracing stardom. Just before *Out from Under* opened in May 1940, all of Vance's insecurities shone through when she revealingly declared, "I hope what they say about [producer] Brock Pemberton having discovered so many famous actors and actresses is really true. Brother, if it is, I'm on my way up right now."

Not helping her was her chosen profession, with all its preoccupation with surface glamour and fantasy. "This world of make-believe is dangerous for an actress," she observed in 1962. "It's easy to slip across the line from reality. . . . And it can get bad. So when you read about a famed actress who commits suicide do so with compassion and understanding. Don't condemn; try to understand."

Vance's conflict was further intensified by the fact that she felt she had selfishly chosen a career in an ego-driven profession. Sure, she may have been active with the American Theater Wing, and had entertained the front-line troops in *Over 21*. Nonetheless, her lack of self-worth was compounded by a sense that she was "making too much money and not contributing anything to mankind."

At least now, as she entered and became deeply immersed in analysis, Vance finally was taking constructive steps that allowed her to understand and work out her ongoing emotional problems.

Vance and Ober were visiting his family in Kennebunkport, Maine, in 1949 when they received a call from their actor friend Mel Ferrer, who wanted them to come to Hollywood to appear in an RKO film he was directing, *The Secret Fury* (1950). "It was the first of several post-treatment tests," Vance recalled. "Fate wasted no time in putting me through the jumps in my new life. . . . I was scared—it was a new medium—but I accepted. It worked out all right."

The Secret Fury was a poorly reviewed melodrama that, ironically, charted the plight of a psychologically tormented woman (Claudette Colbert). Of his and Vance's small roles in this thriller, which featured Robert Ryan, Ober remarked curtly, "We both got killed."

Had Vance and Ober come to Hollywood a decade or two earlier, they more than likely would have signed standard, seven-year, major-studio acting contracts. However, because of the changing economics in Hollywood, there were no such pacts awaiting these two middle-aged latecomers to the screen medium. So when filming of *The Secret Fury* was completed, the couple returned to Maine and spent another year in Kennebunkport.

Vance returned to California for a second screen role in RKO's *The Blue Veil* (1951), a well-received tearjerker about a war widow (Jane Wyman) who loses her own baby and devotes the rest of her life to selflessly caring for the children of others. Given her future disdain for playing the wife of Bill Frawley, Vance's part in *The Blue Veil* is ironic. At one point in the Curtis Bernhardt–directed adult drama, Wyman's character looks after the motherless child of a corset manufacturer. He summarily proposes marriage, but ends up wed to his secretary (Vance) after he is rejected by Wyman's character. So not only was Vance cast as a man's second choice as a mate, but the actor playing the role was no Hollywood hunk. Rather, he was the rotund and homely Charles Laughton.

♥

After filming *The Blue Veil,* Vance and Ober settled in at their New Mexico ranch. Had she not been cast in *I Love Lucy*, Viv might have used the spread as her home base and safe haven, intermittently returning to Hollywood for screen and television roles—and developing an entirely different career as a dramatic supporting player. In fact, during this period, Vance actually did slip off to New York to appear on live television, working with Marc Daniels, her *Counsellor-at-Law* director, who soon would be hired for *I Love Lucy.*

In the summer of 1951, there came a second call to Vance from Mel Ferrer—one that would forever alter her life. This time, he was mounting productions of *The Voice of the Turtle* and *Come Back, Little Sheba* at the La Jolla Playhouse in southern California. Ferrer wished to cast Phil Ober in *Sheba*, opposite screen veteran Una Merkel, and Vance as Olive Lashbrooke in *Turtle*.

Upon hearing the name of the play, Vance recalled, "Everything rushed back at once: nausea, throat constriction, abject terror. But it lasted no more than a minute. Phil was talking to me. I might as well tackle it, all or nothing. I did the play. In the wings, a moment before the curtain rose, I nearly fainted. Then I spoke my first line, and knew I was all right."

Later that summer, Vance and Ober returned to New Mexico to star in *Over 21*, appearing in Santa Fe, Albuquerque, and Los Alamos. However, it was at La Jolla where Desi Arnaz saw Vivian's performance and offered her the role of her lifetime—Ethel Mertz, on *I Love Lucy*.

Part Three

THE MERTZES

Frawley gives Vance a quizzical look. (PHOTO COURTESY OF GLOBE)

Frawley and Vance cavort as "Fred and Ethel." (PHOTO COURTESY OF GLOBE)

Chapter Twelve

FRED AND ETHEL

The roles of Fred and Ethel Mertz on *I Love Lucy* were fated to earn William Frawley and Vivian Vance a celebrityhood that eludes most supporting players—and it is difficult today to imagine any other performers in these beloved characterizations. Yet neither actor was the automatic first choice to play these key TV sitcom parts.

The stories surrounding the casting of Fred and Ethel are by now familiar ones and component parts of the *I Love Lucy* mythos. More to the point, though, they reflect on the backgrounds and careers of Frawley and Vance.

Upon deciding to develop a situation comedy for TV in which they would star, Lucille Ball and Desi Arnaz formed Desilu Productions— which made them the show's once and future bosses. When *I Love Lucy* was in its initial stages of actual development, in 1951, the characters of the Mertzes did not exist.

"I remember in the early days when *Lucy* started, they [Lucille Ball and Desi Arnaz] weren't sure who or what they wanted," recalls actress Sheila

MacRae. "In the first place, they didn't even know if there would be a couple next door [as there had been on *My Favorite Husband*]." *My Favorite Husband*, the precursor of *I Love Lucy*, was Ball's popular half-hour radio series. The domestic comedy was heard on CBS from July 1948 through March 1951 and starred Lucy as Liz Cooper, the birdbrained wife of Midwestern banker George Cooper, played by Richard Denning.

In the original *I Love Lucy* pilot—the test, shot on March 2, 1951, to convince CBS network executives and potential advertisers that Desi Arnaz would make a believable sitcom husband for his real-life wife, Lucille Ball—Fred and Ethel are nonexistent. Originally, *I Love Lucy* was supposed to have a third regular character: Jerry, club performer Ricky Ricardo's talent agent and best friend, played by Jerry Hausner, a forty-one-year-old actor who occasionally had played roles on *My Favorite Husband*. This character even appears in the pilot. Eventually, it was decided that Jerry would be on the show only sporadically—thus depriving Hausner of an opportunity to become a television legend.

At the same time, it was deemed that the evolving TV show should have husband-and-wife supporting characters. As Jess Oppenheimer, the show's producer and head writer, once explained, "And we could pair them off couple against couple, women against men, or haves against have-nots—all setups which had worked for us on the radio series." Indeed, on *My Favorite Husband*, the characters of George and Liz Cooper were supported by a duo who were second bananas/comic foils: Rudolph Atterbury, George's bank president boss, and Iris, Atterbury's wife and Liz's best pal.

It was decided that the new characters on this New York City–set program would be an older couple. Their connection to Ricky and Lucy Ricardo was that they owned the small Manhattan apartment building in which Lucy and Ricky lived; even so, the Ricardos would be more affluent. Their addition also would allow the series to offer differing perspectives on marriage.

And so Fred and Ethel Mertz were born. They were named for a couple from Indianapolis who lived down the street from Madelyn Pugh, one of *I Love Lucy*'s original writers.

Next, the right actors had to be hired for the roles. Character comedian Gale Gordon (who had played Rudolph Atterbury on radio and was to support Lucille Ball in her subsequent TV sitcoms) originally was cast as Fred. This did not work out because Gordon, age forty-five, already was under exclusive contract to appear on the radio version of *Our Miss Brooks* (1948–52) as high school principal Osgood Conklin, a role he would continue playing when the show was transferred to television. He remained on the show for its entire run, which began in 1952 and ended four years later. (There was also the obstacle of Gordon's relatively high salary demands.)

Veteran character actor James Gleason, age sixty-five, was considered and he, as Gordon, would have made an excellent choice. Yet Gleason's demand of $3,500 per week priced him out of the role. After all, the budget originally allotted for each *I Love Lucy* episode was $26,500. Eventually, Philip Morris Tobacco, the show's sponsor, trimmed the weekly production allowance to $19,500. Lucy and Desi's joint salary was to be $5,000 per episode, but that was decreased to $4,000.

Unlike Gordon and Gleason, Bill Frawley was then well into his career slump. He was having difficulty finding steady work and, to pay his substantial bar bill, he even had been accepting quickie minor assignments on radio and TV shows.

In 1951, Frawley was desperately looking for employment in the then-blooming television industry. He put a positive spin on his situation when he recalled, early in the *I Love Lucy* run, that he "got the hang of [the medium] last season when I played a variety of roles on *The Alan Young Show* [1950–53]," a Thursday-night variety program featuring the future star of *Mister Ed* (1961–66).

Having heard about *I Love Lucy*, Frawley, then in his mid-sixties, called to inquire about playing Fred Mertz, and Ball and Arnaz seriously considered him. In latter years, each took credit for receiving Frawley's phone solicitation. In his autobiography, published in 1976, Arnaz wrote, "I got a call from William Frawley," and added, "After I hung up I kept seeing his puss and remembering how good he was at playing the kind of gruff character he usually played. The more I thought about it, the more I became convinced he was Fred Mertz." Yet in 1984, during a seminar sponsored by the Museum of Broadcasting (now known as the Museum of Television and Radio), Ball explained that Frawley had actually called her. She quoted the actor as telling her, "I understand you're looking for a type. And I'm interested in doing some television.

"And so we saw him," Ball continued, "and I said, 'Geez, he's a great guy. He's marvelous. Right age and everything.'"

However, CBS-TV officials, and Philip Morris and its ad agency, were reluctant to cast stocky, bald, cigar-chomping Frawley because of his imbibing habits. "Well, those bastards, those sonsabitches," Frawley said at the time. "They're always saying that about me. How the hell do they know, those bastards?"

Despite his reputation, Ball and Arnaz came to like the idea of Frawley playing Fred Mertz and were determined to sign him. In another oft-repeated anecdote, Arnaz and Frawley met at Nickodell's, a Melrose Avenue restaurant-bar in Hollywood near Paramount Pictures and Desilu that was one of Frawley's favorite watering holes. Here, Arnaz established the rules for Frawley's employment on *I Love Lucy*. If the actor were to miss three workdays for anything but a legitimate reason, he would be permanently written out of the show. In baseball lingo, which sports fanatic Frawley could readily understand, it meant three strikes and he was out, with no appeals to a higher authority. Frawley agreed and *I Love Lucy* had its Fred Mertz, at an economical salary of $350 per week. Yet to Frawley, who was dead-broke, this represented a steady paycheck at more money than he could imagine.

While the irascible Frawley was gratified to have found employment, he also doubted that *I Love Lucy* would amount to much. "I didn't think the thing had a chance," he recalled of its pre-premiere genesis. "We did the lines over and over again, and it was like eating stew every night—stale and not a bit funny."

Of course, *I Love Lucy* was a smash. "The show even has revived an interest in me in my old Iowa hometown," Frawley declared. "People I'd thought had forgotten Bill Frawley have been writing me. The local papers even are doing stories on me."

Frawley never once was absent from the *I Love Lucy* set because of drinking or for any other reason. He was destined to appear as Fred for the show's entire run.

And he even came to be fond of his employers. He would affectionately refer to Lucy as "that kid," and occasionally would call out to Desi, "Hey, Cuban!" "I remember Frawley talking about [how] he loved Desi," notes actor Don Grady, with whom Bill was to appear on *My Three Sons*. "And he loved Lucy, too, but he just thought Desi was the living end."

Yet for the most part, Frawley kept to himself among his co-workers. For example, rather than attend a cast party at Marc Daniels's home in Laurel Canyon on October 15, 1951, the Monday night of *I Love Lucy*'s premiere telecast, Frawley opted to return to his suite at the Knickerbocker Hotel and listen to the fights on the radio.

Despite his perfect on-set attendance record, the actor did not stop his heavy drinking during his years on *I Love Lucy*. It was just that now he imbibed at a low profile, and did his socializing away from the studio. According to Dann Cahn, the sitcom's editor, Frawley spent most of his on-set time in his dressing room. "He didn't take part in a lot of the fun and games that would go on," Cahn states. "Vivian did. There was great fun and action between Vivian and the crew. She was sociable. She always kidded with me."

In Frawley's off-hours, according to Cahn, he hung out at Musso & Frank, a venerable Hollywood Boulevard eatery that has been in business since 1919. "I'd see him there in the evenings having a couple of martinis," Cahn notes. "I liked him, and often sat down and had a drink with him, and we just schmoozed." Two *I Love Lucy* co-workers with whom Frawley did socialize formally were Marc Daniels, the show's director, and his wife, Emily—and this only was during the first season, after which Daniels, as Emily explains, "left to go do another show for more money." Every Friday evening during the 1951–52 season, Mark and Emily dined with Frawley at Musso & Frank, "just to have fun," remembers Emily Daniels.

"Bill would go over to Musso & Frank and sit at the bar with old friends," adds Bob Weiskopf. "He just hung around and went to the saloons and places where men of his age and with his interests went. He had his buddies, and that was it."

His on- or off-set habits aside, the bottom line was that, careerwise, *I Love Lucy* resuscitated Bill Frawley from professional oblivion. After noting that the actor's career then was "spotty" at best and "not earth-shaking," Chuck Stevens, Frawley's ball player buddy, adds, "And then he got that series, and that thing just ballooned, and assured him of work for a long time."

Bea Benaderet—who had played Iris Atterbury on Lucille Ball's radio series, *My Favorite Husband,* and was to become a regular on *The Beverly Hillbillies* (1962–71) and *Petticoat Junction* (1963–70)—was intended to be cast as Ethel Mertz. Yet Benaderet, age forty-six, also had a prior commitment. She already was playing Blanche Morton, another famous 1950s TV sitcom neighbor, on *The* (George) *Burns and* (Gracie) *Allen Show* (1950–58).

For many reasons, the role of Ethel Mertz would be difficult to cast. For one thing, she had to look old enough to be the wife of Bill Frawley (who was sixty-four years old when hired for the show) yet be young enough to perform all the physical comedy the role was slated to undertake. One potential choice was Mary Wickes, a lanky, sharp-featured forty-one-year-old character actress (and longtime Lucille Ball friend), but she did not pan out. (One reason for her not joining the ensemble was Wickes's concern that working too constantly with Ball—now as her boss—would strain their off-camera relationship.) Another possibility was Barbara Pepper, a pal of Ball's for twenty years. They were the same age—thirty-nine—but Pepper was overweight and, from a physical standpoint, was perfect for the part. Yet she was known to have an appetite for hard liquor, and Ball and Arnaz did not want two drinkers working under them. So Pepper was vetoed as Ethel Mertz.

"We were really at a loss," Ball recalled in 1984 at the Museum of Broadcasting. "And so with Bea Benaderet in mind, I had no other picture of anyone. No one seemed to fit."

On September 3, 1951, *I Love Lucy* was set to go into rehearsal. As this production date neared, Ethel still had not been cast. Then one evening— in yet another oft-repeated story—director Marc Daniels brought Desi Arnaz and producer-scripter Jess Oppenheimer to the La Jolla Playhouse. Here, Vance was reprising Olive Lashbrooke in Mel Ferrer's production of *The Voice of the Turtle.*

The actress may have been a complete unknown to Arnaz and Ball, but Daniels already had directed her and felt she had the right qualities to make a perfect Ethel. "I know that Marc suggested Vivian because he'd known her in New York for quite a while before that," remembers Emily Daniels, the director's widow. "Marc thought she'd be marvelous as Ethel Mertz."

Arnaz, Daniels, and Oppenheimer drove to La Jolla, 107 miles south of Los Angeles. Ball did not join them, as she had just given birth to her firstborn, Lucie Arnaz. The date was July 28, 1951, a Saturday evening.

As Oppenheimer noted in his posthumously published memoirs, "By the end of the first act, Desi and I agreed that we had found our Ethel Mertz." At that time, as any *I Love Lucy* historian can recite, Arnaz declared, "I think we've found Ethel." This determination came about despite the fact that the characters of sophisticated, bitchy Olive Lashbrooke and unaffected Ethel Mertz had very little in common.

Vance's first instinct was to decline the TV role. "What do I want to get mixed up in that for?" she asked Daniels. "It's only a television show." Only after Daniels called her a "goddamned idiot" for not jumping at the opportunity to appear in what he knew would be a sensational series did Vance agree to seriously consider the potential assignment.

A quarter century later, Vance recalled, "I didn't know what a TV series meant in those days, but it did seem promising if a star like Lucille Ball was going to take a chance, so I agreed to give it thirteen weeks. . . ."

In 1984, Ball reminisced that "it was important to Mr. Oppenheimer and to Desi that I okay the lady. . . . [They] called me back after the first act of *Voice of the Turtle* and said, 'Lucy, sight unseen, take our word for it, this girl is wonderful.' I said, 'That's all I want to hear. Drive home carefully. Bring her here, and I'll see her Monday morning.'" On the other hand, in his autobiography, Desi Arnaz reported that he signed Vance to play Ethel that very evening—also at $350 per week—without consulting Ball. Moreover, Lucy and Viv were not to meet for more than a month.

After completing her weeklong engagement in *The Voice of the Turtle*, Vance returned to Hollywood and showed up in Jess Oppenheimer's CBS office to read a scene from the show's premiere episode (which, at the time, was to be "Lucy Thinks Ricky Is Trying to Murder Her"). Present were Oppenheimer, Daniels, Arnaz, and Harry Ackerman, general supervisor of Hollywood operations for CBS. Viv read the role of Ethel, while Daniels recited Lucy's dialogue. All present concurred that Viv would make an ideal Ethel. The deal with Vance was made.

Vance and Ball finally met on September 3, at the initial *I Love Lucy* rehearsal. All did not begin harmoniously. Desi introduced the pair, and Viv responded with a friendly hello. At first glance Lucy was unimpressed, as she felt that Viv did not have the countenance of a landlady. She was not plump enough to play Ethel, and their hair colors would photograph the same shade in black-and-white. These, of course, were cosmetic effects, and Vance responded that she looked stocky when photographed and easily could alter the tint of her hair.

The two actresses finally did click at the meeting—after Lucy saw how terrifically Viv read her lines. As Desi Arnaz later observed, "We could have never found anyone to play Ethel any better or even as well as Vivian Vance did."

However, at this initial rehearsal, the ground rules of Vance's and Frawley's relationships to Ball and Arnaz were ever so subtly established. In an oft-quoted account, as the morning progressed, the *I Love Lucy* stars began lunching on fried chicken. They chomped away, oblivious to the fact that there had been no lunch break and without thinking of offering to share the victuals with the others.

Finally Frawley spoke up, asking in his inimitable manner, "When do the peons eat around here?"

This underling status is reflected in the CBS press release dated August 31, 1951—four days prior to the rehearsal—which announced to the world the arrival of *I Love Lucy*. It is headlined, "Lucille Ball and Hubby Desi Arnaz Costarred in New CBS-TV Domestic Comedy, 'I Love Lucy,'" and includes, "Basically, the series will revolve about [*sic*] the hilarious problems arising in a household where the wife is stagestruck, and the orchestra-leader husband doesn't see eye to eye with her ambition for a career in show business. . . ." The release goes on to report that Ball and Arnaz met on the set of the 1940 RKO screen version of the stage musical *Too Many Girls*, and lists their respective professional credits. There is no mention of William Frawley and Vivian Vance.

It cannot be overemphasized that, at this point in time, *I Love Lucy* was an unproven commodity, a show that just as easily might have faded to obscurity. Had this been the case, Ball could have resumed her film career, Arnaz might have arranged a series of tours across the United States with his band—and Frawley and Vance surely would have been thrust back into anonymity and oblivion.

As its premiere approached, those involved in the show were uncertain as to how it would be received. Emily Daniels recalls that, at the party held at her and husband Marc's Laurel Canyon home on October 15, the night of the sitcom's debut, "Everyone watched [the show], and the only one laughing was Phil Ober! At the end, Lucy in particular was saying, 'Oh God, I don't know . . . . Do you think it's gonna go?' And Phil—who was the only one who hadn't been in rehearsal or read the script—he was just jubilant. He thought it was fantastic."

After agreeing that all those present (excepting Ober) were so close to the show that they had lost their critical objectivity, Daniels succinctly adds, "But you must remember, at that point, it was just another television show."

However, this status was fated to be short-lived. And while Ball and Arnaz were the headliners and Frawley and Vance the subordinates, the contributions of all were immediately acknowledged by audiences and critics alike. And, from its debut episode, *I Love Lucy* was a smash hit. The *Variety* reviewer, after calling it "one of the slickest TV entertainment shows to date" and praising the "full-blown exposition of Miss Ball's comedic talents," added that "Arnaz, Bill Frawley and Vivian Vance contribute major assists as the show's four personality components." The *Hollywood Reporter* chimed in, dubbing Ball "America's No. 1 comedienne," Arnaz "the perfect foil for her screwball antics," Frawley "superb as the landlord of the Arnaz apartment," and Vance "a trouper who knows her way around both lines and situations."

More importantly, by the end of *I Love Lucy*'s first season (1951–52), over eleven million households were tuning in to the show on Monday evenings at nine P.M.

So from here on in, the diminished status of Frawley's film career was rendered irrelevant. "I don't mind admitting my movie career was having a bit of a lull when *Lucy* came along," he declared in 1953. "Now the movie moguls are after me again and somehow I can't help but gloat inwardly that I can't make movies while I'm playing Fred Mertz."

Meanwhile, Vance was toasted in a profile in the December 28, 1952, edition of the *Kansas City Star*, which noted that "the former Vivian Jones of Independence and Cherryvale, Kansas . . . has done much to bring [*I Love Lucy*] its No. 1 rating.

"In a little more than a year," the anonymously written piece continued, "TV has made the former Vivian Jones . . . a big-name star. . . . It looks as if [she] has a lifetime job in TV's top show."

In the La Jolla Playhouse program for *The Voice of the Turtle*, the names of costars Mel Ferrer and Diana Lynn had been above the title, with Vance's listed below. Yet after winning fame as Ethel Mertz, Vance would be the draw. Never again would she have to settle for secondary billing because she was not as well known as her fellow actors. This was precisely the case in 1953, during her summer break from *I Love Lucy*, when she returned to the La Jolla Playhouse to star with Ferrer in the musical *Pal Joey*.

On February 18, 1953, midway through its second season, CBS announced the signing of a then record-breaking $8 million contract between Philip Morris and Desilu. The agreement guaranteed that *I Love Lucy* would run through the 1954–55 season. Half the amount would be paid by Philip Morris to Desilu for producing the show, while the other half would go to CBS to cover airtime charges. The per-episode budget would be raised to $40,000–$50,000. And you could bet Lucy's monthly supply of henna rinse that Frawley and Vance no longer were earning $350 per episode. They both were given raises—and each eventually earned $2,000 per show.

In November 1953, Vance visited Washington, D.C.—not as a tourist, but as a White House guest of President and Mrs. Eisenhower, who were *I Love Lucy* devotees. Vance, Frawley, Ball, Arnaz, and an array of other celebrities also appeared on *Dinner with the President*, an hour-long TV special that was broadcast on the CBS network live from the Mayflower Hotel on November 23.

During the trip back East, Vance sent a telegram to Jess Oppenheimer in which she cracked, "I STOOD IN FRONT OF THE WHITE HOUSE AND CRIED THEN IN FRONT OF THE WASHINGTON MEMORIAL [*sic*] AND SOBBED THEN IN FRONT OF THE LINCOLN MEMORIAL AND BAWLED AND THEN I JOINED THE ARMY. KISSES, ETHEL MERTS [*sic*]."

The following year, Vance was quoted as declaring, "When I think of how close I came to turning down that La Jolla [theater] date, I nearly die."

During the run of *I Love Lucy* the Emmy Awards were presented in the winter, awarding trophies to selected qualified shows that had aired the previous calendar year. Perhaps Vance's penultimate moment as Ethel Mertz came on February 11, 1954, at the Hollywood Palladium, when she walked off with an Emmy for Best Series Supporting Actress. Her competition was Bea Benaderet, the original choice to play Ethel Mertz, for her role on *The Burns and Allen Show*, Ruth Gilbert (*The Milton Berle Show*), Marion Lorne (*Mr. Peepers*), and Audrey Meadows (*The Jackie Gleason Show*).

The nominees tensely awaited the outcome of the voting as Ed Sullivan, the evening's host, introduced the award's presenter: Richard Denning, who had been Lucille Ball's radio costar on *My Favorite Husband*. Denning was then starring in a TV series of his own, *Mr. and Mrs. North* (1952–54), based on the play in which Phil Ober had once appeared on Broadway.

Denning read off the nominees. "Exciting, isn't it?" he declared, as he tore open the envelope that contained the name of the winner.

Then he extended the suspense for additional seconds by adding, "The Television Academy's 1953 National Award for the Best Series Supporting Actress is presented to . . ."

Denning hesitated yet again before announcing Viv's name to gasps, and then prolonged cheers.

Upon reaching the Hollywood Palladium stage, Vance uttered "Oh, thank you" several times before giggling girlishly and adding, "Oh, my."

"I want to thank all of you very much," she began, "and I want to thank especially the people who created Ethel Mertz: Jess Oppenheimer and Madelyn Pugh and Robert Carroll Jr." Then, tongue in cheek, she concluded, "And I want to thank the greatest straight woman in show business, Lucille Ball"—a crack that garnered hearty laughter and applause.

That same year, William Frawley was a Best Series Supporting Actor nominee along with Ben Alexander (*Dragnet*), Art Carney (*The Jackie Gleason Show*), Tony Randall (*Mr. Peepers*), and Carl Reiner (*Your Show of Shows*). He lost to Carney.

Frawley would win five consecutive Emmy nominations, but emerged a loser each time. For 1954, the category was renamed Best Supporting Actor in a Regular Series and he, along with Ben Alexander, Don DeFore (*The Adventures of Ozzie and Harriet*), and Gale Gordon (*Our Miss Brooks*)—who had been the first choice for Fred Mertz—again lost to Carney. For 1955, the Best Actor in a Supporting Role Emmy also went to Carney (*The Honeymooners*). Joining Frawley as an also-ran were Ed Begley ("Patterns,"

Kraft Theater), Carl Reiner (*Caesar's Hour*), and Cyril Ritchard ("Peter Pan," *Producers' Showcase*). In 1956, Reiner won for Best Supporting Performance by an Actor, beating Frawley, Carney (*The Jackie Gleason Show*), Paul Ford (*The Phil Silvers Show*), and Ed Wynn ("Requiem for a Heavyweight," *Playhouse 90*). Finally, in 1957, the award name was changed to Best Continuing Supporting Performance by an Actor in a Dramatic or Comedy Series. Reiner again emerged victorious, besting Frawley, Paul Ford, Louis Nye (*The Steve Allen Show*), and Dennis Weaver (*Gunsmoke*).

As it turned out, Vance's 1953 award would be her sole Emmy victory. The following year, she and fellow nominees Bea Benaderet (*The George Burns and Gracie Allen Show*), Jean Hagen (*Make Room for Daddy*), and Marion Lorne (*Mr. Peepers*) were beaten by Audrey Meadows (*The Jackie Gleason Show*). In 1955, Vance did not even win a nomination. The five who did were Ann B. Davis (*The Bob Cummings Show*), Nanette Fabray (the eventual winner, for *Caesar's Hour*), Jean Hagen, Audrey Meadows, and Thelma Ritter ("A Catered Affair," *Alcoa-Goodyear Playhouse*). Vance was back in the running for 1956, but she and Ann B. Davis, Audrey Meadows, and Mildred Natwick ("Blithe Spirit," *Ford Star Jubilee*) lost to Pat Carroll (*Caesar's Hour*). Vance, as did Frawley, won her final Emmy nomination in 1957. That year, the winner was Ann B. Davis. Joining Vance as also-rans were Pat Carroll, Verna Felton (*December Bride*), and Marion Lorne (*Sally*).

So now Vivian Vance and Bill Frawley were multiple Emmy Award nominees—and, in the case of Vance, an Emmy winner!

SECOND BANANAS

Bill Frawley had no difficulty fitting into the character of Fred Mertz, if only because the role was so much like the actor. Plus, he got to mouth wisecracks and express comic disdain for his sitcom wife.

On the other hand, public statements and Emmy nominations aside, Vivian Vance had a difficult time adjusting to playing dowdy Ethel Mertz, ever-faithfully married to curmudgeonly old Fred.

Vance, of course, was a former showgirl who often had played femme fatales onstage. Yet now, she was purposefully deglamorized for her TV role as Ethel. An apocryphal story has her contract including a "fat clause," which stipulated that whenever *I Love Lucy* was in production she had to be at least twenty pounds heavier than Ball (whose own figure had spread a bit through the years). Otherwise, Viv's costumes would have to be padded. Supposedly, if she lost any weight when the show's filming ceased between seasons, Lucy would be sure to remind her to put it all back on before production resumed. As for the "problem" with her hair color, Vance attempted to find a tint that was more complementary to Lucy's locks by frequently changing her shade of blonde. During the first season, her hair color varied from episode to episode, running the gamut from very light to ash- and honey-blonde.

Additionally, Vance would be costumed in frumpy housedresses. Thus, Viv-as-Ethel's unfashionable appearance could be comically ridiculed by Frawley-as-Fred. Yet beyond the wringing of laughter, the purpose of dressing down Viv/Ethel was to make her appear older than Lucille/Lucy, and to accentuate Ball's femininity.

"Vivian wore those dresses," recalls Emily Daniels. "They were really pretty dowdy. The first year, she accepted all that." But as the years passed, Vance felt that her "frumpy Ethel" image was being overplayed at the expense of her talent. On May 12, 1955, she appeared with Frawley, Tony Martin, and Marguerite Piazza in "High Pitch," an hour-long, original, made-for-TV musical that aired as an episode of CBS's *Shower of Stars*. At the time, the *Albuquerque Tribune*—the newspaper of Vance's adopted hometown—ran an article that typically described her as "the homey neighbor on *I Love Lucy*." So caught up was the paper in Vance's break from her Mertz characterization that the piece was headlined "Vivian Vance Will Wear Glamour Clothes on Show."

"I really minded losing my identity on *I Love Lucy* and becoming Ethel Mertz," Vance declared in 1976—sixteen years after last playing the character. "When I die there will be people who send Ethel flowers. I'll get up to heaven and someone will say, 'Hi, Ethel, I see you're still in rerun.'"

Imogene Littell, Vivian's second cousin, offers insight into Vance's perception of Ethel when she observes, "Vivian really didn't like her role as Ethel. But that's who she was on television. That's why she was loved so much. That's what she was good at. But that really wasn't her. It wasn't intended to be her.

"She was good at the character she was playing," Littell continues, "but I think she thought people thought that that's what she was like. They thought she *was* Ethel Mertz.

"And so she lost her identity. But that's all part of the game. That's what an actress is [supposed to do], for heaven's sake."

Sheila MacRae reports that when the cameras were not rolling, Vance "looked very much the same [as Ethel], except that she was better-dressed, of course. She was always well dressed, and well coifed."

Marjorie Lord, Vance's longtime friend, recalls, "One thing about Vivian, she really wanted to be a glamour girl. She loved to dress beautifully. I think playing Ethel was a little hard on her that way sometimes."

From the very beginning of *I Love Lucy*, Ethel's less-than-captivating physical presence was emphasized on the series. The personalities of Fred and Ethel were established on the very first broadcast episode. The title is "The Girls Want to Go to a Nightclub," and the comic contentiousness between the Mertzes is at the crux of the story.

It is the Mertzes' eighteenth wedding anniversary, and the story line has Ethel scheming to get Fred to take her to a nightclub to celebrate the event. Fred will have none of this, as he tells Ricky, "I'd like you to join me in commemoration of an eighteen-year-old tragedy," adding that he would rather attend the fights on his anniversary.

Not too long into the plot line, there is an Ethel fat joke. Ricky suggests that a woman can be manipulated by smooching. "Now look," Ricardo notes, "everybody knows you can get around a woman with a little sweet-talk." Fred then quips, "Well, that's all right for Lucy but it's a little longer trip around Ethel." Vivian, of course, was heavier than Lucille, the star, but if you had not taken a close look at her, you would have thought her character was being played by Kate Smith.

In actuality, Vance was just two years Ball's senior, yet there is a calculated effort to imply that Lucy was much younger than Ethel. As the episode progresses, Ricky and Fred get blind dates for the evening—who turn out to be Lucy and Ethel, impersonating coarse and ill-kempt Mammy Yokums.

Tellingly, Mammy Yokum Ethel is described as the mother of Mammy Yokum Lucy.

Throughout the run of *I Love Lucy*, Ethel's—and Fred's—physical appearance remained a constant source of on-camera humor. This extended beyond the most familiar, half-hour episodes.

The sitcom eventually became *The Lucille Ball-Desi Arnaz Show*, consisting of sixty-minute black-and-white episodes that were aired as segments on CBS-TV's *Desilu Playhouse* (1957–60). The initial show, "Lucy Takes a Cruise to Havana," was extra-special: a seventy-five-minute-long episode that was shot in June 1957 and broadcast the following November.

On the show, Lucy reminisces about how she met Ricky, Fred, and Ethel years earlier. "Vivian and Bill were portrayed the way they were supposed to look in 1940," explains film editor Dann Cahn. "Frawley had that big head of hair. And [Vance] loved that picture, because she got to really dress up. She got a big kick out of that."

In this episode, Ethel's husband is described as "a gay young blade named Frederick Mertz," and is dapperly attired in a striped sport blazer with white silk ascot tied masterfully around his neck and a yachting cap covering his head. He removes the latter, to reveal an incredible toupee. Even his eyebrows are dyed brown.

Escorting him is "his child bride of 1934" who, ever so typically, complains that Fred pays more attention to his hair than he does to her. "Sometimes I wish you were bald," Ethel declares, at which point Fred becomes animated. "Oh yeah," he retorts. "Well, don't worry. That's one thing that will never happen to me!"

Ethel makes quite an on-screen entrance. Wearing an attractive fitted frock, a shoulder-length styled blonde hairdo, and a triple strand of pearls, she swings her hips and shows off a slimmed-down Ethel Mertz figure.

By the time this installment was filmed, Vance had become so disenchanted with playing dowdy Ethel that she insisted in a clause being added to her new contract—at the beginning of each new TV season, her agreement would be renegotiated—stipulating that she would have nicer costumes.

Understandably, Vance was elated when, in October 1959, she appeared as a guest on the popular TV game show *I've Got a Secret*

(1952–67, 1972–76) and Bess Myerson, one of the show's permanent panelists, casually remarked, "Vivian, may I say you look much younger than you do on television." Vance promptly beamed and responded, "You may say that forty-five times, Bess."

Indeed, Vance looked smashing on the show. She was garbed in a fitted, stylish dress, which showed off her bosom. Ethel Mertz never, ever was as alluring.

♥

If Vance was immediately recognizable to the *I've Got a Secret* audience—and she and Frawley each became audience favorites in their ongoing roles as the Mertzes—both she and Bill were destined to remain victims to the Hollywood A-list/B-list mentality.

On November 13, 1952—over a year after the *I Love Lucy* premiere—Ball, Arnaz, Frawley, and Vance, along with an array of talent then associated with CBS-TV, appeared on a comedy-variety special titled *Stars in the Eye*. The program commemorated the opening of CBS Television City, the network's new Hollywood production facility near the historic Farmers Market.

More than two dozen performers were cited in the opening credits, from Gracie Allen and Eddie "Rochester" Anderson to Marie Wilson and Alan Young. Frawley and Vance were *not* listed among them. They were relegated to the second tier of actors, cited at the program's end. Interestingly, one of the latter was Gale Gordon, whose show, *Our Miss Brooks*, had made its CBS bow a month earlier. Gordon plays a CBS executive on *Stars in the Eye*—and has more on-air time than practically anyone else on the special.

Stars in the Eye consists of a series of musical routines and skits. In one of them, Desi appears as himself and announces that he is suing Jack Benny for lousing up the filming of an *I Love Lucy* episode. Arnaz then shows Benny footage of three of the show's "outtakes," on which Benny comically intrudes. Lucy and Desi are in all three, while Bill and Viv appear only in the first.

With regard to Frawley's and Vance's lack of exposure during this period, Sheila MacRae explains that Lucy and Desi "were the stars. They were 'Hollywood.' Frawley and Vance were not—and there always was a big difference in those days."

Even though Frawley had over one hundred feature-film appearances to his credit, he and Vance, according to MacRae, "weren't what you'd call identifiable. When you'd say their names, nobody knew them. After the second year [of *I Love Lucy*], people knew their names much more."

Despite their growing recognizability and popularity, Frawley and Vance never came to rate any kind of star treatment at the CBS network. For example, in "High Pitch," a May 1955 installment of CBS's *Shower of Stars*, Frawley is ideally cast as Gabby Mullins, manager of the Hooligans, a perennial last-place major-league ball club. Viewers had come to expect to see Vance playing Frawley's wife, so she was assigned the role of Mullins's mate; however, her Mrs. Mullins is more of an Alice Kramden type than an Ethel Mertz. Still, the characters of Manager and Mrs. Mullins are strictly secondary, and Frawley and Vance are underutilized in the proceedings. They serve as catalysts in the romantic manipulations and misunderstandings of Ted Warren (Tony Martin), a talented but egocentric baseball hero, and Dorothy Meadows (Marguerite Piazza), a baseball-loving opera star who buys the Hooligans, vamps Warren, and then purchases him for her team.

Despite their proven abilities as musical performers, Frawley neither sings nor dances on "High Pitch" and Vance appears only in a brief number in which she and the athletes' spouses lament "the life of a ballplayer's wife." The routine sounds as if it might have been borrowed from *Damn Yankees*, the smash-hit baseball musical that had just opened on Broadway in 1955. Vance performs the number in a Mermanesque manner, a style of singing she had not displayed since her salad days in 1930s Broadway musicals.

This second-stringer status also extended off-camera in the Hollywood milieu. "The truth of the matter was that if [Frawley and Vance] were invited to any parties, they would have been seated at the 'B' table," notes MacRae. She recalls attending a network dinner in the late 1950s. "I know that Vivian Vance was there," she recalls, "and so was Frawley and all the people connected with the show.

"But they were not at that big table [where Lucy and Desi were seated]."

Despite the passing years and all their acclaim, Vance and Frawley knew all too well that they remained vulnerable to the whims of their bosses. Gene Reynolds recalls that he was acting on an *I Love Lucy* episode later in the series' run. At the time, Keith Thibodeaux (billed as Richard Keith) was playing Little Ricky, the son of Lucy and Ricky Ricardo.

"They had him in a high-chair," Reynolds explains, "scribbling and so forth on a piece of paper they had given him to amuse himself."

Someone said to the youngster, "Richard, what are you doing?" And Frawley, in his familiar voice, grumbled, "He's writing me out."

Chapter Fourteen

OIL AND WATER

To the outside world—and even to many at the Desilu studio in Hollywood where *I Love Lucy* was produced—Vivian Vance and William Frawley were simpatico. One insider was Hugh O'Brian, whose popular Western TV series *Wyatt Earp* (1955–61) also was shot on the Desilu lot. Lucille Ball even let O'Brian use her dressing room from time to time, because the *Wyatt Earp* production company refused to rent sufficient space for the star of its show. So for the final years of *I Love Lucy*, he was a constant presence at Desilu.

"I saw Frawley and Vance quite often [on the lot]," recalls O'Brian. "They were most pleasant, and very kind to me.

"I'd see them occasionally around town. Again, it was always very pleasant. I have nothing but positive things to say about them. *{I Love Lucy}* was a pro show. If there was any wrangling, I certainly didn't know about it."

Roy Rowan, the *I Love Lucy* announcer, concurs with O'Brian. "They were just multitalented," is how he describes Frawley and Vance. "Every now and then I would have a part on the show, and so I was there during some of the rehearsals. At showtime, all these people were so locked into what they had to do [that] they were not going to kibitz around with you at all.

"There has been a lot of talk that [Vance and Frawley] didn't get along," he adds. "But I never saw that. Whether it's true or not, I have no idea."

Keith Thibodeaux began playing Little Ricky in 1956, before he had reached his sixth birthday. Forty-two years later, he recalls, "Bill and Vivian had good relations as far as I knew. They were always nice to me, and we got along great."

Upon coming to television, the cast of *Our Miss Brooks* would rehearse in the studio adjacent to where *I Love Lucy* was ensconced. Robert Rockwell, one of its stars, who played Mr. Boynton the biology teacher, reports that he, too, has only fond memories of Frawley and Vance.

"As far as I am concerned," Rockwell declares, "Mr. Frawley was exactly what he was on the show. He was a most affable person, loved a good joke, and seemed to enjoy life. He wasn't a 'loudmouth,' although his voice was what came across.

"Mr. Frawley was a gentleman and a fun person," Rockwell concludes. He describes Vance as "a refined and gentle lady." And he reports no dissension between them.

♥

The actual truth of the matter was that Vivian Vance and William Frawley were anything but refined and gentle toward each other. It would be difficult to overemphasize their mutual contempt. Yet neither wanted to imperil his/her job, so to the outside world—and even to insiders like Hugh O'Brian, Roy Rowan, Keith Thibodeaux, and Robert Rockwell—they came across as well mannered and behaved in their personal dealings.

A more accurate appraisal of the Frawley-Vance relationship comes from Bob Schiller, who with Bob Weiskopf began penning *I Love Lucy* scripts in 1955, at the start of the show's fifth season. "The two of them together weren't too happy," he explains. "That's been well documented. [Vance] always felt that she was much too young and pretty to have an old fart like Frawley as a husband. And he couldn't stand her, either."

Weiskopf reiterates his partner's point when he notes, "One of the big things on the show was that Vivian was always a little upset that she was playing Bill Frawley's wife when Frawley was considerably older than she was. So that bothered her." Marjorie Lord declares, "She wasn't all that crazy about Bill Frawley. She wanted to be married to somebody handsome. Vivian liked good-looking men." And series film editor Dann Cahn adds, "He was sort of an old goat to her."

Jess Oppenheimer would note in his memoirs that Frawley and Vance initially got along. Perhaps they might even have traded memories of their many years as Broadway actors. For despite the differences in the eras in which they worked, they still managed to be connected to some of the same Broadway luminaries. In 1928, Vinton Freedley had produced *Here's Howe!*, in whose supporting cast was a middle-aged musical-comedy performer named Bill Frawley; four years later, Freedley hired Vance for *Music in the Air*, her first Broadway show. Chubby comedian Victor Moore was one of the stars of Vance's follow-up musical, 1934's *Anything Goes*; three years earlier, he had headlined *She Lived Next to the Firehouse*, which featured Frawley. In 1947, George Abbott directed Vance in *It Takes Two*; fifteen years before, he had directed Frawley in *Twentieth Century,* Bill's biggest Broadway success.

Nevertheless, mutual disdain eventually set in and was irreversible. Frawley and Vance's difficulties started off innocently enough. "He sometimes snapped at her," explains Emily Daniels, who was on the set daily during the show's first season. "It would be some dumb little thing. He was just kidding, and he did this with everybody. He was curmudgeonly, and that was his way of being funny.

"But Vivian didn't like it. [Frawley's humor] was just something she didn't care for. She'd kind of say something back," says Daniels.

Tensions soon escalated. Before the shooting of a nightclub sequence early in the show's run, Vance insulted Frawley by informing the choreographer that she was positive that Frawley—a veteran vaude-ville and Broadway hoofer—would be unable to learn the steps. "Well, for Chrissakes," Frawley declared, "I was in vaudeville since I was five years old and I guarantee you I'll wind up teaching old fat-ass how to do the fucking thing."

Soon Bill was asking Desi Arnaz, "Where the hell did you find this bitch?" And Vance was no more delighted to be working with Frawley. In fact, behind-the-scenes creative force Jess Oppenheimer noted that he occasionally had to be called to the set to mediate disputes between the actors. "Usually it was because Viv had suggested some script changes or additional bits of business," he recalled. "Because it was Viv who had done the suggesting, Bill would flatly refuse to cooperate, often retreating to his dressing room in a pout."

At the Emmy Awards ceremony for calendar year 1953, Vance won a trophy while Frawley was an also-ran. In yet another example of the acri-mony he felt for his costar, Frawley was heard by several who attended the ceremony to mutter, with regard to Vance's victory and his loss, "It goes to prove that the whole vote is rigged."

"Frawley was a grumpy, volatile, mercurial guy," notes Gene Reynolds. "Very Irish. He would get angry, and let you know." Yet Reynolds is quick to add that the actor's behavior "didn't mean anything, for the most part. It was just a little bit of the old sod coming out. But for somebody work-ing with him, it could have been plenty tough."

Frawley's ballplayer pal Chuck Stevens observes that the actor "always carried himself like a gentleman, and he reacted like a gentleman to every situation." He notes that Frawley was "probably one of the nicest men I've ever met, and I knew lots of people in the picture and radio business. He was always one of my favorites, and one of every baseball player's favorites." Still, Stevens also is quick to add, "But I know darn well if the occasion arose, he could be feisty. I really don't know that I ever would have wanted to get him upset. He may have been a handful."

Reynolds remembers a rehearsal of a very physical, comic *I Love Lucy* scene in which Lucy and Viv had a rope around Frawley. "They said, 'Now, look, Bill, you pull here, and then let go, and come back here.' And he's saying, 'I'll knock you both on your asses in a second. . . .' That's the way he'd be popping off. He'd be impatient.

"And of course Frawley was always very upfront with his feelings, saying things like, 'What the hell are you doing, for Chrissakes?' and, 'Well, give me a chance, I'll be there in a minute, for Chrissakes.'

"But at the same time," Reynolds concludes ever so accurately, "the two of them, as the Mertzes, were gold."

When *I Love Lucy* was in production, Vance was tactful not to publicly voice her displeasure with Frawley. "The four of us are like family," she explained diplomatically to the media in 1954. "When we squabble it's a family fight with no hard feelings afterward."

However, the depth of Vance's acrimony was demonstrated later in the sitcom's run, when Little Ricky was emerging as a principal character. The possibility then existed for a spin-off TV series featuring Fred and Ethel Mertz, to be produced by Desilu. Vance nixed the idea, because she could not stomach the notion of costarring on an even more full-time basis with a man as crude and insulting as she found Frawley to be. She would not even film a pilot episode—even after Desi Arnaz agreed to pay her a $50,000 bonus. When Frawley learned of Vance's refusal he was irate, if only because the eternally money-conscious actor—who had a well-earned reputation as a cheapskate—would have been paid a much-higher salary than he currently was earning. Here was one instance where Frawley's nastiness toward Vance detonated in his face like a cheap trick cigar.

Later, in 1962, when Vance agreed to rejoin Ball as her TV second banana on the forthcoming *The Lucy Show*, she made a strong stipulation: she must *never* again be paired with Frawley. "I loathed William Frawley and the feeling was mutual," she recalled. "Whenever I received a new [*I Love Lucy*] script, I raced through it, praying that there wouldn't be a scene where we had to be in bed together."

Post–*I Love Lucy*, Vance would freely express her opinion of Frawley to one and all. On *The Lucy Show*, young Jimmy Garrett (who was cast as Lucy's son) often was assigned the type of crabby dialogue that had once been the domain of Fred Mertz. One time, after spouting one such quip, Vance hugged Garrett and told him, "You got a great laugh on that line— and you're a lot cuter than that old poop."

Nor had the years softened Frawley's view of his former TV wife. Upon being informed of her various post–*I Love Lucy* projects, Frawley quipped, "That's okay with me. . . . She could go to Budapest and I wouldn't care." In a frequently quoted wisecrack, Frawley told the world that Vance was "one of the finest gals to come out of Kansas, but I often used to wish she'd go back there. I don't know where she is now and she doesn't know where I am, and that's exactly the way I like it."

Despite this proclamation, it just so happened that *The Lucy Show* and *My Three Sons* were shooting right next door to each other, on adjacent sound stages on the Desilu lot in Hollywood. Don Grady, who played Fred MacMurray's middle son on *My Three Sons*, prefaces a retelling of a Frawley anecdote by noting that the actor "used to call me 'Goldie.' I don't know why, but that was his nickname for me."

One time, Frawley called Grady over and asked, "You know how to Frisbee? Are you really good at Frisbee?"

Grady, then in his mid-teens, responded, "Yeah, I'm pretty good." So Frawley gave the youngster a film can, and opened a stage door that connected the *My Three Sons* and *Lucy Show* sets.

Frawley then asked Grady, "You think you can throw this film can through that door?"

"Yeah, I think I can," was the answer.

Frawley then instructed Grady: "Okay, I'll tell you when. When I go like this"—and he gave Grady a hand signal—"let me see you throw that thing through the door. And let me see how far you can get it, too.

"I'm going to go through the door," Frawley continued, "and I'll be on the other side, and when I give you the signal, you try to reach me with it."

"So he goes over there," Grady explains, "and he's kind of standing around. He's waiting for something. And finally, he looks back at me and gives me the signal.

"I Frisbeed this thing through the door, and it landed right in the middle of Vivian Vance's take! And he ran off that stage like a little kid, closed the door behind him, and said, 'Good shot, Goldie!'"

Stanley Livingston, cast as the younger brother on *My Three Sons*, recalls a similar incident. "[Frawley] got me involved in one prank," he says. "It was something to get back at Vivian; he'd rag on about her for hours. Anyway, he hatched this plan . . . he got the idea of us going to get all these film cans. So we amassed twenty or thirty cans, and put them in this box. We went on the soundstage, and he waited until he heard [Vance's] voice. I guess they were having a rehearsal or something. And we held on to the box by its flaps and then threw it up in the air. The cans rolled around, and it sounded like twenty hubcaps bashing into each other.

"Vivian probably knew it was him."

Tim Considine chimes in with his own anecdote. While performing on *My Three Sons,* the actor, then in his early twenties, was in the Air Force Reserve. One day, his commanding officer, a lieutenant general, came to visit the set. Considine describes him as "kind of a stick, straitlaced and whatever. But his adjutant was a good guy." Around midday, Considine took both military men to lunch with Frawley.

"Now you never knew which Frawley you were gonna get," Considine declares, "but [the meal] went really well. I mean, he was on his game. He was really terrific and funny and charming."

On their way back to the set, Considine congratulated himself, thinking, "Well, this is just terrific. He's shown them a really good time." Considine was walking with the adjutant, in front of Frawley and the lieutenant general. The quartet was just about to turn a corner on the lot, leading to the set.

At that point, Considine heard the lieutenant general ask Frawley, "Uh, what was Vivian Vance like?"

Considine knew exactly what was coming. All he could do was flinch and think to himself, "Oh God."

The next voice he heard was Frawley's, who responded with three words: "That miserable cunt."

"And I looked back," Considine concludes, "to see this lieutenant general's face go red."

It is no understatement when scriptwriter Bob Weiskopf, comparing Vance to Frawley, notes, "She was a lot more cultured than he was."

In at least one instance, Frawley was not the instigator of an outlandish incident in which Vance found herself a central player. Its perpetrator was a show-business personality whose legendary outrageousness might even have been too much for Frawley: Ms. Tallulah Bankhead.

In the fall of 1957, Bankhead appeared as herself with Ball, Arnaz, Frawley, and Vance on an hour-long Lucy-Desi show titled "The Celebrity Next Door." "We always would go through our notes in Desi's office after a run-through," explains Jay Sandrich, future television director, who then was paying his dues as the show's assistant director. "Vivian had loaned Tallulah a sweater. The notes session still was going on, but Vivian was finished and was dismissed."

As she was preparing to leave Arnaz's office, Vivian asked Tallulah a simple and reasonable question: "Can I have my sweater back?"

Tallulah, who was famed for her unpredictability, quickly responded, "You want your sweater? You can have it! And you can have everything else!"

Sandrich explains that Tallulah promptly "took every stitch of clothes off. We all sat there aghast.

"And that's how Vivian got her sweater back."

♥

In addition to their shared mutual dislike, Vance and Frawley were polar opposites in their approach to their acting craft. "Vivian took acting very seriously," recalls Sandrich, who first worked on *I Love Lucy* during the 1956–57 season. "She was like a method actress. She really examined the lines in the scenes, and would try [to look for] motivation."

"And she's unappreciated," notes Gene Reynolds, "because most of the shtick is going to Lucy. But you've got somebody there who never drops the ball, who keeps the rhythm going, who knows how to feed, who knows when to hold still, who knows when to respond. Vivian was such a pro, very valuable for Lucy to have."

Frawley, on the other hand, was concerned only with his own dialogue. After an initial reading and rehearsal, he never would bring the entire *I Love Lucy* script home with him. More often than not, he could be found with a newspaper sports section or the daily racing form under his arm, rather than the week's script.

"He was the only actor I ever knew," relates *Lucy* scriptwriter Bob Schiller, "who would count the pages and ask for less. That was really wild!" Fellow scribe Bob Weiskopf notes, "He was one of the few actors who loved to be into the script as light as possible rather than as heavy. He always used to say to us, 'Jesus, could you cut it down, guys?'"

Frawley was not at all pleased when *I Love Lucy* became the hour-long *Lucille Ball-Desi Arnaz Show*, if only because this meant double the dialogue. "The scripts for the hour shows were long, a hundred pages or whatever," explains Jay Sandrich. "Bill would come to the [script] readings with eight pages. As the show would be read by the other actors, Bill literally would be nodding off. Somebody would punch him and he'd read his line and get a big laugh from everybody, not really ever understanding that the line he had to read referred to something earlier in the show.

"But it didn't seem to matter. He had his style, and it was wonderful and funny." Then Sandrich adds, "But I think that bothered Viv, too, because she took [her work] so seriously, and he didn't."

If anything, as the years passed Frawley became even more set in his ways. "He never talked about acting," notes Don Grady. "We would sit around, and [*My Three Sons* star Fred] MacMurray had philosophies and ideas about acting. But Bill would say, 'I'm just here to make money and have a good time.'"

Despite such declarations, Frawley's approach to acting should not be misconstrued as being slipshod. However, as he entered his mid-seventies and was appearing on *My Three Sons,* his work began to be noticeably affected by advancing age and declining health. Up until then, he had been a no-nonsense performer who would learn his lines and do his business quickly and in one take. His many years performing in vaudeville made him a master at his craft, and he had impeccable comic timing.

It was just that he had zero patience for long rehearsals.

According to Sandrich, if there was a scene between Vance and Ball, the two really would rehearse. "Lucy loved to know exactly what she was doing and why she was doing it and how everybody else would say their lines," he explains. "Nothing was taken for granted with Lucy and Viv. But if it was a scene with Desi and Bill, they'd sort of go through it one time and the guys would move on.

"Desi, of course, was very involved in running the studio. He had this ability to turn on and off whatever he was doing at that moment. He could be off the stage and come back an hour and a half later and pick right up where he left off." In fact, as the years passed, the role of Ricky Ricardo became smaller and, as Ball and Vance had developed into such a good comedy team, more material was written that spotlighted the on-camera scheming of Lucy and Ethel.

"Bill would just come in, and do his lines, and go back to his dressing room," Sandrich concludes. "Nothing was wrong with this, because he always did good work. It was just different styles of working."

Tim Considine notes, regarding the *My Three Sons* years, "He was a real character who just used his own character, the charming or interesting parts of his character." Don Grady adds, "He never had a problem with character motivation. He was just Bill Frawley. He came on and delivered the line and was funny."

One cannot imagine William Frawley brushing up his Shakespeare at the Actors Studio. So he certainly had no patience for listening to Vance as she analyzed the "motivation" behind a scene. Still, Sandrich reports that Frawley and Vance "would talk if they had to about staging, you know, or if Bill was supposed to make a move and he didn't. But I don't remember Bill and Viv having much conversation about things that didn't relate to the show."

Sandrich has only fond memories of Vance. He would go on to become an Emmy Award–winning director, but when he came to *I Love Lucy* he was young and inexperienced and not the professional equal of any of the veterans in his midst. "Yet Vivian just treated me really well," he says. "It's not an easy thing to be twenty-four years old and really not know what's going on on the stage, much less in life, and be thrown into a situation like that. But she was just terrific to me."

For a woman who seemed to relate so beautifully to so many people, it is both ironic and unfortunate that a person with whom she did not get along was the actor fated to be her television husband and costar for nine long years.

Another source of agitation for both Frawley and Vance was that, to countless *I Love Lucy* fans, they ceased being Bill Frawley and Vivian Vance, professional actors with off-camera lives, and actually *were* Fred and Ethel Mertz. In one of his more perceptive moments, Frawley cited as the reason for this phenomenon the uniqueness of TV as an entertainment medium. "That's what's so fascinating about television," he declared. "The people think you're just one of them coming into their living rooms to visit with them. They go to a movie or to a stage show and they expect to see actors, but not on television."

On one occasion in 1955, while he was dining at the famous Chasen's restaurant in Beverly Hills, a gaggle of Texas tourists surrounded Frawley, requesting that he autograph their menus. One of them remained after the others had left the table, to query the actor on how to break into television.

Frawley asked if he was a performer. "No," was the response, followed by a question: "Do you gotta be an actor to get on a television show?"

"It helps," Frawley replied. "It sure helps."

"Gee, I didn't know you were an actor," the Texan declared. "I thought you were just yourself."

Needless to say, as the Texan and his fellow tourists departed Chasen's, they directed Frawley to "give our love to your wife. We think she's wonderful, too."

Vance encountered similar real-life episodes. On more than one occasion, she would be made to feel uncomfortable while in a restaurant or other public place with then-husband Phil Ober. "The women give me suspicious looks as if they've caught me stepping out," Vance explained. "I can't always stop and tell them that Phil is my real husband."

Not surprisingly, Vivian was particularly irked by such recognition as Ethel Mertz. "[Ethel] was everything I didn't want to be," she declared, years after playing the role, before adding that "it just galled me when strangers on the street greeted me as 'Ethel.'"

On another occasion, Vance noted, "Why, my own father back in Kansas said to me, 'Why can't you use your own name on that *Lucy* program? Fred Mertz uses HIS name.'"

Chapter Fifteen

PROFESSIONALS

Despite the rancor Bill Frawley and Vivian Vance felt whenever they were mistaken for real-life spouses, it is a tribute to their talents—and their professionalism—that they *were* Fred and Ethel to the hordes of *I Love Lucy* fans.

Many of those with whom they worked and who were on the Desilu lot, including Bob Schiller, Hugh O'Brian, Keith Thibodeaux, and Roy Rowan, attest to the duo's professionalism.

Marjorie Lord notes, "[Vance] didn't make a big deal of [her feelings]. You never saw it on the screen. When Danny [Thomas] and I didn't get along, you'd see it right up there on the screen. But I never noticed it with her and Bill."

In particular, whenever Vance-as-Ethel called Frawley-as-Fred an "old goat" or some similar age-related insult, there never was a sense of personal animosity or added sarcasm as Vance delivered her lines. Bob Weiskopf adds, "I don't think any of the Lucy fans knew that Vivian was pissed off that she was playing the wife of someone who was much older than she was."

Furthermore, Lord observes that, during the *I Love Lucy* years, Vance "didn't feel that it was always real happy [for her]. I think she had challenges on the *Lucy* show. I know I had my challenges. You don't do a series week after week and year after year without certain challenges. But she always seemed chipper and wonderful."

At the same time, whenever Frawley-as-Fred called Vance-as-Ethel "honeybunch," he delivered the endearment sweetly, and with the joviality of a loving husband.

Even though Fred and Ethel Mertz were not conceived as musical roles, Vance as well as Frawley often were called upon to utilize their stage backgrounds. "A few weeks after we started production," remembered Jess Oppenheimer, "we had a story idea that depended on Bill and Vivian being able to sing and dance a little. I went down to the stage where they were rehearsing and sheepishly asked them if they thought they could handle it."

Frawley and Vance each informed Oppenheimer of their respective song-and-dance credentials. Even though Viv's questioning of Bill's dancing ability was to be one of the biggest sparks that lit the fire of the Frawley-Vance hatefest—professionally speaking, at least—as Oppenheimer concluded, "a whole unexpected, wonderful new area fell into our laps as a gift."

In particular, *I Love Lucy* offered Frawley an opportunity to directly tap into his vaudeville background. As the character evolved, Fred Mertz—born in Steubenville, Ohio, which for biographical purposes might be a clone of Burlington, Iowa—became an ex-vaudevillian. The initial mention of his theatrical roots occurs in "Drafted," the episode that aired on Christmas Eve, 1951. In this installment, Ricky is searching for appropriate material to perform at an army camp, and Fred advises him of a suitable routine left over from his vaudeville trouping.

As Fred's character further developed, it was established that he had been one-half of a song-and-dance team, the name of which varied. In the episode "The Ballet," which aired in 1952, Fred's vaudeville partner is called Ted

Kurtz. In the "Mertz and Kurtz" episode, from 1954—the show that most closely explores Fred's vaudeville background—he is Barney Kurtz, and their billing is "Laugh 'til It Hurts with Mertz and Kurtz." In "Ricky Loses His Voice," from 1952, Fred produces "the whole act—words, music, orchestrations, gags, routines—everything" from *Flapper Follies of 1927*, in which he appeared at the Palace, "the best theater in Jamestown, New York," with his vaudeville partner—Ethel! Indeed, the words "Mertz and Mertz" may be found later, printed on an old trunk from their vaudeville days.

"When we were doing a 'show within a show,' and felt that Bill and Vivian should do something, we would ask them if they had [any specific number] in mind," remembers series writer Bob Weiskopf. "Then they'd come up with something. Bill was an old, experienced vaudevillian. He was always funny, you know. He used to make me laugh." Film editor Dann Cahn adds, "He was adorable when they'd do those little song-and-dance things. My God, when he'd get into doing that vaudeville stuff, he was on. All his old vaudeville days came back in a rush."

The harmonious on-screen chemistry shared by Frawley and Vance also shines through on a number of specials in which the pair appeared, including their brief scenes together in "High Pitch" in 1955 on CBS-TV's *Shower of Stars*.

This is especially the case in the 1953 TV special *Dinner with the President*. The occasion was the fortieth anniversary of the Anti-Defamation League of B'nai B'rith, and the guests of honor were President Dwight D. Eisenhower and first lady Mamie.

Frawley and Vance joined Ball and Arnaz on the TV program. The quartet was introduced by Rex Harrison, who captured the spirit of the occasion as he noted, "It seems there was an Irishman, a Cuban, a Welsh-Irish-English lass, and a redhead from Jamestown. These four people, all with different national backgrounds, decided to make people laugh. These four Americans . . . created the most successful TV show since, well, since ancient Greece. . . . That's why we love *Lucy*."

The skit in which the quartet appears opens with Viv-as-Ethel singing the end of "Carolina in the Morning," a number in which she and Bill-as-Fred performed on more than one occasion on *I Love Lucy.* "It's the same key we sang it in twenty years ago," he observes. The crux of the sketch involves the preparation of a vaudeville routine, complete with corny jokes, that will be performed for President and Mrs. Eisenhower, with Lucy being miffed because she thinks she will not be part of the show.

As the skit progresses, Fred teaches Lucy "Under the Bamboo Tree." Then Ben Grauer, one of the show's hosts, introduces "Fred and Ethel Mertz in one of their old-time vaudeville favorites"—and the pair perform their rendition of "Carolina in the Morning."

He is garbed in striped coat and matching hat, while she wears a 1920s-style flapper outfit. And Frawley and Vance work magic in their brief moments in the spotlight; while listening to them, even at this late date, you really do get a sense of Frawley's honey-toned, old-style stage tenor. He and Vance might easily have been a real-life veteran vaudeville act who had done thousands of shows together on hundreds of stages across the decades.

A scant two years before, Frawley had been a washed-up movie character actor and Vance had been a relatively little-known stage actress. Now here they were performing for the President of the United States, and in the company of luminaries from their pasts: Ethel Merman (the Broadway legend whom Viv had understudied two decades earlier), Helen Hayes (the wife of Charles MacArthur, co-author of *Twentieth Century*), Richard Rodgers (who wrote the music for *She's My Baby*), and Oscar Hammerstein II (the lyricist of *Music in the Air*).

Another special Frawley-Vance TV appearance came on Ed Sullivan's *Toast of the Town* CBS broadcast of October 3, 1954, which was the eve of the start of the fourth *I Love Lucy* season. One of the highlights of the skit featuring Ball, Arnaz, Frawley, and Vance has Viv and Bill, in period costume, dueting on an endearingly silly gibberish song and performing a brief soft-shoe dance together. The routine is a delight. Here again, Frawley's and Vance's consummate professionalism is on full parade.

And their "all for one and one for all" public facade is ever-present. As part of the sketch, Viv and Bill (who play themselves rather than the Mertzes) separately pay a visit to Lucy and Desi. "Is that Vivian?" Bill playfully laughs, upon spying Viv. He then trots over to her, and the pair greet each other warmly.

On *I Love Lucy*, Vance might have had to ignore her and Frawley's age difference. But here, as they banter over singing a 1913 tune, Vance could emphasize that she was considerably younger than her TV spouse.

Vance and Frawley's functions on *Dinner with the President* and *Toast of the Town* were directly related to *I Love Lucy*. So was their appearance on *The Bob Hope Chevy Show*, broadcast on NBC-TV on October 24, 1956. It included a comedy routine featuring Ball and Vance as their usual Lucy Ricardo/Ethel Mertz characters, but with Hope impersonating Ricky Ricardo, Arnaz playing Fred Mertz, and Frawley cast as Captain Blystone, a seal trainer.

In the Hope outing, the difference in Vance's and Frawley's age, and Frawley's sexual unattractiveness, are the butt of some mildly racy humor. Lucy observes that Desi/Fred looks like a "new man" who "took off a little weight, put on a little hair." Ethel responds, "That's my Freddie. He's my poopsie-woopsie." She then showers Desi/Fred with more kisses then she ever gave Frawley/Fred, and announces, "Hey, you're right, he has changed." Lucy observes this scene and no longer can maintain her growing agitation. "Break it up," she comically pronounces. "Let's not overdo it."

Later on in the TV fun, Fred and Ethel sleep in the Ricardos' apartment. Lucy suggests that the girls take over the bedroom and the boys make do in the living room. Ricky/Hope asks, "Wait a minute, Ethel, wait a minute, honey, don't you want to sleep here with your husband?" Ethel smiles and responds with a provocative, "Well . . ." Lucy butts in and declares, "No, she doesn't," and pulls Ethel into the bedroom.

Vance may well have preferred a younger and more dashing actor as her TV husband. Yet if someone more appealing had been cast as Fred, the dynamic of *I Love Lucy* would have been seriously altered—and all the humor that derived from Fred's and Ethel's idiosyncrasies might very well have never been.

Chapter Sixteen

A BACHELOR'S LIFE

On *I Love Lucy,* the characters of Fred and Ethel Mertz were the epitome of an old married couple. Yet for years Bill Frawley lived alone, or with one of the few women he could tolerate for any length of time—his younger sister, Mary, who died at age fifty-nine in 1957.

De-De Ball, Lucille Ball's beloved mother, may have been fabled for never missing an *I Love Lucy* filming, but she had a rival in Mary Frawley, who also savored watching the show's shooting on the Desilu lot. Mary described Lucille Ball as "a wonderful, wonderful person. I'm crazy about her," and characterized Desi Arnaz as "a mighty fine fellow."

At the time Bill Frawley signed to play Fred Mertz, he and Mary were sharing a suite at the Knickerbocker Hotel, located on Ivar Street just off Hollywood Boulevard. Frawley lived in the hotel for many years before spending the final portion of his life in an apartment at 450 North Rossmore in Hollywood. In fact, at one point in "High Pitch," the 1955 television musical in which Frawley appeared as a major-league manager, newspaper headlines flash across the screen. One of the fictitious papers is *"The Rossmore Journal."*

Two years before her death, Mary Frawley returned to Burlington for the first time in over two decades to visit friends and relatives. Mary reported that, while in Burlington, Bill and Paul Frawley phoned her from Los Angeles and "were anxious to hear about Burlington." "I told Bill there was no smog here," Mary revealed. "That's the favorite topic of conversation on the Coast."

As the years passed, a favorite topic of Frawley's remained sports. To his great pleasure, his obsession with athletics also was incorporated into scripts of *I Love Lucy*. In fact, in "The Girls Want to Go to a Nightclub," the sitcom's very first broadcast episode, the comic complications revolve around Fred's desire to spend his eighteenth wedding anniversary at the fights rather than with his beloved Ethel. On "Lucy Is Enceinte," the classic 1952 episode in which Lucy tells Ricky she is pregnant, Fred enters with a ball, bat, glove, and New York Yankees cap. He hands the latter three to Lucy, "for my godson."

Regarding the baseball, he adds, "And wait'll you see the name on this. That's the name of the best ballplayer the Yankees ever had."

"Uh, Spalding," Lucy blurts out, after glancing at it.

"C'mon, honey, turn it around," Fred instructs.

"Oh, Joe DiMaggio," Lucy declares.

"You betcha," Fred responds, taking a mock batting stance. "Ol' Joltin' Joe himself."

During his *I Love Lucy* years, Frawley supplemented his income by making occasional appearances in promotional films. For example, in *Shopping Around*, a twelve-minute sales film produced for Chevrolet in 1954 by the Jam Handy Organization, he discussed how automobile-purchasing conditions had changed since the end of World War II. This bit of casting is ironic in light of the fact that Frawley did not drive!

He also guest-starred by himself on television variety shows. One such part came in January 1959, when Frawley performed what he described as "a number or two" from his record album on singer Patti Page's TV show.

He showed up on a Thanksgiving 1958 edition of *The Red Skelton Show*, playing a coldhearted restaurateur who becomes the Turkey Day nemesis of Skelton's Freddy the Freeloader. As the skit was presented in pantomime, Frawley—fabled for opening his mouth both on and off camera—remained silent for his entire performance.

Quite a few of his non-*Lucy* projects also involved baseball. In the summer of 1954, he accepted a role as a major-league scout on *Great Scott*, a new radio series. He also donned a baseball uniform on television in 1955's "High Pitch" and "Comeback," a drama in which he costarred with Dan Duryea, which aired on *Desilu Playhouse* in 1959.

Frawley was a willing recruiter for the sport. In 1955, he appeared in *Take Me Out to the Ball Game*, a short promotional film in which he, Humphrey Bogart, Bob Hope, and baseball commissioner Ford Frick extol the virtues of the national pastime. Segments of the film were televised during the World Series, which pitted the New York Yankees against the Brooklyn Dodgers.

In Frawley's segment, he is first shown as his Fred Mertz character, on the phone with Ethel. He tells her that he is "goin' to a ball game," and is delighted when Ethel tells him she wants to join him. Then Frawley appears as himself and explains, "This is Bill Frawley . . . and I want you to know what baseball means to me. It's a wonderful game. Of course, a man's wife wants to go. It's a game for the whole family. Ya have the fun of being in there with the kind of people ya like, and rooting until you're hoarse. And in the American Way, you even give the visitors a hand. . . . " At which point Frawley snappily claps his hands.

"Television is fine," he continues, "but it can't give you the thrills and the fun ya have at the game, getting the sunshine and fresh air and being a real part of our national pastime. So let's all forget our worries and have fun at the ball game whenever we can get to one."

Frawley concludes his spiel with a robust, "Whaddya say?" followed by an equally hearty, "Let's go!"

While Frawley mostly maintained his privacy on and off the *I Love Lucy* set, he, Desi Arnaz, and scripters Bob Schiller and Bob Weiskopf occasionally would attend sporting events together. "We were sports buddies at that time," Schiller recalls. "[Frawley] was my partner's hero. . . . He and Frawley got along great because they're both big sports fans. . . . When you talked sports with him, you were on safe ground."

Weiskopf echoes his writing partner's interpretation. "[Frawley] was just an old curmudgeon-type fellow," he says. "That's the way I am, too, so he and I got along fine."

Weiskopf adds, "Schiller and I were sports fans. And Bill Frawley was an old sports fan. So we used to discuss sports. He knew a man named Fred Haney, who played in the big leagues for a while and played out here and then managed for a while. He was only one of them. But he knew all the names, you know."

Frawley frequently would mix his knowledge of sports with his salty humor. "He did a thing at a rehearsal [of *I Love Lucy*] once," says Weiskopf. "They were doing a show about a mountain, the side of a mountain. He had a line about how high the place was. And at rehearsal he [quipped], 'This place is as high as [basketball player] Goose Tatum's ass.' He turned to me and Schiller and said, 'I did that for you two guys.'"

♥

Frawley still generally preferred the company of sports figures to Tinseltown types. During the run of *I Love Lucy*, Vivian Vance—who never would have found herself joining Arnaz, Schiller, and Weiskopf at a sporting event—tactfully told a reporter, "None of us see much of Bill except when the show's being prepared. He likes to pal around with Joe DiMaggio and the baseball crowd." Vance also was careful to remind the reporter that she was not Frawley's real-life wife when she added, "Don't forget, he's a bachelor." She also once observed, "Playing Fred Mertz on the top-rated show in television was a nuisance to Bill. It interfered with his hobby of sitting in bars, chewing the rag with baseball players."

Just as Frawley back in the 1930s had a clause in his Paramount contract specifying that he be allowed to attend the World Series, a similar provision was included in his *I Love Lucy* agreement. Only here, the clause stipulated that he could frequent the Fall Classic whenever the American League pennant winner was the New York Yankees. As the Bronx Bombers were October perennials during practically the entire *I Love Lucy/Lucille Ball–Desi Arnaz Show* run, winning seven of nine American League pennants, Frawley attended quite a few Fall Classics.

Actor/director Gene Reynolds describes Frawley as being "crazy about the New York Yankees." He adds, "I remember I was with him one time and we were doing a kitchen scene [on *My Three Sons*]. In between shots, we'd turn on the radio because it was getting right down to the World Series. The Yanks either were trying to get into the World Series, or were in the World Series and losing. Some guy would get up and dribble a ball down to second or strike out, and Frawley, if he happened to be near a pot or a pan, you know, he'd let it fly. There would be a tremendous crash— and there'd be a little obscenity to go with it."

When Frawley visited New York during the 1950s, he could be found lunching with Dan Topping, co-owner of the Yankees, or at a select seat at Yankee Stadium. The Bronx Bombers' Hall of Fame catcher Yogi Berra remembers meeting Frawley and describes him as "a great fan."

Throughout his tenure on *I Love Lucy,* Frawley also remained a frequent presence at Hollywood Stars games. "I was with the Stars in 1954," declares Gene Karst, the team's former publicist, "and saw Bill Frawley there many times, as well as Walt Disney, Rita Moreno, and others in the film world." The ballclub even made its way into an *I Love Lucy* script. In "In Palm Springs," which aired in 1955, Fred and Ricky plan to attend a Stars game, which is rained out.

Upon the arrival of the Dodgers from Brooklyn for the start of the 1958 major-league season, the Hollywood Stars moved on to Salt Lake City while the Los Angeles Angels headed to Spokane.

As a quarter-century-long southern California resident, Frawley would not have concurred with Pete Hamill's claim that the three biggest villains of the twentieth century are Hitler, Stalin, and Walter O'Malley. The latter, of course, was the owner of the Dodgers and the man responsible for the team's abandoning the "Borough of Churches" for the orange groves of southern California—and thus rechristening Frawley as a Dodgers rooter.

When the Dodgers first came to California, they played in the Los Angeles Coliseum, a cavernous arena wholly unsuited to baseball. Clearly, a more fitting ballyard had to be built. On June 3, 1958, a referendum was held on whether to allow the city of Los Angeles to sell to O'Malley three hundred acres of land in Chavez Ravine, on which a new stadium would be constructed. On the Sunday before the vote, Frawley, Danny Thomas, Jeff Chandler, and other Hollywood luminaries joined O'Malley on a special five-hour-long show, aired on Gene Autry's local TV station. The program essentially was a paid political announcement in which the stars urged the populace to "vote yes for the Dodgers." Perhaps it did convince just enough voters to approve the measure, which was narrowly passed, 345,435 to 321,142.

Frawley was further elated when major-league expansion in 1961 resulted in the creation of the American League Los Angeles Angels, which eventually were rechristened the California and then the Anaheim Angels. He was delighted to be named a member of the team's seven-man honorary board of directors. "Having the Angels and Dodgers here is great," he enthused in 1961. "I was very happy when the Dodgers moved to Los Angeles."

By now, the seventy-four-year-old actor was a beloved Hollywood senior citizen whose fame extended wherever *I Love Lucy* was broadcast.

Chapter Seventeen

A TROUBLED STATE

Despite the continuing inner turmoil that was a vestige from her nervous breakdown, Vivian Vance was able to maintain her high-spiritedness and sense of humor while on the *I Love Lucy* set.

Her quick wit was apparent to those with whom she worked. And her cracks could be quite risqué. "Viv had one of the great lines of all time," notes scriptwriter Bob Schiller. "In those days, we both were in analysis and we used to share our stories. One day, she called me down to the set and she was laughing."

Vance told Schiller, "I'm in that part of my analysis where I'm talking about my relationship with my father, and nudity, and all that kind of thing." Then she added, "I was so ashamed of my body that I spent half my life hiding it under men."

Even as she was smiling on the outside and cracking up America as she cavorted with Lucy and company, Vance was confronting her demons through psychoanalysis. Of her years playing Ethel Mertz, she reminisced,

"I'd go from the couch to the studio every morning." Yet her problems in no way impeded her performance. Whatever Vance may have been feeling on any given day, she kept those sentiments to herself and gave her all during the *I Love Lucy* rehearsals and filming.

At Christmas, 1953, Lucille Ball presented Vance with a special gift: an album of photos, programs, and press clippings, which Ball called *This Is Your Life—Vivian Vance*. "And when she presented it to me, before the whole company," Vance dramatically noted, "whatever fears were still plaguing Vivian Vance were wiped away forever."

Vance remained married to Phil Ober for the entire *I Love Lucy* run. By now he was well into his fifties, but he was no William Frawley. "He was a handsome man, kind of posh, you know," recalls Bob Weiskopf. "He was an elegant fellow." Sheila MacRae adds, "Phil Ober was a very presentable, nice-looking gentleman. Very well spoken, with this great voice and wonderful presence."

Vance and Ober had what Jay Sandrich describes as a "nice home" in Pacific Palisades, a particularly lovely area of Los Angeles adjacent to the ocean and south of Malibu. When they were not working, the Obers retreated to their New Mexico ranch, where their neighbors were Mexicans and Laguna Indians rather than celebrated Los Angelenos. "We're living two lives, Phil and I," Vance explained during her lengthy *I Love Lucy* run. "When we work, we're part of the pressure and speed and concentrated effort that goes with television and the stage. But we're only a few hours away from our own large, generous slice of peace. I've found that if we have a decision to make, it usually becomes quite simple to make the right one if we just go to our desert home to think about it."

On another occasion, Viv noted, "It's a casual life. Everyone for miles around comes to our campfires . . . ranchers, cowboys, and Indians. It's a wide place in the road and a place which draws us away from the city, and makes us appreciate our city home more when we return."

The Obers also passed their time away from Los Angeles visiting Viv's parents (who still resided in Albuquerque) and traveling. In February

1953, *I Love Lucy* went on hiatus after the birth of Desi Arnaz Jr. A chatty item in the *Albuquerque Journal* reported that "the Obers came to Albuquerque by way of Carmel, Cal., and Las Vegas, Nev. While in the Southwest, they will go shopping in Santa Fe for dining furniture for their California home. From Albuquerque the couple will continue their vacation in Rome, Italy."

Apparently, Vance and Ober were not spending enough time away from the Hollywood rat race, or making the right decisions about their relationship. As the years passed, their marriage deteriorated. There always had been a competitive edge to their union. While Ober had been steadily employed on the stage—he was somewhat of a name on the Broadway boards—his New York fame meant nothing on the West Coast.

Just as his wife was beginning her run on *I Love Lucy*, Ober declared that he hoped to put his stage work behind him and continue his career in Hollywood. "You hear that remark about the stage being the only real medium," he declared in 1951. "That's just not true. In pictures, things can be done much better. When you have to do a love scene and you whisper, you can speak low and you're heard. It's the most honest medium."

The fifty-something Ober, though, was fated to play few celluloid love scenes. While he began appearing regularly on-screen in the 1950s, he was quickly relegated to character/supporting roles and never won Hollywood stardom. Through the next two decades, he was cast in a couple dozen movies. They ranged in quality from highly prestigious—*Come Back, Little Sheba* (1952), *North by Northwest* (1959), and *Elmer Gantry* (1960)—to highly forgettable—*The Girls of Pleasure Island* (1953), *Escapade in Japan* (1957), and *The Ghost and Mr. Chicken* (1966).

Perhaps his most familiar role came in *From Here to Eternity* (1953), in which he played Deborah Kerr's coldhearted spouse, who is more concerned with winning a military boxing championship than with offering his wife the affection she craves. Nonetheless, thinking of the Fred Zinnemann-directed Oscar-winner, one recalls Kerr, Burt Lancaster,

Frank Sinatra, Montgomery Clift, Donna Reed, Ernest Borgnine—but *not* Phil Ober.

Ober also appeared on *I Love Lucy*, playing various roles. On one episode, "The Quiz Show"—the fifth *I Love Lucy* to be aired during its first season (1951–52)—he was Lucy's bogus long-lost first husband. In another, "Don Juan Is Shelved," broadcast in 1955, he was cast as then MGM studio boss Dore Schary (who was supposed to appear as himself, but backed out before the episode was filmed). Yet here Ober was just one of dozens of mostly anonymous actors who played parts on the show.

Throughout the 1950s, Phil made non–*I Love Lucy* TV guest appearances. Yet here, too, his roles were unmemorable. A typical Ober television part was on a *Ford Theater* episode titled "Sheila," which aired in May 1956. Ober plays Kirk Adams, a widower who is clueless as to how to give his wayward adolescent daughter Laura (Stephanie Griffin) his understanding and love. Laura attends a boarding school run by the title character (Irene Dunne), while Elinor Donahue plays Sheila's well-adjusted offspring. The show's opening credits may have read, "Irene Dunne in 'Sheila' with Philip Ober and Elinor Donahue," but it was Dunne, Donahue, and Griffin—without Ober—who were featured in the show's promotional clip.

When "Sheila" aired, Vance had long been recognized by millions as Ethel Mertz. What's more, there she was winning Emmy Award nominations and performing on national television in front of the President of the United States. The culmination was that Ober felt professionally resentful of his wife, to an obsessive degree. Reportedly, he even refused to allow Vance to display her Emmy Award in their home.

Marjorie Lord remembers that Vance's fame "was hard on Phil. He was a rather important leading man in New York, and I think that Vivian's tremendous success was a bit [too much for him]. He never quite equaled it in pictures although he worked a lot, he worked all the time. But she became extremely famous. Everybody knew her, but wouldn't know him, necessarily."

Sheila MacRae concurs with Lord. "[Phil] used to be as important, or more important [than Vivian]," she says. "Perhaps her fame was too hard for him to take. If they were in different businesses, perhaps it wouldn't have mattered."

"He was very possessive," notes Irma Kusely, the *I Love Lucy* hairdresser, "and also kind of a womanizer. He also seemed to be very jealous of her friends. I know that I [would go out to] their house in Pacific Palisades, and he wondered what the heck we were doing and what was going on and why was I there. I sensed that he just wanted her not to have a lot of friends.

"She was just really a great gal," Kusely adds. "I think a man should have been very proud to have her as a friend, [much less] a wife. She was just wonderful. She was capable of doing a lot of things that most people in the business weren't. She was a very good cook, and a good entertainer. She was just a regular gal. She had no illusions of grandeur about herself at all."

Film editor Dann Cahn knew Ober well and recalls, "Phil used to come to the [filming of the *I Love Lucy*] shows and he'd roar, in the beginning. I'm talking about the first couple of years. Whatever happened happened, and then he didn't come anymore."

Vance and Ober were separated in February 1958 and were divorced fourteen months later. Their split reportedly was encouraged by Lucille Ball, who was then ending her own turbulent marriage to Desi Arnaz. It is no secret that Desi was cheating on Lucy, and that he shared with Bill Frawley a fondness for alcohol.

At this point in time, the off-set tensions were becoming apparent to those on the inside. "There were not a lot of laughs around," remembers Jay Sandrich. "I do shows where we laugh all day at rehearsals. But here, there wasn't a lot of laughter."

Nevertheless, Sandrich emphasizes that, despite the upheavals in the personal lives of Lucy, Desi, and Viv, "The shows always were hilarious."

"There we were," Vance remembered a half decade later, "two miserable women, commiserating, even crying together, then bucking up to go in front of the cameras and make the whole country laugh."

To Sheila MacRae's way of thinking, however, any conversations between Vance and Ball regarding marital woes had to have been one-sided. "All of that stuff I don't think [Lucy] ever shared with Vivian," says MacRae. "You see, she couldn't. It was different." For after all, Vance still was an employee. Ball was her boss. And Ball's marital difficulties were with Vance's other boss. Ball did confide her problems to MacRae, who understood all too well what she was going through because—as MacRae readily admits—she was experiencing similar difficulties with her own husband then.

"My husband liked to dominate and discipline me," was how Vance once described her trouble with Ober. "I kept trying to please him, but nothing I did was right." Rumors even circulated that Ober would hit her and that, on one occasion, she arrived on the *I Love Lucy* set with a black eye. He also allegedly humiliated Viv by scolding her for acting touchy-feely with Ball, as though they were a pair of lesbians.

Yet it was Ober who sued Vance for divorce, claiming cruelty. In her response, she declared that she and Ober "could never agree on how to handle my success," that Ober was jealous of her fame, and that he insisted they fritter away her earnings.

"He seemed to have a compulsion for high living and often told me about the futility of saving money," Vance declared. She added that she readily would have quit *I Love Lucy* in order to save her marriage, but that Ober forbid her to do so.

All of this was told to Los Angeles Superior Court Judge Burnett Wolfson on April 24, 1959, at their divorce hearing. Wolfson granted her a default divorce while observing, "Damon Runyon used to say that 'they never had to hold a benefit for a man who saved his money'—Mr. Ober might well hark those words." Judge Wolfson also noted, "It might be that I am very naive, but if there ever was a case of killing the goose that laid the golden egg, this is it."

In order to be rid of Ober, Vance—on the advice of her attorney, Payson Wolff—waived her right to alimony and gave him one-half of their community property, valued at $160,000, while maintaining their Pacific

Palisades home. When asked by Judge Wolfson if she thought this fair, she responded, "No, sir, I think the terms are pretty liberal. After all, I made and saved all this money."

Ober was not present during the proceedings. His lawyer, Milton M. Golden, was, and he declared, "My client is not a super fool or a plain fool. It was his astuteness in buying stocks which contributed to the community property."

Whatever the facts, one thing was certain: the Ober-Vance divorce was anything but amicable. "It was a shame that [their marriage] didn't last throughout her lifetime," declares Marjorie Lord, who was on the scene when the pair first met and fell in love.

Eventually, Ober married Jane Westmore, an NBC press agent. He left performing and settled in the beach resort of Puerto Vallarta, Mexico, where he acted as emergency United States representative for the American consul. "I visited him in Mexico," notes Dann Cahn. "He had a house down there near the Burtons [Elizabeth Taylor and Richard Burton]. We spent a wonderful evening together. He'd become kind of the unofficial mayor of Puerto Vallarta. He'd get American kids who'd gotten in trouble, out of trouble."

Ober eventually returned to the United States. He died in Santa Monica of a heart attack in 1982, at age eighty. He was survived by his wife, Jane.

♥

As the close-to-eighteen-year marriage of Vance and Ober crumbled, so did the almost twenty-year union of Ball and Arnaz. On March 2, 1960, Ball filed divorce papers, professing that her off-camera life with Arnaz had become a "nightmare." She submitted the petition one day after completing filming of "Lucy Meets the Moustache," the very last episode of *The Lucille Ball–Desi Arnaz Show*, which featured comedian Ernie Kovacs and his wife, Edie Adams, as guest stars. The episode ended with the Ricardos sharing a final kiss. From now on, and forever more, the Ricardos and Mertzes would appear on television screens only in rerun.

Eight and a half long years had come and gone since the launching of *I Love Lucy*, and so much had happened to its four principal actors. The circumstances of their lives, both personal and professional, now were so different. From here on in, each would go on to other projects and savor other accomplishments. Yet one thing was certain: The thrill of the making of *I Love Lucy* never, ever could be duplicated.

Part Four

WILLIAM FRAWLEY
AFTER FRED

Frawley in a publicity still for *My Three Sons*. (PHOTO COURTESY OF GLOBE)

Frawley and Vance at it again. (PHOTO COURTESY OF GLOBE)

Chapter Eighteen

"BUB"

Bill Frawley hoped to continue playing Fred Mertz for "as long as they'll tolerate me." Yet in the late 1950s, his run in the role was destined to begin winding down. Frawley, who by now was well past retirement age, might have considered embracing a life of leisure, living off his *I Love Lucy* residuals (which he once described as "beautiful") and hanging out at his favorite Hollywood saloons. Instead, he chose to continue working in television.

When *I Love Lucy* became the *Lucille Ball–Desi Arnaz Show*, Frawley reported that he was considering roles in two potential sitcoms. "One would be a series in which I play a football coach and the other is an adaptation of [the] George McManus comic strip, 'Bringing Up Father.' I would play Jiggs." Neither came to fruition.

Frawley did star in the pilot episode of *Fit as a Fiddle*, an unsold comedy in which he was paired with fellow ex-vaudevillian Eddie Foy Jr. and Florence Halop (in a dual role) as four characters who operate a combination dance academy–gymnasium–charm school. He also was cast with Gale Gordon—choice number one to play Fred Mertz—in yet another failed pilot, *Mr. Harkrider and Mr. Sweeney.*

And he guest-starred (along with Andy Devine) in *No Place Like Home,* a sitcom starring Gordon and Sheila MacRae as a show-business couple. "The whole idea here was that Gordy would be a cowboy star," explains Sheila MacRae. "They didn't want us to emulate Lucy and Desi. Yet they wanted us to capitalize on Lucy and Desi." Unfortunately, *No Place Like Home* could not find a place on any network schedule.

Frawley hit pay dirt with an altogether different new half-hour comedy. It was *My Three Sons,* which debuted on the ABC network on September 29, 1960—scant months after the March 8, 1960, air date of "Lucy Meets the Moustache."

On the new show, set in the Midwest, Frawley was cast as Michael Francis "Bub" O'Casey, the curmudgeonly father-in-law of consulting aviation engineer Steve Douglas (Fred MacMurray), a widower attempting to raise the title trio: eighteen-year-old Mike (Tim Considine), fourteen-year-old Robbie (Don Grady), and seven-year-old Chip (Stanley Livingston). Bub's purpose within the framework of the show was as a combination housekeeper/den mother to the Douglas clan.

My Three Sons was a reunion of sorts for Frawley and MacMurray, a fellow former Paramount studio contractee. "I was in the first movie Fred ever made for Paramount," Frawley recalled a year into the series. "It was called *Car 99* [1935]. We starred in another old-timer, too, *The Princess Comes Across* [1936], with Carole Lombard. Fred played a bandleader on a ship and I played his manager." Frawley was in no way exaggerating when he added, "There isn't another guy in show business as nice as Fred MacMurray."

Series production manager John Stephens recalls that Frawley was the first person hired for *My Three Sons*—even before MacMurray. "Don Fedderson [the show's executive producer] was a gambler," he says. "We made the first show as a pilot, with very little publicity. He got Frawley and then Fred MacMurray on a very unusual deal. He guaranteed them and the entire cast one year's salary, which back then was thirty-nine episodes.

He gambled that he'd sell it. We had no backing from an agency, or anyone. He invited a few people to see the dailies, and the second day Chevrolet bought the series."

During their years together on *My Three Sons*, Frawley and Stephens became close friends. Yet his introduction to Frawley, which predated *My Three Sons'* debut by several years, was less than auspicious.

Stephens was working for Fedderson on a sitcom called *A Date with the Angels*, which starred Betty White and Bill Williams and was aired between May 1957 and January 1958. "We were filming it at Desilu Gower," he recalls. "I certainly knew who Bill Frawley was, but had never met him.

"I used to go into the commissary and he'd be in there having a bowl of, say, split-pea soup. He'd have on a suit and tie. He'd take his spoon and put it in the soup, and as he was lifting it up to his mouth the entire spoon would wind up being spilled over his shirt, his tie. Occasionally, he'd manage to get some of it up to his chin."

Stephens looked at Frawley and thought, "Oh boy . . . wow, poor guy, how much longer is he going to last? I'm certainly glad I never worked with him."

"But then," he notes, "a year or so later, *boom*—I was working with him."

As he got to know Frawley, Stephens became fond of the old actor. "He really was much more of a person than an actor," Stephens explains. "You could talk to him about anything, and be yourself [around him]. He had no air of, 'I'm a star and don't bother me.' It was not like that at all with Bill.

"Character actors are mostly insecure," Stephens continues. "They're the people who really need the most pampering. But not Bill. He never really asked for that.

"He never tried to act. He was just himself—he was enough of a character himself. If you see him in any of his old movies, he really virtually was always the same. . . . What Bill Frawley would do is bring the character to Bill Frawley. He wouldn't say, 'Gee, what would Bub say?' He never went out of character. He was the same on-screen as off-screen. What you saw was what you got."

Additionally, Frawley did not come to *My Three Sons* as a second banana and an employee of the star. While Fred MacMurray was the show's primary headliner, Frawley received the deference that was due him as a veteran performer—and star status in his billing. At the beginning of the show's first episode, which was titled "Chip—Off the Old Block," a voice announced, "*My Three Sons*, starring Fred MacMurray and, as Bub, William Frawley."

The installment opens with a salesman ringing the Douglas doorbell and asking, "Well, is the lady of the house in?" Chip yells into the kitchen, "Bub, somebody wants to see you." Then Frawley makes his initial appearance, garbed in an apron and muttering to himself, "Cook the dinner, clean the house, wash the dishes, answer the door. I don't know what they do around here. . . ." Bub asks the salesman, "Watcha peddlin'?" The answer is cosmetics. "Oh boy," he laughs. "Have you got the wrong house! I'm the nearest thing to a lady around here. Come back when somebody's married."

And so we have the introduction of the all-male *My Three Sons* household.

The scenario of this premiere show involves young Chip feeling harassed by the friendly overtures of Doreen Peters, a "dumb girl," and an attempt by some of his father's friends to hook Steve up with a marriage-minded woman. Throughout the episode, Bub is forever slaving over the stove, and forever wearing an apron. "That should have been donated to the Smithsonian, along with Archie Bunker's chair," declares Stanley Livingston, more than thirty-seven years after the fact.

To emphasize Bill Frawley's place in future *My Three Sons* episodes, the program's final shot is of a smiling Bub.

♥

During the *My Three Sons* years (1960–65), Frawley came to caricature himself. Now more than ever, he would not so much speak, explain, declare, or utter, as growl. Reporters from around the country who interviewed him during this period described him as "a friendly man with a voice like a foghorn coming closer" (Ron Burton); an "ancient actor [with] a voice that rattled the windows in the Brown Derby" (Vernon Scott); a "salty, cantankerous, outspoken actor" and "gravel-voiced star" (Kay Gardella); and a character with a "strutting manner, growling voice, [and] hard-jawed face" (Murray Schumach). Schumach added, "[His] tough features seem to have been carved out of stone to illustrate Damon Runyon short stories." During their interview, Frawley "tossed a side-mouthed greeting and a debonair wave to a passing acquaintance, exchanged a bit of banter with [a] solicitous restaurant manager, and then traced his cockiness back to his Iowa roots."

However, this self-confidence was, at least in part, the result of Frawley's elevated status in the show's on-camera hierarchy: a standing that is reflected in *Variety*'s review of the show's premiere episode. In the first line of the piece, *My Three Sons* is referred to as "the new Fred MacMurray–Bill Frawley comedy." The critic labeled the show "an amiable, leisurely family comedy," adding that "Frawley was perfectly cast as [MacMurray's] wry father-in-law who acted as chief cook and bottle-washer."

"As it is," Frawley noted of his part on the show a month after its bow, "I berate the kids and a dog named Tramp. . . . I spend a lot of time in the kitchen and cleaning up the house. I can't fry an egg in real life. But on the show I turn out layer cakes and prune whip. I also sweep the dust under the rugs."

Ethnicity was one of the key ingredients of Bub O'Casey's makeup. If his last name had been Cohen, he surely would have been a master at stirring up chicken soup for his charges. If it was Cirillo, he would have been adept at baking lasagna or manicotti. Being that it was O'Casey, the character was an expert at concocting mulligan stew—a dish which, Frawley explained, "has everything in it but a leprechaun."

Frawley quickly grew to relish playing Bub. "Nothing to it at all," he declared at the close of the show's first season. "I'm equipped with all the things this old character has to have. I can wash dishes, make a bed, cook some coffee, fry an egg or two with ham, whistle an Irish tune, sing a song."

The blending in the public eye of the personalities of television characters and the actors who play them was to further plague Frawley when he became Bub on *My Three Sons*. Because Bub was a cook, Bill frequently would receive letters from housewives requesting kitchen tips. A typical one came from a woman in New Jersey. "I am Italian, my husband is Irish," she wrote. "I know how to make spaghetti, but he doesn't think I make good mulligan stew. Will you send me your recipe?"

Only trouble was, Frawley's occasional declarations about brewing coffee and frying eggs aside, he also admittedly barely knew how to boil water, let alone muster up a tasty mulligan stew. Off-camera, he was as adept in a kitchen as Julia Child would be if she attempted to slide into second base.

"To me, the funniest scenes in the world were the kitchen scenes where Bill was making dinner," recalls John Stephens. "[The] Bill Frawley I know could pour himself a drink. But other than that, I never saw him do anything in his life that had to do with cooking. He didn't even know how to shred lettuce. He'd put carrots or celery in the salad, and instead of cutting [the vegetables] he would saw them. Instead of chopping, he would move the knife back and forth. He had no idea of what he was doing.

"If you see any of the old episodes [with] him in the kitchen, you'll notice this. It was absolutely hysterical," says Stephens.

Tim Considine adds, "All during rehearsals, he [actually] would pour the coffee or make the cereal. He'd dirty these cups and glasses, and they finally had to beg him to please just fake it during rehearsals. So now, he got that down. But then when we went to shoot [the scene], he did the same thing. He'd now trained himself not to pour anything, so he continued doing it like a mime when we were actually filming. I remember that was good for a laugh."

Frawley's lack of concern for acting craft or character motivation remained with him as he began playing Bub O'Casey. He was especially irked by one incident that occurred during the show's first season (1960–61). The director, Peter Tewkesbury, was shooting a scene in which Bub purchased a pair of shoes. John Stephens recalls that Tewkesbury said, "Okay, I'm ready for a take. Now, are there shoes in the shoebox?"

Was the box going to be opened anytime during the scene? No.

Still Tewkesbury commanded, "I want shoes in the shoebox."

Stephens found a pair backstage and placed them in the box. Tewkesbury then asked, "Wait a second, are those Mr. Frawley's shoes?"

They were not, and Tewkesbury continued, "I can't shoot this scene unless he has his own shoes in the shoebox. I'm having a hard enough time getting him to act the way I want him to act."

Luckily Frawley lived only five minutes from the studio, so a driver was dispatched with the actor's keys to retrieve the needed footwear. According to Stephens, Frawley just shook his head and grumbled, "We gotta get rid of this guy, John. We gotta get rid of this guy." Tewkesbury ended up leaving the series at the end of its first year.

Four years into the run of *My Three Sons*, upon the start of the 1963 television season, the show was reevaluated by *Variety*. If by then the sitcom seemed to have gone stale, it was not because of its veteran stars. "The series has, of course, a great deal going for it in a couple of old hands, Fred MacMurray and Bill Frawley, who have real comedy style and, amazingly, can still go through the hackneyed paces as though genuinely inspired," wrote the *Variety* critic. "Some of their professionalism seems to have rubbed off on MacMurray's three video sons, Tim Considine, Don Grady, and Stanley Livingston. . . . Frawley has his moments too [in the season premiere episode], most of them centering on his diligent housekeeping, a sort of running gag.

"His is perhaps the key role in *Three Sons*, the one that gives the series its uniqueness on television, and he plays it on the soft pedal with comic charm."

Chapter Nineteen

NEW FRIENDSHIPS

Sheila MacRae recalls an occasion back in the 1950s when she was attempting to teach her young children how to properly tip in a restaurant. She was doing so in the presence of Frawley, who was hanging out with her husband, Gordon, and their cronies. Sheila was stressing the need to tip generously, and Frawley told her, "Jesus, look at this. The kid got a $7 hamburger and she's giving a $5 tip. That's no good. These kids are gonna be brats."

One of those brats-in-training grew up to be Meredith MacRae, who came to *My Three Sons* in 1963 and played Sally Ann Morrison, the fiancée of Mike Douglas.

Frawley welcomed her presence on the show. After all, when *My Three Sons* began, there were no female regulars. "So far, the only girls who have shown up are romantic interests for MacMurray," Frawley growled just after its premiere. "There aren't any girlfriends written into the script for me, though. Maybe it's just as well. I might wind up with another old-crow type.

"On the other hand, it wouldn't be bad if they brought in some young chick for me to chase around the set," he added.

The following year, 1961, the ever irascible Frawley still was grumbling that there were "no dames" on *My Three Sons*. "That's what our show needs—more dames!" he pronounced. "Even *Mutiny on the Bounty* would be better with women in it. Anyway, it's asking an awful lot to expect people to watch a show with three kids and a couple of old guys without any dames in it."

Here again, Frawley was just mouthing off and enjoying listening to himself talk. For at the same time, upon her joining the cast, he managed to thoroughly captivate Meredith MacRae.

"I loved Bill Frawley," she notes. "It was impossible to know him and not to just adore him. He was absolutely one of the most delightful people I have ever known. And for me, it was such an honor to have my first real job in show business working opposite him and Fred MacMurray.

"I really consider myself very blessed and lucky because they were just both such consummate professionals. They were wonderful actors, and delightful people as well off-camera. You couldn't imagine or fantasize a better first job, to suddenly come into this family that had already been together for several years and to be made to feel welcome."

Meredith remembers Frawley and MacMurray reminiscing about Old Hollywood and the movies they had made together. "Everybody had a good rapport," she recalls, "and Fred and Bill especially." John Stephens concurs: "It was a great cast. Everybody got along. That's because Fred MacMurray, I think, set the pace."

MacMurray had a customized contract that allowed him to shoot all his scenes in a clump and then take off for months at a time to make future films or to relax. According to Meredith MacRae, MacMurray's deal "was great for him, but more demanding on the rest of us. They would shoot the master scene with Fred, and then Fred's close-up. Then they would take Polaroid stills of us, and the wardrobe lady and the hair and makeup people would save them and match them [for when the scenes would be completed with the other actors].

"But nobody minded and nobody complained. And especially Bill. He was pretty old by that time. But he was always a professional."

On the *I Love Lucy* set, Frawley also had maintained his professionalism. Yet Dann Cahn uses the words "loner" and "recluse" to describe him during those years, noting that Vivian Vance was the one with the sense of humor. On *I Love Lucy*, Frawley had felt a tension among the personalities. He and Vance came from two different worlds and, despite his fondness for Lucy and Desi, they were not really colleagues but employers: bosses who could replace him or write out his character in an instant. The difference now was that Frawley's personality was not reined in and, as a result, his love of laughter was able to thrive.

And no longer were there any restrictions on the actor's drinking habits. In fact, John Stephens states that, in the five years he knew Frawley, "There was not a single alcoholic beverage that I didn't see him drink. I mean everything. He was amazing."

In fact, Frawley was savoring a martini on the rocks when he gave an interview to journalist Vernon Scott (United Press International) a couple of weeks after the *My Three Sons* premiere. Scott asked Frawley if he missed his former costar. "Only because I don't have a nagging wife to bounce the comedy off of," Frawley was quick to quip. "There's nothing better than a battle-ax as a foil for laughs."

Once the *My Three Sons* cameras stopped rolling, there was no longer a need for Frawley to retreat into his private world. "He was at all the Christmas parties and things that we had," notes Meredith MacRae. "Bill also used to go every single day and have lunch at Nickodell's, have lunch and a couple of drinks. Every Friday, we used to all go and join him in this big red leather booth in the back of Nickodell's. It was on the left side, the biggest booth there. And we'd have lunch with him. That was really a treat."

Don Grady adds, "It was like Frawley and Nickodell's, they just went hand in hand." Nickodell's, of course, was the Hollywood restaurant in which the actor had interviewed with Desi Arnaz for *I Love Lucy*.

Meredith MacRae in particular was a sports fan, and was an enthusiastic listener when Frawley shared athletic anecdotes at their Friday lunch table. When she married at the end of her tenure on the show in 1965, she recalls that Frawley "sent me a letter and with it was a check for $100. And he said something like, 'I wish you kids the best. Here's a little something I earned myself to get you started.' I thought that was so wonderful. That letter was my favorite wedding gift. And of course, $100 at that time was like $1,000 now."

This was the type of thoughtful act the young cast members savored reciprocating. Tim Considine reports that Frawley "had made a big fuss over a dessert he had in New York, some chocolate-creme something, a very special deal." So for his birthday one year, Considine had the treat flown in from the East Coast. It was served on the set, and a good time was had by all.

When in the company of the opposite sex—especially younger females, such as Meredith MacRae—Frawley usually would be well mannered. And in his old age, he became fond of one particular woman: actress Patricia Barry, who did guest shots on *My Three Sons* and appeared with him on-screen in *Safe at Home!* (1962), his only post–*I Love Lucy* feature film. Barry was even in the *My Three Sons* premiere, cast as the potential girlfriend of series lead Fred MacMurray.

Red-haired, brown-eyed Barry was born in 1930 in Davenport, Iowa, making her forty-three years Frawley's junior. She had studied acting with Maude Adams at Stephens College and, during the late 1940s, appeared on-screen using the stage name Patricia White. In 1950, she wed Philip Barry Jr., son of the noted playwright, and the pair eventually had two daughters; they remained married until his death in 1998. During the late 1950s and early 1960s, she was one of the busier television-series guest stars, appearing on *Route 66, Thriller, General Electric Theater, Ben Casey, Dr. Kildare,* and many other programs. "I guess you might call me the queen of the guest stars," Barry once observed.

While recalling Frawley's general disdain for women, Don Grady also readily acknowledges Frawley's special, uncharacteristic fondness for

Barry. "I knew that he liked her," Grady says. "And she was very pretty. It wasn't until years later that I found out there was a lot going on there. When [the impact of their friendship] hit him, he must have fallen pretty hard. She must have found a crack in the fortress."

My Three Sons costar Stanley Livingston confirms Grady's report. "The lady who was playing Fred MacMurray's girlfriend on the first show, Patricia Barry, he got involved with, to whatever degree," Livingston explains. "He used to be very fond of her. I remember him talking about her constantly. I think it was probably an infatuation [with a younger woman] that an older guy gets.

"At [his] age, you still like to look."

Gene Reynolds adds, "She was very close to Frawley. I think he really liked her. They were real pals, really close. There was a real friendship there. She knew him terribly well."

Frawley's feelings for Barry were a matter of public record. "One of Patricia's most recent conquests is Bill Frawley," wrote Hal Humphrey in a profile of the actress published in the *Los Angeles Mirror* in January 1961, four months after the *My Three Sons* premiere. Humphrey noted that Frawley "joined the redhead's fan club" when she appeared on the pilot episode. "He calls her frequently," the journalist continued, "and even goes over to the Barry household to watch Patricia's two young daughters put on a puppet show."

Frawley also did whatever he could to hype Barry. Later on in 1961, Zuma Palmer wrote in the *Hollywood Citizen-News* that Frawley "has so much faith in the acting ability of Patricia Barry, one of today's young TV actresses, that he thinks someone should give her a 'billion dollar contract.'" At one point, the Frawley-Barry friendship appeared to chill. "I just remember her being around quite a lot," notes Stanley Livingston, "and then something must have happened, and she wasn't around quite as often. I don't know whether that had to do with the relationship cooling or her probably not [being] interested [in Frawley] outside of [his being] a father figure."

"He was certainly fond of her," recalls John Stephens. "I can tell you this much, which is not any big secret. She did break it off for a while, because obviously word got around that she was his girlfriend. She came to me shocked [about it]. But no one on the set ever discussed it."

Tim Considine offers further insight into the Frawley-Barry rapport when he notes, "I think he was encouraged, in a funny way. I think she enjoyed it. Now, how far it went, I don't know. But I had the feeling there was some encouragement. . . .

"It's always a compliment when somebody makes a fuss over you," he continues. "She was an attractive woman, but here was a guy who was very popular and, certainly, a dynamic personality. On a show on which she worked, [he] made a tremendous fuss over her. My impression as I recall was that there was some encouragement [on her part], that it wasn't put down [by her] or anything like that. That's the way I'd leave it. As I say, I don't know if there was any hanky-panky or anything, but I'm sure she enjoyed it."

Across the years, John Stephens notes that "a lot of people would ask me about [the situation], and this is all I can say: I'm not here to approve or disapprove of what anybody does or doesn't do. The only thing that I know is, whether she's bad or whether she's awful or whether she's gold-digging, whatever, she makes him happy. And as far as I'm concerned, I'll leave it at that. I don't want to pass any judgments.

"It wasn't a scandal," Stephens emphasizes regarding the Frawley-Barry friendship. "Everybody knew about it, and nobody cared about it. She made Bill happy, and that's what was important as far as I was concerned. What else was he going to spend his money on?"

Another actress whose company Frawley fancied was Joan Vohs, John Stephens's attractive thirty-something wife, who appeared as a guest on *My Three Sons*. "Bill knew her well and liked her a lot," Stephens says, "and he would always give me this line, 'If it wasn't for Joan, you'd be in the gutter.'"

One time, when Vohs was on *My Three Sons*, she called Stephens down to the set.

"I think you better talk to Bill," Vohs told her husband.

"Huh?" was Stephens's response.

"I don't know if Bill really knows who I am," Vohs explained.

"What do you mean?" Stephens asked.

Vohs implored him, "Please, just come."

Stephens went up to Frawley and, before he could say anything, the actor asked, "Johnny, have you seen that redhead working today?"

Stephens responded, "Well, yeah."

"Oh boy," Frawley retorted, "would I like to fuck her!"

Then, in an instant, Frawley snapped to it and realized his gaffe.

He looked at Stephens and said, "Uh, is that Joan?"

Stephens answered, "Yeah, Bill, it is."

Frawley exclaimed, "Oh, what have I said?!"

And Stephens reassured him, "Well, it's okay."

"Joan didn't mind it," Stephens concludes. "She just thought I should come down before it got out of hand.

"But you never knew what he was going to say or what he was going to do."

Chapter Twenty

ONE LAST SCREEN ROLE

A decade prior to signing on as Bub on *My Three Sons*, as he became ensconced in his role as Fred Mertz, Frawley remained embittered that producers had refused to hire him for movies. Just after the death of Mary Frawley, his sister and roommate, in 1957, Frawley declared, "I'm all alone now. I sit at home and watch television, collect residual checks for *Lucy* reruns, and take great pleasure in saying no when the movie studios call me now. I don't intend to make another movie."

Despite this promise, he did appear in one post–*I Love Lucy* feature—and that was only because of its baseball theme. The film was *Safe at Home!*—shot at Columbia Pictures between the 1961 and 1962 major-league seasons, while Frawley was on hiatus from *My Three Sons*. The seventy-four-year-old actor played what, for him, was the tailor-made role of Bill Turner, a cantankerous yet sympathetic lifelong bachelor and New York Yankees coach.

In *Safe at Home!* Frawley's character is a variation of crotchety but lovable Fred Mertz and crotchety but lovable Bub O'Casey. Particularly in his scenes with young Bryan Russell, cast as Hutch Lawton, a boy attempting to get Yankee stars Mickey Mantle and Roger Maris to show up for a Little League function, Bill appears to be rehashing his role on *My Three Sons.*

Also in *Safe at Home!* Frawley gets to play out his real-life camaraderie with ballplayers. In one scene, Coach Bill, Mantle, and Maris play Scrabble in a hotel room, and the M&M boys gently rib their instructor, telling him he cannot spell.

"Who says so?" Coach Bill not so much asks as barks.

"Webster," Mantle responds.

"What club's he with?" is Coach Bill's response—and it easily might be a line improvised by Frawley.

Throughout his on-screen time, Coach Bill grunts at Hutch. He grumbles at Hutch's teammates. He growls at the Yankee ballplayers. He grouses at Mantle and Maris, telling them, "No wisecracks from you guys," and, "Now don't you be shovin' me and pushin' me around. . . ." He also calls Mantle and Maris, then the reigning major-league home-run tandem, a "bunch of mangy rookies." Coach Bill apparently is a former ballplayer, and at one point he utters to Mantle and Maris what for Frawley must have been a dream line: "I could still outhit you two if it wasn't for my lumbago." And Maris jokingly tells Coach Bill that he and Mantle "grew up [and] joined the Yankees just to give you somebody to holler at."

"Bill Frawley was good people and a major baseball fan," notes Tom Naud, the film's producer and story co-author. "He loved being cast in *Safe at Home!* He loved calling Ralph [Houk], Mickey [Mantle], Roger [Maris], and Whitey [Ford] by their first names." Frawley even brought his *My Three Sons* friend John Stephens an autographed Mantle-Maris baseball, which he possesses to this day.

Walter Doniger, the sports film's director, describes Mantle and Maris as being "pretty arrogant and ego-driven." To get them to respond to his direction, he decided that "the best thing I could do would be to pretend total ignorance of baseball, and not know who they were. One time, I said to them, 'I'd like in this scene for you to run not counterclockwise but clockwise around the bases.' They looked at me and said, 'You can't do that in baseball.'

"I would deliberately get their names reversed, so that they kept trying to prove to me that they were important. I thought the best thing to do would be to make them ordinary people to me, and not big baseball stars and world heroes. So I did that, and it seemed to work."

Doniger had no such problems with Bill Frawley. "He was a nice man, a sweet man, the nicest man in the world, and lovely to work with," Doniger notes.

While on the *Safe at Home!* set, Frawley hung out only with the big-name Yankee players. "I wouldn't have been invited to talk baseball with him," explains Jim Bouton, then a rookie hurler on the team, who worked in the movie as an extra. "That was for Mickey Mantle and Roger Maris and the big guys, like Whitey Ford. I was just happy to be asked to be an extra in the movie, for which I got paid the munificent sum of $50.

"But it was nice to meet Fred Mertz," Bouton adds. "He was just a fun foil, and a perfect grumpy character."

Bouton and his fellow cast members were charmed by the actor's now legendary irascibility. "I remember one moment when there was this scene where William Frawley had to come out of the tunnel leading from the locker room into the dugout," Bouton says. "It had to be coordinated with other people coming and going. It really was a simple thing. It should have been done in two or three [takes], but it had to be shot about twenty times. One time it was the lights. One time it was the camera. Another time it was a couple of extras. . . .

"In any case, about the nineteenth time, Frawley hollered from the back of the dugout to the director who was outside waiting to call 'Action.' And this voice comes from out of the dugout: 'Sid!' or 'Harry!' or whoever was the director.

"'What is it, Bill?'

"'Hey,' [Frawley] said, 'I quit.'

"That may not sound funny now, but it was funny at the time. Everybody got a laugh, including Mickey and Roger."

♥

As he aged, Frawley remained the ever-rabid baseball fan. The sport constantly would make its way into his everyday conversation. "The series is going great," Frawley declared of *My Three Sons* in 1961. "We're very proud of it. I guess the only thing that could disturb me would be having baseball televised on Thursdays, the night of our show."

After moving from Brooklyn and New York to Los Angeles and San Francisco respectively, the Dodgers and Giants maintained their close rivalry. For Frawley, a Giants-Dodgers game was an unusually hot ticket.

Gene Reynolds reports that, on one occasion, Frawley was unable to procure tickets to one such contest at Dodger Stadium. Because the game was sold out, it was blacked out on local television. It so happened that Frawley had a couple of days off from his *My Three Sons* chores.

"To hell with it," he exclaimed. "I've got an idea." He and Phil Tanner, his friend and right-hand man during the final years of his life, headed for the airport. They flew to San Francisco, booked a hotel room, and watched the game on television. Then they flew back to Los Angeles.

One day, a number of San Francisco Giants visited Frawley on the *My Three Sons* set. "There was a guy named [Jim] Davenport, a wonderful third-baseman for the Giants," Reynolds notes. "Frawley's saying, 'We're getting you down here. You're gonna play for the Dodgers.' Then he says it to me as if it's a done deal. He says, 'We're gettin' this guy, we're gettin' this guy.'"

Of course, this was Bill Frawley's fantasy. Jim Davenport was not traded to the Dodgers. Simply put, Frawley's zealousness as a baseball aficionado had taken hold of his imagination.

Indeed, Frawley's enthusiasm for all things athletic would skewer his sense of reality. "They were playing the [National Football League] Pro Bowl out here at the L.A. Coliseum," explains John Stephens, "and there was a receiver [in the game] for the Philadelphia Eagles called Ray Walston." (Actually, the footballer's name was Bobby Walston.)

Stephens continues. "At that time, I was also doing a pilot for Don Fedderson called *The Devil Made Me Do It*, starring the actor Ray Walston—who knew nothing about pro football."

Stephens and Walston walked into the Desilu commissary, and Frawley was sitting there with Phil Tanner.

Stephens said to Walston, "Ray, would you like to meet Bill Frawley?"

"Oh yeah, sure," he responded.

The pair walked to Frawley's table, and Stephens said, "Bill, this is Ray Walston."

"Frawley by that time didn't follow Broadway or anything," Stephens explains. So he had never heard of this Ray Walston—even though, in 1955, Walston had originated the role of Mr. Applegate on Broadway in *Damn Yankees*.

Stephens quickly realized Frawley's lack of recognition of the actor and picked up on the fact that Frawley thought this Ray Walston was the football player. For laughs, he decided to go along with the misconception.

First Frawley told Walston, "Yeah, yeah, well, sit down, Ray. It's great to meet ya."

Then he added, "Geez, you're awfully little to be a pro end."

Walston, obviously confused, blurted out a one-word response: "What?"

"I just can't believe you're that great receiver," Frawley continued. "I mean, you just don't look like a receiver."

Walston attempted to set Frawley straight by telling him, "Well, I'm not."

Frawley, however, would not acknowledge Walston and declared, "You're one of the best there is."

"They're going on and on like this for fifteen minutes," Stephens notes. "I could never even bring myself to tell Bill what I'd done.

"When we walked away, Ray asked me, 'Is that guy crazy?' If you saw the look on Frawley's face, and the way he was talking. . . . To this day, wherever he may be in heaven, I'm sure that Frawley thinks he met

Walston [the football player]. And if he were to meet [the football player] Walston up there, he'd say [and Stephens growls], 'What? You've suddenly changed!'"

♥

During the *My Three Sons* years (1960–65), Frawley often would attend sporting events with his colleagues. Stanley Livingston recalls visiting Dodger Stadium with him. "I have no particular memory of it, other than of him being a vocal fan, really into the game," Livingston says. "I remember Bill jumping up and down and cursing and being the Bill that I knew. He was loud and really into it, and there was a lot of cursing going on.

"We must have had a box seat. We ate quite a few hot dogs. I think he even bought me a hat, a blue Dodgers hat."

During this period, championship fights would be broadcast live on the screens of Los Angeles movie theaters. "We used to always go," notes John Stephens. "[Frawley] would take [Phil] Tanner, Fred MacMurray would go with us occasionally, and we'd get a couple of the kids. We'd have dinner at Nickodell's. He loved that."

On many a Friday night, reports Stephens, you could find Frawley at Hollywood Legion Stadium watching the fights. "It was a small place," Stephens declares, "similar to the old St. Nick's [St. Nicholas Arena] in New York. And he really loved that. He and Tanner would sit there smoking cigars. He loved smoking cigars. But he'd really get upset if he'd pay his money and go to a fight and it would be a one-round knockout. He'd go crazy.

"He knew everything there was to know about prizefighting. I would say that prizefighting and baseball were his two favorites."

While one hardly can imagine an adult Frawley actually swinging a bat in a ballpark or pounding away at an opponent in a boxing ring, the actor did not even partake in golf, the one athletic pastime then savored by men of his age and station. Bill Frawley was strictly a fan.

"He used to go to [the] Lakeside [Country Club] with Gordy," notes Sheila MacRae. "He'd never play in any of the golf tournaments, but would hang out and wait. Then he'd say, 'Hey, come on, come on' [if the game was lasting too long].

"He and Gordy hung out with a bunch of Texas millionaires, high-rollers who savored gambling and kibitzing. They were the guys who gambled, bet on the games, loved sports."

When not at a ballgame or boxing match, Frawley often could be found at the racetrack, betting on any and all nags. In fact, older brother Jay, upon his retirement, became an admission-gate executive at the Santa Anita racetrack about twenty miles northeast of downtown Los Angeles near Pasadena. Previously he had worked for Burlington's Kelly Sand and Fuel Company, organized Lions Clubs out of Chicago, and moved to California where he worked for the Radio Corporation of America.

"Frawley loved to gamble," recalls John Stephens. "During the race season, he would come to me and say, 'John, you gotta put down a bet for me . . . a real hot tip on the third race, the horse that Shoemaker is riding.' I'd say, 'Yeah, okay. What do you want, a hundred to win?' And he'd say, 'Two dollars across the board.' There were always bookies around to take [the bets]."

In 1964, with $15,000 received in a residual check, Frawley purchased a racehorse, sight unseen. It was an English racer, oddly named French Evidence, which had won twice and placed second in its three races across the Atlantic. Bill had the animal shipped to Hollywood, to run him at Santa Anita and other local tracks.

"Yeah, I spent enough dough to buy 'em all, but this is the first one I've owned," he declared at the time of the nag's purchase. "I'm not going to tout my friends on French Evidence, but I might telephone some producers who refused to hire me and say he's a cinch to win every race. I'd bet on the horse myself, but I suppose he'll flop down in the middle of the stretch and say, 'Bring me some milk.' I'm used to horses behaving like that."

Frawley did not restrict his gambling to the nags. Gene Reynolds reports that he frequently would wager on the New York Yankees, especially during and around World Series time. He also recalls, "Notre Dame has this annual [football] game with USC. It's a very highly contested game, with a great tradition to it. Ever since I was a kid, I'd go down to the [Los Angeles] Coliseum and see these games.

"One particular year, when I was on *My Three Sons*, Notre Dame was playing here in the West. SC had a tough team and was strongly favored. It was not one of the great years for Notre Dame. So the betting was favoring SC."

A Notre Dame booster who was in town for the game wrangled an invitation for Frawley to a pre-game dinner with a bunch of Notre Dame players.

"Well, I guess you're gonna have a tough time tomorrow," Frawley told them. "What do you think is gonna happen? You're up against a pretty rough team."

The Notre Dame players responded with bravado, telling Frawley, "Ah, these guys, they're not so great. We're gonna knock 'em off."

Frawley was encouraged by the players' confidence. "Evidently he went out and bet heavily on Notre Dame," continues Reynolds. "And Notre Dame lost. The next day, he was pretty salty.

"I remember he was in the kitchen [on the *My Three Sons* set]. He was throwing some pots and pans around, and he said, 'I think I had dinner with a bunch of Presbyterians!'"

Chapter Twenty-one

CRANKY BUT LOVABLE

During the *I Love Lucy* years (1951–60), Bill Frawley did not become pals with Keith Thibodeaux, or Lucille Ball and Desi Arnaz's children. Yet just the opposite was the case with regard to the child actors on *My Three Sons*.

"He never had children, and I don't know if that hurt him or not," observes John Stephens. "But he loved kids. He was real, real good to the kids." Gene Reynolds notes, "The kids all loved him. He cracked the kids up. He was always grumpy around them, but he loved them. They were always very bemused by him.

"One time, there were some tough little kids working on the set," Reynolds adds. "Redheaded, freckle-faced little guys. I remember he got a big kick out of them."

Fred MacMurray's long absences from the filming of *My Three Sons* made Frawley the senior performer on the set of the TV series and left him in the company of the show's young actors. They loved his jocular tone and respected his reputation as one of Hollywood's most prolific and surefooted character actors.

Clearly Frawley felt the warmth that these young colleagues were putting out toward him. In fact, all were carefully cast, with as much an eye toward their off-camera personalities as their on-camera charisma. Don Grady, in fact, was a replacement Robbie. The first actor selected was Billy Chapin, brother of Lauren Chapin, who played Kitten on *Father Knows Best* (1954–60). "But [Fred] MacMurray didn't like him," Grady recalls. "The director, Peter Tewkesbury, had just come from directing *Father Knows Best*, and I guess it was his idea to bring Billy on the show. But [Chapin] was a little too rebellious, and MacMurray wouldn't have that."

Had a nonconformist youngster been cast on the show, Frawley might have remained distant. Yet this was not the case here. "I'm bossy and mean as ever," the old actor declared with a twinkle in his eye one month after the show's premiere, "but I'm loved, too. Those three boys—Tim Considine, Don Grady, and Stanley Livingston—are my buddies. We get along just fine."

"He was one of the funniest people I've ever known," recalls Grady. "He loved to make people laugh. That was his turn-on. He would do anything he could to make you laugh." Stanley Livingston observes, "If they could have just let Bill be Bill, you would have had the funniest show on earth. All the stuff that would come out of his mouth, all of his ad-libs—he'd have everyone just falling on the floor."

Grady adds, "I was an easy target for him. He could make me laugh so easily." On one occasion, he and Frawley played a scene detailing the aftermath of Chip's pet frog escaping its quarters and hopping around in the bushes outside the Douglas home. The time was midnight, and no one in the household could sleep because of the loud frog noise. So they all were outside the house, attempting to recapture the pet.

"I was on one side of the house," Grady continues, "going in the bushes on my hands and knees, going toward the corner of the house making a frog noise. Frawley was on the other corner side, coming toward the same corner as I was. He's also making a frog noise. So each thinks that the other is the frog.

"As we get closer, we each think we're gonna get this frog. And at the very end, what we have to do is part the bushes and, nose to nose, look at each other and at the same time go, 'Ru-her.' It was so funny to look into his face. When he would do it, his jowls would move and wiggle in the wind. His face was so rubbery; he had just a funny face to look at.

"And he knew he had me. Each time we did it, I kept cracking up. I wasn't supposed to crack up, I was supposed to be mad."

It took twenty-three takes to complete the shot. And what did one-take Bill Frawley think of doing twenty-three takes? "Oh, he loved it," Grady responds. "He was making somebody laugh. He would do anything he could just to cut a caper."

On occasion, the joke would be on Frawley. While in his dressing room on the Desilu lot between takes, he sometimes would fall asleep. He and Tim Considine had dressing rooms in the same corner of the stage. When they were needed back on the set, it was Considine's job to walk by Frawley's cubicle and make sure he responded to the call.

"This one time, I heard [Frawley] calling us," recalls Considine. "I looked in on him, but he was gone. So I went to the set, but he wasn't there. So I walked back, and looked in [his room]. There was nobody there. I walked back around the corner to see if he'd gone into my room."

Then Considine heard the famous Frawley grumble, "Tim, Tim, where are you?"

"Bill, where are you?" Considine responded.

"In here," was the reply. "In my room."

Considine again looked in Frawley's dressing room, but could see no one. He repeated, "Where are you?" and was answered, "I'm right here."

Finally Considine walked into the room and discovered Frawley stuck in a newly purchased reclining chair.

"I'm in this fucking chair, and I can't get out," Frawley told him.

"It was real low," Considine continues, "and his legs were raised up, and he literally could not get up. But he was hidden behind the door, so I never saw him.

"He was a hoot. A real hoot."

Unlike Meredith MacRae, the "three sons" report that they spent all their lunch hours with Frawley at Nickodell's. "He'd go down there, and he had his booth and everything," notes Don Grady. "They'd set him up, and he'd start drinking his lunch. We'd just sit down there and have a great time with him.

"We were alert enough to know that we'd have to get back [to the set] at the end of the hour," he continues, laughing. "And we'd always come back without him." Grady then grumbles, in imitation of Frawley, and says that the actor would tell them, "You boys go ahead, I'll be there in a couple of minutes."

Grady and Stanley Livingston, of course, were minors then, but Tim Considine was old enough to drink on his own. "So it was sort of my task to bring Frawley home every day from Nickodell's," Considine explains. "He'd have a drink after lunch, and maybe two, and I'd start tugging on him." Considine, more often than not, would fail in his appointed task. Grady notes, "A half hour would roll by, and they'd have to send somebody over to bring him back." John Stephens adds, "He really didn't eat that much. He'd kind of pick at his food. But boy, he drank."

Livingston notes, "I actually went to lunch with him every day for about four years. There was a booth we used to sit at, and [for years afterward] I swear to God there was an impression on the seat where he used to sit. This was years after he passed away, but you could tell it was from Bill. It was him. The exact amount of weight!"

Despite Frawley's fondness for forgetting the time while lunching and imbibing at Nickodell's, Grady stresses that the old-timer was a hard worker. "He'd be on the set as late as he needed to be," he says. "Bill wasn't lazy at all." It was just that Frawley enjoyed his lunch hours, the Nickodell's ambience, and his booze.

Frawley and Nickodell's eventually came to a sudden and bitter parting. John Stephens was with him on that fateful evening, when the pair came to the restaurant after the completion of the day's shooting.

"A highball then cost about eighty-five or ninety cents," Stephens notes. "Frawley had a couple, and was given the bill. He says [and Stephens grumbles, in imitation of Frawley], 'What's this? What's this?' They'd upped the price ten cents. Ten cents! And he said, 'I'm not putting up with this.' The two owners came over, and he created this whole riot. He left the restaurant—and never went back there, ever." In the very last years of his life, Frawley instead frequented Musso & Frank on Hollywood Boulevard.

"When Nickodell's lost him," concludes Stephens, "they lost a big customer."

♥

Another reason for Frawley's popularity among the youngsters was that he did not censor himself in their presence. And he taught the younger boys how to drink. "How many [kids] have an older figure like that who you could go drink with?" asks Grady. "You weren't of age, yet he would show you how to drink. It was just great fun for a kid."

Frawley also kept a stash of booze in his dressing room. Livingston remembers Frawley instructing him, "Don't tell anybody about this. It's my medicine." Grady then laughs, "It definitely wasn't medicine."

Additionally, X-rated language constantly would spew from Frawley's mouth. This, of course, was during an era when "darn" was considered too harsh a word to be spoken in the presence of a minor. "When he would swear," notes Gene Reynolds, "he would really cut loose. For a little kid, this is shocking and thrilling and completely amusing. They found him very quaint, and very funny."

Stanley Livingston concurs, declaring that Frawley "knew some really cool words. He was famous for his profanity."

John Stephens notes, "We had a welfare worker on the show. I had to say, 'Look, I really need special permission with Bill. There's no way that I can teach this man who's been swearing his whole life to ever change his language. So please give me a break.' Frawley was such a goodhearted man, and he really meant well, but he knew no other language."

"In those days," adds Livingston, "I was, what, nine or ten years old? And there was a studio teacher there, who was a holier-than-thou person. It really wasn't her jurisdiction to monitor what went on around the minors. [But] she took offense to the fact that if not every other word, then every third word out of Bill's mouth was some sort of curse. He was basically like a sailor. I remember that she tried to intercede. But it was hopeless. That was Bill, and they were not going to try to make him more couth."

Livingston notes that a typical Bill Frawley phrase was "double-barreled asshole." On another occasion, while filming a Thanksgiving show for the series, Frawley was supposed to be carving a turkey. "He just could not get this line out. So all of a sudden, he started stabbing that turkey and [yelling], 'Goddamn fuck. Who wrote this shit?' That was his usual line: 'Who wrote this shit?'"

The latter, or a variation, would in fact be exclaimed by Frawley whenever he had trouble remembering dialogue. Gene Reynolds recalls Frawley frequently taking the script and throwing it against a wall as he uttered the rhetorical question. The line even was quoted in *TV Guide*, but with a G-rated twist: "shit" was replaced by "trash."

Furthermore, Don Grady adds, "It wasn't beyond him to do something fairly lewd to evoke some laughter."

He continues, "Once we had this [American] Indian on the show, a real Indian, actually. Frawley was just trying to crack the Indian up. It was very difficult to make him laugh, and he would not crack a smile. It was becoming increasingly funny to everybody else, what Frawley was going through."

Cut to the final day of shooting, during a close-up of the Indian. "Frawley and a couple of us boys were off-camera," Grady continues, "delivering the lines to the Indian. At one point [the Indian] says, 'Chief Running Water wants to thank the Douglases for letting us stay on your lawn.'

"And when he said 'Running Water,' Frawley whipped out his weenie and pretended to pee on the lawn. And you saw one side of the lip of this very stoic Indian start to tremor a little bit. Then it tremored a little more. Now the other side started to tremor. It was like watching one of those buildings fall—and he finally erupted in this huge laugh, as if he had never before laughed in his life. It was such a coup for Frawley."

As Stanley Livingston explains, the *My Three Sons* cast members were "forced contractually to do commercials for the sponsors. For a while, we had Hunt's ketchup. Bill must have hated ketchup. He wouldn't call it ketchup; he kept calling it 'ket-chap.' I know he was doing it on purpose. So they had to cut, and do it again. And right in the middle of the thing, he would just come out with these [outrageous lines], or spit out [the ketchup] and say, 'Shit, this is awful.' I was just rolling on the floor."

All of this would transpire in the presence of the product and advertising agency honchos. Frawley didn't care. And when he did Quaker Oats commercials, according to Livingston, Frawley was supposed to be merrily cooking up the product. Instead, he would make up and blurt out jingles: "Quaker Oats is for the goats. Cream of Wheat is really neat."

On other occasions, Frawley's uncensored responses were not premeditated. One time, the *My Three Sons* script called for a lion to be present on the set. During the shooting, the animal got loose. "Now, don't anybody move," its trainer instructed the actors and crew. "Everybody just freeze, and we'll get the lion under control."

Despite this pronunciation, the trainer could not get near the animal for a good ten to fifteen minutes. It eventually was shuttled off the set, around the side of the stage, and into the narrow alleyway where all the dressing rooms were located.

"Then we heard Frawley coming back on the stage," Grady explains. "He always used to go for a whiz about every hour—he had to go to the men's room. We heard him whistling or humming or something, coming through one of the doors. And we went, 'Oh, my God, it's Bill!' And he ran right into this lion—and we heard [him exclaim], 'Holy shit.'

"And we thought that was it. . . . But the lion turned and ran the other way! Frawley went into his [dressing] room—and it was, of course, a good excuse to take a drink break."

John Stephens takes responsibility for the incident. "I should have told Bill that there'd be a lion working on the set," he declares. "But I heard about it from him right afterwards."

♥

Barry Livingston, who joined the *My Three Sons* cast in 1963 as Ernie, a neighborhood kid who is Chip's friend (and who eventually is adopted into the Douglas family), was simply too little to remember Frawley. "I really didn't have much contact with William Frawley," Livingston admits. "My recollections of Bill were sitting on the sidelines at lunch with my brother."

However, Barry's older brother Stanley, perhaps more than any of the "sons," has an extra-special attachment to the actor. "I never really knew either of my real grandfathers," he explains, "and by the time we were doing *My Three Sons* he was kind of my surrogate grandfather.

"We took to each other immediately. Some of my fondest memories are of the scenes I did with Bill."

At the time, one of Stanley's favorite actors was Peter Lorre, who then was in the twilight of his career, starring in Roger Corman–produced American International Pictures horror films. Stanley used to imitate Peter Lorre, and Bill would get a big kick out of his mimicry and fall over laughing.

Livingston adds, "I remember I got into surfing when I was about twelve or thirteen. I used to go down to the beach and surf with friends. For my thirteenth birthday, they had a party on the set for me. It was really neat. And Bill, on his own, had his own surprise. I had no idea what it was."

Frawley told Stanley, "I've got something really special for you." And Stanley thought, "Oh yeah, right. What is it, a dog or something?"

"Anyway, I went back to his dressing room. I don't know how he did this, but he had found out enough about surfboards to know that a Dewey Webber was the best surfboard you could get. In his room was a nine-foot-long coral-colored Dewey Webber surfboard. I was completely blown away."

What Stanley found particularly funny about the incident was what he describes as "the incongruity of Bill Frawley in a surf shop, trying to pick out a surfboard." Yet he adds, in all seriousness, that this is one memory of Frawley that evokes real emotion within him. "A lot of times, adults don't really tune in to what kids are into," he says. "The fact that he was that in-tune, and went so far out of his way . . . he probably had to go to some trouble to find that surfboard."

Before he met Frawley, Livingston already was an admirer of the actor from his work on *I Love Lucy*. "I was a big fan," he says. "I liked Lucy, but I really loved Fred. He was so cranky and lovable.

"I didn't even realize until the day we started shooting [*My Three Sons*] that William Frawley was going to be the grandfather." Livingston, in fact, recalls the moment he met Frawley. "It was on the set. It was the first day of shooting, and I immediately knew who he was. I had probably a million questions for him, because I loved [him as Fred Mertz]. To be honest, I probably knew less about Fred MacMurray than Bill Frawley. Being the age I was, TV was the medium I was a little more familiar with, and I already was watching Bill on *I Love Lucy* for two or three years.

"You know how you meet people in a group, and after a while the ones that get along sort of pair off? We just paired off. When I wasn't doing anything, I'd go in his dressing room and just hang out with him."

Of all those who knew him during this period, it is Stanley Livingston who offers the most incisive observation about Frawley. "I'm sure he had his cronies, and then there was that Patricia Barry thing," he observes. "But to have some sort of companionship, outside of Phil [Tanner], [was essential for him] at that age.

"I'm just hypothesizing, but I really did get this sense of loneliness, and that may have been why we would talk or hang out. He may have had regrets that he didn't have any kids. . . . That was probably something he needed in his life. I'm sure that just as I adopted him as a surrogate grandfather, I was sort of like a surrogate grandson or son to him.

"Here he was on a family show, and he didn't have family, didn't have kids. Everybody would go home at night to their own families. And he probably would head out to a bar, or to a card game or something.

"You know, what I really had a sense of was the fact that he just seemed very lonely."

During the later stages of his life, Bill's one constant companion was Phil Tanner, whom he knew from his vaudeville days and who did double duty as his assistant and straight man.

Tanner also served as Frawley's driver. Desi Arnaz believed that Frawley had had his driver's license revoked because of his propensity for obtaining traffic tickets, and even was arrested for driving under the influence. John Stephens, on the other hand, is convinced that, back in the 1930s, Frawley had been in a serious auto accident. "He never would discuss it in detail," he notes, "but someone was injured, and he lost his license, and he never would drive again."

"He [Tanner] used to do everything for Bill," recalls Don Grady. "I think that he and Bill could drink the same amount. He always had this cherubic look on his face. His cheeks were always red, and he was always smiling. [He was] a really nice guy, quiet but with a cheerful nature.

"He was always where Bill was," Grady continues, "and Bill always would humorously put him down. And this guy would just sit there and smile and take it."

Gene Reynolds describes Tanner as "very nice, a very sweet guy. And Frawley was very salty, and he'd always be pretty tough on the guy, contradict the guy and so forth. He always would be arguing about sports trivia. 'He never hit .360 in his life,' Frawley would say."

When the Brooklyn Dodgers relocated to Los Angeles after the 1957 baseball season and made it to the World Series in 1959, 1963, and 1965, baseball fanatic Frawley could view the Fall Classic right in his own "backyard." In 1963, the Dodgers and Frawley's beloved New York Yankees were facing each other in the series. Reynolds recalls that Frawley had procured tickets, and Tanner drove him to Dodger Stadium.

"I'm gonna see the game," Frawley declared, "and then I'm meeting the players at the Bounty [a Wilshire Boulevard restaurant-bar]."

"They go to the ballgame," Reynolds explains, "and they park and watch the game. Then they come out, and [Tanner] forgot where he parked the car! You go out of Dodger Stadium, and there's twenty thousand auto-mobiles sitting around.

"So Frawley begins groaning that he is supposed to have dinner with the Dodgers, and is swearing at poor Tanner."

"To hell with it," Frawley finally muttered, and he and Tanner hailed a taxi which took them to the restaurant. Afterward, they took a cab home.

The following day, Tanner cabbed it to Dodger Stadium. "Of course," notes Reynolds, "there's this enormous parking lot. And sitting all by itself is the car. That's how they finally found the car."

Late one evening, John Stephens received a phone call from Frawley.

"Johnny, ya can't believe what that damn Tanner did to me," Frawley grumbled.

Stephens inquired as to what had happened.

"I can't believe it. He *died*. How about that, that son of a bitch."

After Stephens expressed his condolences, Frawley added, "Aah, ya can't trust anybody anymore."

Chapter Twenty-two

DECLINING HEALTH

In the early 1960s, Frawley was approaching his mid-seventies—and his advancing years began seriously exacting their toll. Tom Naud, the producer and co-author of *Safe at Home!*, reports, "Unfortunately, I believe he may have suffered a slight stroke before he joined us in Florida." He adds, "While doing his last big scene with the players, in front of about ten thousand fans who came to watch from the stands, I believe he had another stroke. It took two hours to shoot some dialogue that should have taken twenty minutes."

Walter Doniger, the film's director, vividly recalls the experience. "One day we had a scene which takes place in the stadium [in Fort Lauderdale]," he notes. "He had to get up and talk to the team in front of five thousand people. To get the five thousand people, you had to put ads in the paper because you couldn't pay for that many [extras]. So they'd come out of curiosity, and they'd sit for a while and then they'd leave.

"The day we did this, Bill evidently had some sort of minor heart attack or something, or a minor stroke. He got in front, and suddenly he couldn't speak."

Eventually, Frawley blurted out, "Now, fellas, when are we gonna jump on the monkeys, the monkeys, the monkeys . . .?"

Doniger kept correcting the actor and telling him, "Bill, the line is, you know . . ." Yet Frawley kept blowing the dialogue.

While this was transpiring, the crowd was becoming restless and gradually thinning out. "We thought we'd postpone [the shoot] to another day," Doniger continues. "But Frawley said, 'No, no, no, I want to do it today.' He insisted on doing it. But he just kept repeating the same line, over and over. Finally, we got it somewhat correct, but just as the last of the people left. We had to piece it together [in the editing room]."

Anyone who had worked with Frawley would have found this last account depressing, especially given his well-earned reputation for always knowing his lines and doing his business all in one take.

Even back in 1960, when he joined the cast of *My Three Sons*, Frawley was not in the best of health. "He had a tremor," recalls Don Grady. "Most of the time, his hands were shaking. If you look at [the show], you'll notice that most of the time something is shaking. His nervous system must have been in pretty bad shape."

Frawley's health problems were fated to only worsen. He remained with the show until halfway through the 1964–65 season, when he was forced to leave.

"Unfortunately, Bill wasn't with us for all that long," notes Grady. "He didn't pass the insurance test, and it really broke his heart."

John Stephens accompanied Frawley to that crucial physical. "It was with a fellow called Dr. Gerson," he recalls. "If in five minutes you could take one breath, he would say, 'He's fine. He's fine. He's passed. He's in perfect health.' We always joked that Gerson would pass anybody."

After this particular examination, Dr. Gerson told Stephens, "John, can I see you?"

Out of Frawley's presence, he declared, "John, I've done everything in the world for you and everyone else in Hollywood, but I can't pass this man."

"What?" was Stephens's response.

"I can't pass him," Gerson explained. "This man should have been dead a year ago."

"You passed him last year," Stephens retorted.

And Gerson responded, "I gave him the benefit of the doubt, but everything is getting worse. I can't believe that he's still walking."

"I didn't say a word to Bill," Stephens notes. "Instead, I went to Don Fedderson. We had quite a decision to make, because we were just about to start the season. We couldn't get insurance [for Frawley] anywhere." Fedderson decided to gamble on Frawley for thirteen episodes, which would allow for sufficient time to find a suitable replacement.

If *My Three Sons* were aired today, Bub O'Casey might have died and an episode or two would be devoted to the impact of his demise on the other characters. Yet back in the 1960s, when sitcom characters remained terminally healthy, Bub's absence was explained by having his character "depart" on a journey to Ireland. He was immediately replaced by Bub's brother, Uncle Charley O'Casey (William Demarest), a former sailor with a cranky disposition. Like Frawley, Demarest was a veteran performer: a former vaudevillian, carnival performer, and boxer who played character roles in scores of films. Most memorably, he appeared to merry effect in a series of Preston Sturges comedies, playing a political hack in *The Great McGinty* (1940), a disbelieving valet in *The Lady Eve* (1941), a tough Marine in *Hail the Conquering Hero* (1944), and a hot-tempered father in *The Miracle of Morgan's Creek* (1944). Any of these screen parts might have been performed by Frawley. So was the role that won Demarest his lone Academy Award nomination: the cello-playing vaudevillian who becomes Al Jolson's manager and advisor in *The Jolson Story* (1946).

Tim Considine recalls that Frawley had grown increasingly tired during his last year on *My Three Sons*. "Toward the end, it was pretty sad," remembers Don Grady. "He would forget his lines. It got worse and worse. The last year, we had off-camera cards that Bill would read. Then after a while, he couldn't read the cards. So they would shoot him a line, and he would say the line, and they'd cut it right later." According to John Stephens, the ever-prideful Frawley never requested the cue cards.

The situation declined further. "Then his energy started going, and his mind started going," continues Grady. "They'd shoot him a line, and he'd forget it. They'd shoot [it to] him again, and he might say it. Then somebody else would have a line, and it would come back to him, but he might have fallen asleep in that fifteen seconds.

"So somebody would lay on the floor and have a hand on Bill's pant trouser—which I think he probably secretly enjoyed. When they sensed he'd be falling asleep, they'd pull on his pants and it would wake him up."

In master shots in which the Douglas household was depicted as a group, Tim Considine would be placed right next to Frawley. In case he fell asleep standing up, Considine would squeeze Frawley in the back to awaken him just before he was to speak his line. The camera would be angled so he would not be recorded sleeping. If he started to snore, the scene would have to be reshot. "If he didn't have any words [in a scene], he'd doze off," Considine recalls. "His head would go down, and he would be asleep. So they used to give him dialogue in strange parts of scenes, just to keep him awake."

Grady observes that Frawley still could remember who hit a triple in the 1934 World Series, and in what inning. John Stephens notes that Frawley still could name the guy who used to play shortstop for the Hollywood Stars. Yet crew members now had to pull on his pant legs to keep him awake and help him recall his lines. "That was the last season that Bill did the show," Grady adds. "Especially during the last several months, that's how we did the show. He went down real fast. The show was never the same after he left, [even though] it went on umpteen more years."

Stanley Livingston declares simply, "I was pretty upset [by] the fact that he wasn't coming back. Until my brother came aboard, he probably was the person I was closest to.

"I don't know what liability the doctor would have had, had Bill dropped dead during the production year," he said. "But this was not unheard of. I remember being really pissed off that they couldn't have him [continue]. So what would have happened had we been shooting [and he died]? So we would have not been able to finish one of the episodes, and they would have done exactly what they did anyway and bring someone else in.

"I just felt it was kind of heartless, to [do to] somebody that age. And when you're the age that I was, you have a different feeling for the people you're working with. As you get older, it's just a job and half the time you know you're never going to see [your costars] again, even though you're close with them [during the shoot]. That's the way it is. But at the age I was, [the *My Three Sons* cast and crew] really were like a second family."

♥

Frawley may have professed that playing Bub O'Casey had become little more than a job to him—despite the fact that it was a job at which he excelled. "To tell you the truth," he explained in 1961, "I don't give much thought to television as a field of endeavor. It's a place—an art, let's call it—where I'm making a livelihood." Nevertheless, he was heartbroken when he was forced off the show.

Don Grady describes the situation as "pretty sad." Stanley Livingston remembers it as "really painful."

It was left to John Stephens to give Frawley the bad news. "I didn't until the end of the twelfth show," he says. "It was one of the most difficult things I've ever done in my life. We originally had a script written where he and his supposed relative, Bill Demarest, were going to meet. That didn't work, because they both hated each other."

After leaving the show, Frawley still visited the set—and made it clear to one and all that he had no love for Demarest. Grady adds, "He was really ticked off that Demarest took his role, and he wasn't working. And it's not like he was smoldering in the background. He'd come out and [grumble], 'Jesus Christ, I wouldn't have said the line like that.' Nothing subtle.

"Demarest did his best to try and ignore him. But Demarest was not a subtle person, either, and there were words and bad feelings." Grady recalls that Frawley eventually had to be told that he was no longer welcome to come and observe the shooting.

"He was very depressed after he had to leave *My Three Sons*," recalls John Stephens. "Very depressed. He became very bitter. But there was nothing we could do."

From that point on, Frawley's health declined even further. He began experiencing heart-, kidney-, and prostate-related ailments, and hired a male nurse to care for him.

Frawley was destined to have one last acting role. That came on an episode of *The Lucy Show* (1962–68), Lucille Ball's post–*I Love Lucy* sitcom. The show, titled "Lucy and the Countess Have a Horse Guest," aired on October 25, 1965. The plot involves Lucy and her old friend Rosie (Ann Sothern), a count's widow, who has inherited a horse. The women visit the animal at its stable, and who comes ambling out with broom in hand but Bill Frawley, playing the horse's trainer.

The countess announces herself using her full name, at which point Frawley's character—in typical Frawley fashion—yells out, "Hey, boss, there's a dame here to see ya." Lucy stares at him with a quizzical expression on her face and eventually remarks, "You know, he reminds me of someone I used to know."

In the closing credits, Frawley's name appeared last in the billing. His acknowledgment—"And our own Bill Frawley as The Trainer"—was warm and heartfelt.

It should be noted that Vivian Vance was nowhere to be found in "Lucy and the Countess Have a Horse Guest."

On the evening of March 3, 1966, Frawley and the nurse were strolling down Hollywood Boulevard after seeing a movie. Near the corner of Hollywood and Vine, Frawley was stricken with a heart attack. The nurse carried the actor into the lobby of the nearby Hollywood Roosevelt Hotel, where Frawley soon passed away. He was pronounced dead on arrival at Hollywood Receiving Hospital.

Frawley had become so linked to *I Love Lucy* that, despite his more recent success on *My Three Sons*, he was initially described in his *Burlington Hawk-Eye* obituary as "a veteran entertainer who in recent years was known as Fred Mertz on Lucille Ball's *I Love Lucy* television show. . . ." His involvement with *My Three Sons* is not mentioned until the very end of the piece.

In his *Variety* obituary, Frawley was depicted as "Very Irish in his ways [and] a great teller of tales [who] enjoyed cheerful company and a nip now and then. His high sense of honesty reportedly caused him to lose a number of acting parts and friends. But his open, brisk manner endeared him to his fellow actors." Added the *New York Times*, "When William Frawley strutted around a room, hands on hips and complained in a gravelly voice, he usually brought smiles to the faces of his listeners, for he had the ability to growl with warmth."

"Oh, I'm terribly sorry. I've lost one of my dearest friends," declared Lucille Ball upon learning of Frawley's passing. "Show business has lost one of the greatest character actors of all times." Desi Arnaz took out a full-page advertisement in the *Hollywood Reporter*, which included a photo of Frawley, his birth and death dates, and the words "Buenas Noches, Amigo!"

Fred MacMurray characterized Frawley's demise as "a great loss," adding, "I'm so terribly sad." He and Arnaz, along with old pal Bob Cobb, ex-boss Don Fedderson, actor William Lundigan, and actor-producer-director Richard Whorf, were the pallbearers at Frawley's funeral, held at the Church of the Blessed Sacrament in Los Angeles. A photo of the pallbearers carrying Frawley's casket even made the front page of the *New York Post*.

Bill Frawley was buried in the San Fernando Mission Cemetery, located in Mission Hills, northwest of San Diego. Also interred there are a cross section of celebrities: William Bendix, who starred in *The Babe Ruth Story*, which featured Frawley as Baltimore Orioles manager Jack Dunn, and with whom he shared some funny scenes in *Kill the Umpire*, with Frawley an umpire school head who attempts to break in novice arbiter Bendix; Chuck Connors, whose company Frawley would have appreciated because of Connors's pre-acting career as a professional baseball player; as well as Lee DeForest, Walter Brennan, and early rock 'n' roller Ritchie ("La Bamba") Valens.

Frawley's headstone is simple and flat, and features the words "IN LOVING MEMORY/WILLIAM C. FRAWLEY/FEB. 26, 1887 MAR. 3, 1966." In between the birth and death dates is a small cross.

Frawley's gross estate totaled $92,446, a tidy sum back in 1966, and his assets were on track to continue growing after his death. "I know that Bill Frawley had the most unique deal ever on *I Love Lucy*," explains John Stephens. "He had a deal where he was paid in perpetuity. Now, I've never known the biggest of stars to [have] a deal like that.

"In those days, when you started [on a series], after six runs you got certain residuals," Stephens continues. "If [the series] went into network syndication, they could play the shows as often as they wanted, but I don't think [the actors] would get very much money. But [as a result of Frawley's deal] every time *I Love Lucy* would run for a number of years, the estate was paid. Each episode has been run almost a thousand times. I would guess that there was good money coming in probably for the first two hundred to three hundred runs.

At the time of Frawley's death, both his brothers still were alive, and their plight was especially sad. John Stephens recounts that Paul and Jay Frawley "were at St. John of God Hospital [in the Los Angeles area]. They were paid for by [Bill] for life. That was an alcoholics' hospital. They were both in pretty bad shape." Stephens never met either Frawley sibling, but adds that Bill often spoke of his brothers and occasionally would visit them in the hospital.

It has been said of Frawley that he was an alcoholic. If so, he was a functioning drinker—unlike his brothers, who in their advanced years were incapable of caring for themselves. If they had serious drinking problems, Bill had what Stephens describes as "a drinking opportunity. He didn't consider it a problem."

One might venture a guess that Paul, the former "singing juvenile" of Broadway who frolicked onstage with Marilyn Miller and Gertrude Lawrence and Ginger Rogers, was unable to accept his obscurity once his fame faded. After the demise of his Broadway career, he surfaced in Hollywood and had a bit role as a reporter in the Tyrone Power–Loretta Young–Don Ameche comedy *Love Is News* (1937) at Twentieth Century-Fox. He remained in Hollywood and lived to be eighty-four years old. When he died in January 1973 he was long-forgotten on Broadway—and for years had remained on the sidelines as his big brother earned everlasting fame on *I Love Lucy*.

In his will, dated and signed October 2, 1964, Bill Frawley bequeathed $5,000 to St. John of God Hospital "to be used in the Operating Account or Care of Patients Account." The patients, of course, were Jay and Paul Frawley. He left $2,000 to his "dear friend" Phil Tanner, who had predeceased him.

The surprise of the will was that Frawley bequeathed $1,000 each to Miranda Robin Barry and Stephanie Ann Barry, the daughters of Patricia Barry. The will continued, "I hereby devise and bequeath all the rest, residue and remainder of my estate to PATRICIA BARRY, the mother of Miranda Barry and Stephanie Barry. In the event PATRICIA BARRY should predecease me, I bequeath all the rest, residue and remainder of my estate to JOHN GALLAUDET [Frawley's old actor pal]."

According to John Stephens, Walter Meyers, Frawley's longtime agent, contested the will. The main thrust of Meyers's complaint related to the fact that Frawley's siblings were incapacitated alcoholics, and Meyers wanted Stephens to testify on their behalf. "His brothers could not have gotten out of the hospital [to do so]," Stephens states. "But I think he felt that he, Walter, who did a lot for Bill, and the brothers were entitled to part of the estate." However, the will was deemed valid—its probate number is P506609—and there is no evidence at the Los Angeles County Records Center that Meyers's suit was ever brought to trial.

This last incident is a minor footnote in the life of William Frawley. As a vaudevillian, Broadway actor, and movie and television performer, he bridged the history of American show business in the twentieth century.

He always was able to earn a living at his chosen profession, even when he started out in the business and even when his screen career was fading in the late 1940s. He was well known among his peers and was a familiar face to moviegoers—until the role of Fred Mertz came along, making Bill Frawley a small-screen legend.

Part Five

VIVIAN VANCE
AFTER ETHEL

Vance in her study at home, circa 1950.
(PHOTO COURTESY OF ARCHIVE PHOTO)

Vance in a publicity still for *I Love Lucy*.
(PHOTO COURTESY OF GLOBE)

Chapter Twenty-three

ESCAPING THE SHADOW
OF ETHEL

On one level, the Lucy Ricardo–Ethel Mertz relationship is of historical significance in that it served as a model for countless future television situation comedies. On them, the star of the show (Gale Storm, Mary Tyler Moore, Ellen DeGeneres, Cybill Shepherd) is given a female buddy (respectively, ZaSu Pitts, Valerie Harper, Joely Fisher, Christine Baranski) who serves as a fellow laugh-getter/comic co-conspirator. While the star *is* the star, to the point where her name often is her show's name—*The Gale Storm Show* (1956–59, which was also known as *Oh! Susanna*), *The Mary Tyler Moore Show* (1970–77), *Ellen* (1994–98), and *Cybill* (1995–98)—much of the chemistry that makes the on-camera comedy so effective is provided by the second banana.

Occasionally, a second banana can become a star. Valerie Harper did just that on *Rhoda* (1974–78), the *Mary Tyler Moore Show* spin-off, where she now had her own comic sidekick in the person of her younger sister (Julie Kavner). Yet Vivian Vance was not fated to topline a TV series of her own, not as Ethel Mertz or as any other character.

In 1959, as she was completing her final chores as Ethel Mertz, Vance made the pilot of a proposed new comedy series. It was to be titled *Guestward Ho!*, and was based on a book by Patrick Dennis, the author of *Auntie Mame*, and Barbara Hooten. In it, she played Babs, whose husband, Bill, is a New York advertising executive; the pair flee their harried New York City lifestyle and open a dude ranch in New Mexico. The part of Bill, played by veteran actor Leif Erickson, was much-coveted by her actor husband, Phil Ober. His casting opposite Vance would have been disastrous, given the state of their marriage.

On *Guestward Ho!*, Vance was to have been the top-billed female. "Right now I'm hoping to star in my own series," she explained at the time. "The pilot already has been filmed."

Yet when the cameras first began rolling, Vance—who reportedly was intimidated by being Lucyless and the real focus of the show—became paralyzed with fear, and the entire shoot did not go well.

Guestward Ho! was produced by Desilu, the parent studio of *I Love Lucy*. Upon the rejection of the Vance-Erickson pilot by ABC, Desi Arnaz offered to refilm it. Notwithstanding, network executives demanded that different actors be used for the revamped project. So when *Guestward Ho!* premiered in September 1960, Joanne Dru—who previously had starred in an unsuccessful Desilu pilot, *Adventures of a Model,* and was fourteen years Vivian's junior—had replaced Vance while Mark Miller took over for Erickson.

"I think I was fated to do this series," Dru observed around the time of its debut. "I almost signed for it three years ago, when CBS owned the property. I read some of the scripts then and didn't think it was for me. Later, Vivian Vance did a pilot and it didn't come off. I became interested again when Desi Arnaz got the property and had it rewritten with a little boy, making it a family show. Now I think it's got something special."

Despite Dru's optimism, *Guestward Ho!* lasted only one season on ABC-TV.

Beyond Vivian's less-than-stellar performance in the pilot, Sheila MacRae offers additional perspective on why Vance did not star in

Guestward Ho! "They wouldn't want her because she was too associated with playing Mrs. Mertz," MacRae declares. "It was the same thing with Art Carney. Art Carney went on to win an Oscar [in 1974, for *Harry and Tonto*], and he's done many plays. He's a brilliant actor. But [after playing Ed Norton], he couldn't get any more good TV roles."

There are exceptions, of course. After starring as affable sheriff Andy Taylor on *The Andy Griffith Show* (1960–68), Andy Griffith eventually reinvented himself as wily criminal-defense attorney Benjamin Matlock on *Matlock* (1986–95). Dick Van Dyke went from writing a hit TV comedy series as Rob Petrie on *The Dick Van Dyke Show* (1961–66) to solving mysteries as Dr. Mark Sloan on *Diagnosis Murder* (1993–). Carroll O'Connor played comedy as lovable bigot Archie Bunker on *All in the Family* (1971–83) and then went on to become police chief Bill Gillespie on *In the Heat of the Night* (1988–94). Even a character man like William Frawley could fit into another small-screen venue, playing variations of irascible Fred Mertz—which is exactly what he did on *My Three Sons*.

Yet these are the aberrations, rather than the rules. "It can be tough," adds MacRae, "and it was for Viv and a lot of other people."

♥

Certainly, upon leaving *I Love Lucy*, Vance did not find herself unemployed. One report had her appearing on a new comedy series with Jackie Gleason, but nothing came of this potential project. However, as she explained in 1962, "I played the Jack Paar [TV talk] show, summer stock; I kept as busy as possible. There was a special reason for this. I had to find my own identity. I was so submerged in Ethel Mertz that I was afraid I would never again be recognized for my own self. But, being a creative person, I was worried that I would be stuck doing the same role all my life."

Her appearance on the Paar show was especially jolting for anyone who tuned in expecting to find Viv in a housedress. Just as with her turn on the TV game show *I've Got a Secret*, viewers found a bright and quick-witted woman who was as stylish as ever in a designer ensemble and mink. It was during this time that Vance also had a face-lift, and surgery to straighten the curve of her nose.

One of her acting roles—altogether different from that of Ethel Mertz—was on the television Western drama *The Deputy* (1959–61), which starred Henry Fonda. The episode was titled "Land Greed," and Vance played a feisty widow who approaches lawman Simon Fry (Fonda) with documentation that she and her son are being driven off their land by neighboring ranchers who covet her property.

"The woman I play is a strong individualist who rides horses and drives buggies," Vance remarked. "It's given me a new lease on life." Prior to that outing, she'd made her *I've Got a Secret* appearance and declared that she had just signed for what she described as "my first dramatic role" on *The Deputy.* "I'm a little bit nervous about it," she added. "I've been playing comedy for so long." Garry Moore, the *I've Got a Secret* host, responded, "I'm sure that the audience will be delighted to see you as a serious actress once again."

Another challenging part came onstage in *Marriage-Go-Round*, Leslie Stevens's sophisticated sex comedy which Vance performed in February and March 1961 at two stylish resort theaters, the Nassau Playhouse in the Bahamas and the Coconut Grove Playhouse in Miami. Her costars were John Baragrey—an attractive actor almost ten years her junior—and Sylvia Miles.

In *Marriage-Go-Round*, Vance played a discerning and chic middle-aged wife whose mate is an erudite, reserved college professor—and the polar opposite of Fred Mertz. (On Broadway in 1958, Vivian's role was played by Claudette Colbert, and in the 1960 movie, by Susan Hayward.) A battle of wits results when the couple's marriage is shaken upon the arrival of a conniving and voluptuous Scandinavian bombshell. At the crux of the story is the loving bond between the husband and wife. The emotions comprising the heart of their relationship would have been completely alien to the natures of Mr. and Mrs. Mertz.

Critics and audiences who were expecting Vance to reprise Ethel Mertz onstage were in for a letdown. "Vivian Vance, playing the wife, does not have the opportunity in this play to display the broad comedy talents which have made her a nationwide favourite in American television," wrote Jack Jordan, theater critic for the *Nassau Guardian*. Jordan displayed his ignorance of Vance's pre-*Lucy* career when he wrote, "Her forte in acting appears to be in fast-moving, brittle situation comedy." He then added, "However, she is most convincing in, of all things, the tender and touching love scenes with her husband, in which her wonderful smile, and depth of feeling, warm up the entire audience. She should sometime star in *The Rose Tattoo*. She would be great because I believe she has tremendous dramatic abilities which have not been given a fair showing."

Another commentator, also writing in the *Nassau Guardian*, was more blunt. After complementing Vance on her "vivacious sparkle and very adroit comedy style," he felt compelled to add, "I had a sneaking feeling that she was still Ethel Mertz of *I Love Lucy* somehow caught in a situation that was too sophisticated for her by far. Which is a shame because she is a warm and wonderfully amusing woman on a suburban level."

George Bourke, writing in the *Miami Herald*, had the proper perspective on her professional plight when he wrote, "Miss Vance, the pro that she is, gets her full measure of laughs—but her exposure on TV for so long in *I Love Lucy* may have conditioned some patrons to think of her chiefly as the wife of a plain Joe named Fred."

The irony is that, had she not been Ethel Mertz, Vance never would have been headlining in *Marriage-Go-Round*. Yet many of her fans could see her only as Ethel, or an Ethel-like character. She still had to convince critics and audiences that her talents transcended her trademark role on *I Love Lucy*.

♥

At this juncture, according to veteran actress Sylvia Miles, Vance apparently had been so used to playing second banana—not just on television but in her years on Broadway, with such powerful leading ladies as Ethel Merman and Gertrude Lawrence—that she was unable to adjust to being a gracious star. Miles describes her working relationship with Vance as "grotesque in terms of what happened to me." She adds that she "not affectionately used to call [her] 'Vivian Vonce'"—*vonce* being the Yiddish word for "bedbug."

To appear in *Marriage-Go-Round*, Miles took a leave of absence from her role in the legendary Off-Broadway production of Jean Genet's *The Balcony*. "I had a reputation for being a part of what really then was the avant-garde, before Andy Warhol," Miles explains. She adds that she also was "this Off-Broadway sex bomb. I don't know how else to describe it. And my part [in *Marriage-Go-Round*] was a Swedish sex bomb. I'm in my twenties. I had a gorgeous figure. [Vance] had already heard about me." Suffice to say, even though she was no longer tied to a contract that obligated her to gain weight, Vance—who then was in her early fifties—had not been able to recover a stylish figure.

Miles describes Vance as "this television second banana who now had the chance to be first banana. Traditionally, in situations like that, they're monsters when they get the opportunity to star by themselves and don't have to take second place or kowtow to somebody else.

"I now get this job," she continues. "It was a big thing for me to be able to go to the Coconut Grove and make $350 to $400. That was a lot of money. It certainly was more than the $38 a week I was making at Circle in the Square [in *The Balcony*]."

Miles's role in *Marriage-Go-Round* called for her to wear spiked heels. "I was not accustomed to wearing very high heels," she explains. "So I had to start wearing them right away to get used to them. I wore [them] at the first rehearsal in New York, and Vance [tells me], 'I don't want you to wear those high heels.' Every day I'd get a note from her regarding my looks. She was very, very judgmental during the rehearsal period. Rather than being into the thing, she'd be watching what I did.

"I enjoy creating a role," Miles adds, "and she spoiled my process."

To Miles's way of thinking, was Vance on a power trip? "Yes," she says. "I was sexy. I was a threat. She was competitive with me."

As the time passed, did Vance warm up to Miles? "No," is her response. She also declares, "Actually, I was more than threatening to her. I was frightening to her."

Years later, Vance had remarried—and Miles was back in New York City shooting *Midnight Cowboy* (1969), for which she would win an Academy Award nomination for Best Supporting Actress. "And all of a sudden," the actress remembers, "Vivian and [fourth husband John] Dodds were around. I remember meeting them both at the Pierre Hotel, at a big party hosted by Jann Wenner [of *Rolling Stone*]. At this party it was like I'm her best friend.

"I was always polite, I was always nice to her. Of course, I knew what it was [all about]. She didn't have largesse. I understood it, though. I know what it means, having been a comedienne myself, to be a second banana. I know what it means to have to feed the star, which was what she had to do for many years, probably.

"I don't hate Vivian Vance. I can't hate her. But I do feel sorry for her. And it's just that she spoiled what could have been a very nice time for me. In retrospect, that's very painful. I was not given the opportunity to really enjoy [the experience in *Marriage-Go-Round*]."

♥

During this period, Vance also toured in George Oppenheimer's comedy perennial *Here Today,* playing a Dorothy Parker–like character (as she also had done during World War II in *Over 21*). In fact, Ruth Gordon, the author of *Over 21*, created the role in *Here Today*'s original 1932 Broadway production: a fabled writer who takes steps to rekindle a romance with her former husband—an action that Vance would never, ever consider in real life.

Still, it is no coincidence that Vance, the former New York showgirl who had never seen a college campus and who had so hated playing Ethel Mertz, was selecting stage parts in which she could appear sophisticated and intellectual. The roles she was accepting mirrored the person she wanted to be in real life: the highbrow New Yorker and insider among the city's literati.

This self-image was to extend to her choice of a fourth and final husband.

Chapter Twenty-four

A NEW MARRIAGE, A NEW LIFE

Upon divorcing Phil Ober in 1959, Vance was eager to remarry. For one thing, she was used to having an attractive man in her company (even if he was a louse!). The last time she had fallen in love, she had been young and attractive. Now her situation was much different. She was a middle-aged woman with a matronly figure and a history of psychological instability.

Now that Viv was alone, evenings were especially difficult—and she craved somebody special at her side. What did she have to offer the kind of man she wanted to attract? She had a celebrity name and was financially solvent. In this regard, she knew she had to be very protective of her pocketbook and her emotions.

One potential romantic partner, at least in Viv's eyes, was *I Love Lucy* writer Bob Schiller. "I got a divorce when I was working on *Lucy*," he explains, "and Vivian suddenly became a Jewish mother. She really thought I was hurting, which wasn't necessarily true. So she was trying to fix me up with everybody in town—including herself, I might add."

On one of her visits back to New Mexico to attend the annual Opera Ball in Santa Fe, fifty-one-year-old Vance became acquainted with John Dodds, a literary agent, editor, and publishing executive who was twelve years her junior. They first met at a party at the residence of their mutual friends, Bill and Barbara Hooten—the same Babs Hooten who was the co-author of *Guestward Ho!*, which had become the TV series *without* Vivian.

It was quickly apparent to Vance that Dodds would make an ideal husband. He was bright. He was attractive. He had all the social graces. He was a nice guy. And he was an integral part of the world to which Vance was enamored. The pair entered into a whirlwind courtship and, on January 16, 1961, Vance and Dodds were married in the Hootens' home in Santa Fe. "At first, we decided to keep the wedding a secret," Vance declared right before the nuptials. "But then we decided to let everybody know, and we told [syndicated gossip columnist] Hedda [Hopper]. She broke the news."

It was the first marriage for the forty-year-old Dodds, who was a well-liked and -respected fixture in the New York book world. During the course of his career, the Sacramento native edited or represented the likes of David Niven, Jackie Robinson, Elliot Roosevelt, and Sterling Hayden; among his more prestigious assignments was the editing of Lyndon Johnson's memoirs.

After three failed marriages, Vance felt she finally had found her true life partner. Dodds, unlike Ober, was secure in his place in the world. And also unlike Ober, he appreciated Vance's successes and did not compete with her. The pair shared the same kind of smart humor and enjoyed a warm and loving rapport.

"He was very flamboyant," explains Roslyn Targ, a New York literary agent and Vance-Dodds acquaintance. "He was a very charming [man], definitely the life of the party. You absolutely had to like John."

"It seemed to me he was one of those bright, sharp people around town in the 1960s, in the literary world," notes Sylvia Miles. She then refers to Dodds as a "gay blade," and points out that he had not been married prior to wedding Vance.

"Oh, he was AC/DC," confirms Targ. "And I think he became totally the other way when [Vivian] died."

Apparently, even though he was married—and a loving husband—Dodds still indulged in sexual affairs on the side. "[Vivian] would call up my husband [William, an editor-in-chief at Putnam] when [Dodds] wouldn't come home sometimes," notes Targ. "It would be eight P.M. and she would call us [wanting to know] where was John. Bill always would cover for him. He'd say, 'Look, Vivian, you know an editor has to take authors out for drinks and that sort of thing. They have to discuss the manuscript.' In other words, 'He'll be home. Be patient.' But he never seemed to call her [even to] lie and say, 'I'm still with an author.' She would always call us.

"I can't believe that she didn't know. I can't believe it, [because] she was sophisticated. But she was madly in love with him." Once again, Viv had entered into a union that was fraught with an underlying tension. Despite all they had in common, and there were so many good feelings between them, Dodds's sexuality prevented him from being monogamous—and resulted in increased insecurity for Viv.

Irma Kusely describes the Vance-Dodds marriage as "a strain on [Vance]. I think he was gay. But he adored Vivian. He really did. They got along very well as far as getting along. I think she knew the people who knew, you understand. And so when you go to gatherings, it's a little awkward."

One evening at a party, Roslyn Targ had a conversation with Vance that she describes as "touching." "I was sitting and talking to Vivian and she said to me, 'Johnny, Johnny, I love him so much. God, I don't know what I would do if he died.' Of course, she died before him."

"I know there are lots of stories about [Dodds]," notes Marjorie Lord. "But I don't think that entered into their marriage. He had a nice way, and a nice presence about him."

Sheila MacRae met Dodds on several occasions and describes him as being less prepossessing than Phil Ober. However, weighing the pluses and minuses of their relationship, Dodds's ability to love Vance in a giving way was exactly what she needed in a marital partner. After all, they really meshed as a couple. Even if there were occasions when Vivian desperately struggled to keep her husband from straying, most of the time they delighted in each other's company.

The Vance-Dodds marriage was unusual, to be sure, but it worked. And after all, this was the first time in many years that Viv was to be a part of a really cheerful home, which she did not have as a child, and had only fleetingly in her marriage to Ober.

♥

Upon their marriage, Vance settled in and started a new life for herself as Mrs. John Dodds. The couple resided in a 125-year-old white frame house in Stamford, Connecticut, which came complete with garden and pets. Their framed marriage license quaintly decorated the wall over their canopied bed.

"I visited her up there," recalls scriptwriter Bob Schiller. "She was very happy there. It was very homey." Gene Reynolds recalls, "Bob Schiller and I happened to be in New York at the same time. He said, 'I'm gonna go up and visit Vivian. Would you like to come along?' I said, 'Sure.' This was when she was first married. We went up to their house in Connecticut and spent some time there. She and John seemed to be very happy. They had an idyllic setup back there, a beautiful house. They seemed to appreciate each other enormously."

"Our house is full of writers all the time, and I've always loved writers," Vance observed of this period. Unlike too many performers who act as if they and they alone are the sole creators of their roles, Vance readily acknowledged the creative input of those who put pen to paper when she noted, "As an actress, I'm so beholden to writers. Without the word, we are nothing." She also observed, "A wise actor knows he's completely dependent upon the writer. You can add the velvet, but bad lines can make you look like a bad actor."

The couple also maintained an apartment on Manhattan's upper Fifth Avenue, where they entertained writers and editors. One typical soiree, in the 1970s, was held to commemorate the publication of *Burke's Steerage,* a compilation of celebrity interviews by Tom Burke (which was dedicated to John and Viv). On hand were typical guests at a Dodds gathering: a blend of New York literary figures and journalists, among them Patricia Bosworth, then working on her Montgomery Clift biography, Seymour Peck of the *New York Times,* Jill Goldstein of *Viva,* Arthur Bell of the *Village Voice,* Don Erickson of *Esquire,* and Larry Eisenberg of *Cosmopolitan.*

When not entertaining at home, Vance and Dodds would attend events at chic New York eateries. One such occasion came in 1965, when they were present at a luncheon at the Ginger Man restaurant in honor of novelist Edna O'Brien's new book, *August Is a Wicked Month.* After interviewing Vance, Radie Harris wrote in the *Hollywood Reporter,* "I know it is the kiss of death to say that two people are divinely happy, but it's no ill omen to print this truth about Vivian and John."

Viv really fit into this East Coast upper-crust environment. Literary representative Roslyn Targ, who met Vance during this period, describes her as "dynamic" and adds, "She [once] came to a party I gave where there was Jacqueline Susann and this British duchess or something. Well, you should have seen those three babes vying for attention! It was a riot."

Nonetheless, Vance regarded the company she now was keeping with great admiration. Sixteen years into her marriage, she declared, "I like writers better than actors, so being the wife of an editor is a wonderful life for me. I suffer if their books don't sell and I love hearing them sit around and talk."

In the latter stages of her life, Vance attempted to become an author herself when she began penning an autobiography. "I loved writing," she declared. "Even if you usually find writing difficult you'd be surprised at how easy it is when you're writing about yourself. Putting it on paper was actually very healthy for me. But then I decided that I didn't want the book published. My husband tells me, 'Someday, Viv, you'll get it out.' And maybe someday parts of it will be published, but whether they are or not, I had a good time writing."

In her lifetime, "The Vivian Vance Story" never did make it into bookstores. Had it been published, the book would have been called, simply, *VIV.* At one point it was scheduled to be titled *Go Home, Your Eyes Are Too Close Together*, which, as Vance reported, she once had been told by a Hollywood talent agent after declaring that she was completely unphotogenic for the big screen.

It was around the time that Vivian married John Dodds that she became an aggressive advocate of mental-health programs. Upon moving back East, she became co-chairperson of Operation Friendship, a volunteer recruitment program sponsored by the Connecticut Association for Mental Health.

Vance did more than merely lend her name to a worthy cause and make token appearances. She surfaced at mental-health–related functions where she gave recruitment speeches. She visited patients in hospitals and lobbied to increase state funding for mental-health programs. The fact that she—a celebrity—was willing to talk openly about her own problems and offer compassion to strangers allowed her to connect with sufferers of all ages and backgrounds.

Her activism came quite unexpectedly, as a result of an experience while appearing as a guest on TV's *Candid Camera* (1948–67) in 1960. Vance's role on the show was to act the part of salesperson at a Los Angeles department-store lingerie counter. The camera then would record the reactions of her customers as they realized the famous face with whom they were dealing.

Vance asked one of the customers, a young man, why he was purchasing a nightgown. As tears welled up in his eyes and he explained that the garment was for his wife, who was in a mental hospital, she ordered the camera to stop rolling.

"All I wanted at that moment was to help him," Vance recalled. "I asked if his wife would like to talk to somebody who had been sick, too, and who was well now." She eventually visited the woman, and came to realize that she had an affinity for relating to individuals who were experiencing mental and emotional stress.

At another time, Vance described working in hospitals and talking to patients as "my particular joy." On another, she observed, with much emotion, "This is the most fulfilling work I have ever engaged in."

She also declared, "Nobody knows what talent she has until somebody asks her to use it." And she added, "I do it because it makes me happy. Everybody wants to be loving and giving. It just takes some of us a long time to learn."

On another occasion, Vance noted, "It's difficult for people to know what they really want until they've been successful at what they chose in the first place." In the same conversation, she observed, "Whenever my sisters sigh about the glamour of the life I live, I remind them what it cost.

"After all, I'm the one who had the crack-up."

Chapter Twenty-five

VIVIAN BAGLEY

Despite the comfortable lifestyle she enjoyed as Mrs. John Dodds, Vance was lured back to television by her old boss, Lucille Ball, who was planning a new weekly TV situation comedy.

Viv and Bob Hope had been scheduled to appear with Ball in a television special, *Lucy Goes to Broadway*, to air in December 1961. The show would have centered around Lucy's starring role on the Great White Way in *Wildcat,* a musical that opened one year earlier, but a fatigued Ball left the show six months into its run and the special was promptly canceled.

For Lucy, the ideal career move now would be a new TV sitcom. Yet how could she return to television without Vivian Vance, her beloved comic cohort?

In early 1962, Lucy visited Viv in Connecticut. "She told me she had a script for a new TV series in her purse," Vance explained. "I said, 'Lucy, don't take it out. I won't read it.'" Yet several months later Vance was back in Hollywood, costarring with Ball in the new CBS sitcom, to be known as *The Lucy Show.*

Ball was cast as Lucy Carmichael, a widow who resided in Danfield, New York, with her two children, an adolescent daughter named Chris (Candy Moore) and younger son called Jerry (Jimmy Garrett). Who better to play her co-conspirator in mischief than Vance, who was cast as Vivian Bagley, a divorcée who lived in Lucy's home with her ten-year-old son, Sherman (Ralph Hart).

On *I Love Lucy*, Ball's and Vance's characters were solidly married— but much of the comedy on *The Lucy Show* derived from Lucy's and Viv's obsession with bagging new husbands.

Rehearsals for the show's debut episode began on July 12, 1962, two years and four months after the shooting of the last installment of *The Lucille Ball–Desi Arnaz Show.* The episode was titled "Lucy Waits Up for Chris," and its script centered around Lucy's paranoia as her daughter begins dating.

If one of the most cherished *I Love Lucy* episodes spotlighted the birth of Little Ricky, by now the menopausal Lucy could not be believably cast as the mother of an infant. She was more fitting playing the parent of a teen.

The Lucy Show was produced for Desilu, and by Desi Arnaz. He was present on the set at that first rehearsal. In an often-repeated story, Arnaz's eyes welled up with tears as he stood on a catwalk and watched Lucy go over a telephone scene.

As he dried his eyes, Desi realized that Viv had joined him—and also was crying.

Vance once observed that, on this occasion, Desi "was on the outside looking in and it wasn't fun anymore. He wasn't acting. He was divorced. I'd been divorced, and I was married again. And Lucy was married again [to comedian Gary Morton]. So much had happened to so many people, but most of all to Desi, leaving him alone and a little sad, although he tried to hide it."

From the initial *The Lucy Show* episode, which aired on October 1, 1962, Lucy Carmichael and Vivian Bagley are portrayed as pals; the program even ends with an animated Lucy and Viv bowing to the viewer. On "Lucy Waits Up for Chris," Viv—who then was in her early fifties—clearly is a slightly chunky middle-aged lady whose excess weight reflects her years and her lifestyle. Yet throughout the show, she is attractively clothed in various stylish outfits including a dark-colored V-neck frock and a skirt with patterned blouse. There would be no frumpy housedresses for Vivian Bagley.

Given Vivian's sensitivity about playing the wife of old Bill Frawley on *I Love Lucy*, it is intriguing to note that one of her first jokes on *The Lucy Show* relates to her character's reluctance to acknowledge advancing age. It seems that *Camille*, the 1937 feature starring Greta Garbo, is scheduled for airing on TV's *Early Show*. Jerry asks, "Who's Greta Garbo?" Sherman responds, "I don't know. She's before my time." He then begins to ask his mother, but Vance breaks in with a hasty, "She's before my time, too."

There also are several blatant, ironic references to *I Love Lucy*. On *The Lucy Show*, Lucy is the homeowner while Viv pays the rent. And in one scene, Lucy and Viv are playing gin rummy. At the end of their game, Lucy owes Viv $3.40.

"I'll take it off your rent," Lucy says.

"Okay," Viv quips, "but don't go blabbing it around town."

Lucy asks, "What do you mean by that?"

Viv responds, "Well, if it ever gets back to that cheapskate ex-husband of mine, he'll deduct the $3.40 from my alimony."

There is no indication that Viv's ex is named Fred Mertz Bagley. (Actually, his name was Ralph.)

On the show, Jimmy Garrett was assigned what Vance would characterize as the "Fred lines." "[That was] because my character was kind of an obnoxious cheapskate," Garrett recalls. "After the [premiere] show, Vivian gave me a big hug in the excitement of the moment and told me I really delivered my 'Fred line' wonderfully."

Practically all the *Lucy Show* episode titles spotlighted Ball. Typical among those that aired during the show's first season were "Lucy Digs Up a Date," "Lucy Becomes an Astronaut," "Lucy Is a Kangaroo for a Day," "Lucy Becomes a Reporter," and "Lucy Is a Soda Jerk." However, Vance got her share of attention in "Vivian Sues Lucy," "Lucy and Viv Are Volunteer Firemen," "Lucy and Viv Put in a Shower," "Lucy and Viv Become Tycoons," "Lucy and Viv Learn Judo," and "Lucy and Viv Take Up Chemistry."

While Viv again was playing second fiddle to Lucy, Vance wanted to establish a clear distinction between herself and Ethel Mertz. So she insisted that it be written in her contract that her character be called Vivian. "Now people will know me by my real name and not as Ethel Mertz," she explained. And when fans approached her in a restaurant, perhaps they would greet her as Viv and not "Ethel."

"I wanted [Vivian Bagley] to be more like me," Vance stressed, "to get to wear pretty clothes, to smile and laugh a lot, to be open and optimistic and *not* older than I."

Vance also came to relish playing the mother of a ten-year-old. "Since Vivian didn't have any kids of her own," recalls Jimmy Garrett, "[she developed] a special attachment to Ralph Hart. That was very touching."

"When you have the misfortune, as I have had, of being childless, I don't think it's wrong to try to find a substitute," Vance once declared. "Playing a mother was a great release for me. They chose Ralph Hart to play my son because he looked like me and I really got to love him." Then, Vance tellingly added, "In fact, I ended up pleading with his mother to take him out of show business."

Yet to many, Vance and Mertz still remained inseparable. "One day," Viv recalled, "a famous columnist came on the set and asked me if I thought people would have trouble accepting me as a different character. I said I had come to TV from the stage and that I had made all sorts of different characters believable and that Vivian was going to be as different from Ethel as possible."

"Well," the columnist chided Viv, "you're using her voice!"

"I don't believe I'd have started this show without Vivian," Ball declared during the early run of *The Lucy Show*. "And I didn't know how I could start it *with* her. After all, Vivian had settled into another way of life since we last worked together. She'd gotten married, she had a home in Connecticut, her garden, her pets, her new interests—all the things she loves.

"She was willing to come back if it was okay with John," Ball continued, "and even though it would involve five years of long-distance commuting, he agreed. John felt it was doing him a favor because it made Vivian happy."

In light of his reported sexual proclivities, Dodds may have been thinking of himself when he encouraged Vance to accept the role. Her being on the West Coast would have allowed him sufficient space in which to pursue his own private affairs. Additionally, he had his own career in New York, and an active social life amid the Manhattan literary whirl.

On the other hand, Dodds was a loving partner who wanted the best for his wife. Unlike Phil Ober, he was threatened neither by Vance's celebrity nor by her status as an Emmy-winning television actress. If appearing on a TV series with Lucille Ball—or, for that matter, working in any professional venue—would make his wife happy, then he was all for it.

In fact, when Vance was asked to sign up for *The Lucy Show*, Dodds was in Chicago on business. She decided that he would have the final say on whether she accepted or rejected the offer. Vance phoned Dodds and told him her news. "His reply," she reported, "was just about the sweetest thing that has been said to me in my life."

"Honey," Dodds declared, "I am the greatest fan you have. I think you are the greatest actress in television."

For a good portion of the early 1960s, Vance commuted between Connecticut and Hollywood. While in California, her life consisted of waking up, heading for the studio, rehearsing and filming *The Lucy Show*, and then returning home. She and Dodds never were apart for more than two weeks, and in the process spent countless dollars on airline tickets.

As the years passed, Vance tired of the bicoastal lifestyle and the pressure of preparing a weekly TV show. At the beginning of the 1964–65 television season, she made it known that she wished to exit *The Lucy Show*, and relinquish an $8,000-per-week salary. "I'm quitting the series this year," she announced in September 1964. "I want to live at home with my husband. I'm tired of commuting."

Vance filmed her episodes for the fifth season of *The Lucy Show*, and then kept her promise. During negotiations for her upcoming contract renewal, she made what she thought would be outlandish requests, including a huge salary increase—to a half million dollars a season—and the opportunity to direct, write, and produce. Lucille Ball was willing to accede to all this. Yet in the end, Vance's demands reportedly became so excessive that they were nixed, which also helped usher her *Lucy Show* exit.

"We've got chickadees, nut hatches, and cardinals, and they all love peanut butter," Viv smiled that spring, after jamming peanut butter into a pair of bird feeders in the backyard of her and Dodds's home. Then she added, "If a woman is wise and she has a good husband, she'll live with him and enjoy it. I've seen enough lonely women with big houses and big careers and absentee husbands. I'm not twenty-five anymore and I've reached a point where it just isn't worth it to be away from John."

Vance's devotion to her husband now would be the priority of her life. She frequently would make such declarations as, "Between a home and a career, always take the home," "I never wear anything on stage or off that John doesn't think is right for me," and "I'm able to be a wife and to feel that I'm a good wife. My husband comes first—his comfort and his happiness."

Vivian knew all too well that career and celebrity were meaningless if they resulted in despondency, in being separated from the man she loved. Certainly, her experience with Phil Ober and her years of analysis had taught her to be honest with herself and to maintain her priorities. In the mid-1960s, Vance's actress friend Martha Scott observed, "She has joined the world with a vengeance. And now she is about the happiest woman I know."

Vivian might have been reiterating what she had learned about herself in analysis when she noted, "I have always felt that there was another, more real, kind of life and that I was being pushed and shoved away from it. I had to be one hundred percent at everything. I was miserable if I wasn't the best. I had to be the life of the party, but first I had to cook a fabulous dinner for everyone. I wanted to please so much. . . . I simply had to be liked by everybody." Her willingness to quit *The Lucy Show* was a victory for Viv and her sense of self. She might have stayed with the TV show simply to please Lucille Ball, or the CBS network executives, or her legion of fans. Yet, in the end, she chose to do what was best for herself.

Added to this equation was Dodds's bisexuality. With him three thousand miles away, Vivian often could not help but wonder what he was doing, and with whom he was spending his evenings. Nevertheless, Dodds's public response to Vance's decision came in one word: "Jubilation." Upon her leaving *The Lucy Show*, Dodds explained, "Vivian's decision was too important for me to try to pressure her. But I can't deny my joy that she made it."

Ball was none too pleased when Vance exited the series and, as a result, the pair had a falling-out. Scriptwriter Bob Schiller had no firsthand knowledge of the quarrel, but he reports that he heard all about it. "Lucy was pissed off that Vivian didn't want to come back," he says. "She wanted to live in Connecticut with her husband, who was very nice to her. It was a happy marriage, from what I could see. She just wanted to come back on occasion, which she did.

"They did have differences, but they did reconcile," he continues. "They were pretty close with each other, you know. Lucy didn't have a hell of a lot of friends to confide in. Vivian was with her every day, practically. So they knew a lot about each other."

When Vance departed *The Lucy Show*, Ball immediately altered its format. Lucy Carmichael moved to Los Angeles, with Vivian Bagley remaining back East and occasionally showing up for a guest appearance.

Lucy's new female buddy was played by another old colleague: Mary Jane Croft, who had been cast as Connecticut next-door neighbor Betty Ramsey on *I Love Lucy*.

In 1968, Ball further altered the format of *The Lucy Show*, changing its title to *Here's Lucy* and her character's surname from Carmichael to Carter. In this newest version, Lucy still was a widow, but she lived in Los Angeles and her two children now were played by her real-life offspring, Lucie Arnaz and Desi Arnaz Jr.

The 1964–65 season finale of *The Lucy Show* was titled "Lucy and the Disc Jockey." Its air date was April 12, 1965. Ball and Vance were to appear together on television on several future occasions. However, this episode marked the final instance in which the duo would share credit as official TV sitcom regulars.

Chapter Twenty-six

LUCY AND VIV

The defining factor of the twenty-eight-year-long, on- and off-camera relationship between Vivian Vance and Lucille Ball is that it was multi-layered, hard to pinpoint.

In 1951, when Vance signed to play Ethel Mertz, she had never met Lucille Ball. As the TV series emerged a hit, the hype regarding the pair was that they had become best pals off-camera. "Vivian took immediately to the born trouper she recognized in Lucille Ball . . . ," wrote *TV Guide* in 1954. "It is doubtful that any two working people in all television get along better or have more mutual respect and admiration than these two."

The truth of the matter was far more complex. For all the talk about Lucy and Viv being bosom buddies, and all the respect Lucy had for Viv as a performer, Ball was definitely the star (not to mention overseer) of the show, while Vance was the second banana/supporting player/employee.

At the time, Sheila and Gordon MacRae socialized with Lucy and Desi. "We had a great camaraderie, the four of us," Sheila explains, adding that "During the first [*I Love Lucy*] season, I do not remember

Vivian Vance or Phil Ober or Frawley being invited to the [Arnaz] house. She only had her same old pals. We all played poker until four or five in the morning, and Lucy baked all the cakes." This should not be considered in any way discourteous on the part of Lucy and Desi. After all, Vance and Frawley were their subordinates, and how many bosses invite their underlings home with them to socialize?

Furthermore, particularly at the beginning of the *I Love Lucy* run in 1951, before Ball was fully aware of Vance's capabilities as an actress, Lucy was highly skeptical of her second banana. Would Viv in any way appear too alluring? Would she not weigh enough? Did she have the proper instincts to pull off a scene? Viv was ever mindful of this uncertainty, which Lucy would in no way disguise. So from the very beginning Vance decided, as she once explained, that for her own self-preservation she was "going to learn to love the bitch."

Yet in the early days of *I Love Lucy,* as Vance was to quickly learn, loving "the bitch" would not be easy. *I Love Lucy* expert Bart Andrews related an occurrence on the *Lucy* set in 1952, when Ball was pregnant with Desi Jr. Lucy's dressing room was situated right beside the stage. Viv's was relatively far away, on a different sound stage.

During one particular costume change, Lucy easily switched attire while Viv had to make a frantic dash while avoiding cables, props, and other backstage paraphernalia. Lucy already was in place when Viv arrived back on the set. Andrews has Lucy telling Viv, "You almost missed your cue. You're late," and Viv responding, after taking a deep breath, "I'd tell you to go fuck yourself if Desi hadn't already taken care of that."

As any lover of *I Love Lucy* will know, Lucille Ball and Vivian Vance became as funny a comedy team as Laurel and Hardy, Abbott and Costello, or Martin and Lewis. If Lucy's on-camera antics brought laughs, Viv's wide-eyed, slightly miffed expressions only compounded the zaniness. Lucy was no fool, and she soon came to realize that Viv was an intricate, indispensable part of the show's success. The two also had a similar approach to acting in that they loved rehearsing and honing their comic timing. Jay Sandrich, who worked with Ball and Vance during their final years as Lucy Ricardo and Ethel Mertz, notes simply that by that time "Vivian adored working with Lucy." Hence, when Lucy was planning *The Lucy Show*, she insisted on casting Vance. And during Viv's stint on *The Lucy Show*, she and Lucy were as recognizable a pair as Lucy and Desi—and Ozzie and Harriet, Kramden and Norton, and any other legendary television duo.

By the time Vance began appearing on *The Lucy Show* in 1962, she was a television veteran who knew what worked and what did not in front of the camera. When necessary, she had the self-confidence to be firm and demanding.

The Vance-Ball working relationship at this stage of their careers is subject to interpretation. On the one hand, not only were Viv and Lucy veteran sitcom partners, but they had gone through so much together once the cameras stopped rolling—beginning with the heartache of their marriages simultaneously crumbling.

Lucy no longer had Desi as an on-camera creative partner, and so she depended on Viv for counsel more than ever. At their weekly script run-throughs, Lucy, of course, would be at the head of the table. Yet Viv would be directly at her left. They sat in canvas chairs with the names Lucy and Vivian imprinted on the backs.

"I did notice, in the last format," remembers actor Elliott Reid, who guest-starred on both *I Love Lucy* and *The Lucy Show*, "that [Vivian] and Lucy did have a very close and trusting relationship and, apparently, Vivian was free to offer whatever directorial ideas or guidance she felt moved to contribute. Lucy, naturally, was numero uno, but Vivian was no shrinking violet."

When asked if Vance and Ball were creative partners on the show, Jimmy Garrett, who played Lucy's son, responds with a firm, "Oh, absolutely. In my opinion, yeah. I can't tell you how many times I remember sitting around the set and reading through lines and having Vivian say, 'Well, you know, honey, if I did so-and-so, and then you did so-and-so, let's give that a try because I think that would get a bigger laugh.'

"Between the two of them, it definitely was a collaborative effort to [create] the funniest possible situation. I don't think people realized how much they were a team."

Ball was to publicly acknowledge Vance's off-the-set abilities. "And then the other thing about Viv, she was a great show doctor," Lucy declared in 1984 at the Museum of Broadcasting seminar. "She could look at something and say, 'Hey, I know what's wrong with this. Let's go talk with the writers 'cause, boy, we really learn from our writers.'"

Garrett reports that Vance as well as Ball was present during the auditions for the show's supporting roles. While that is not surprising considering that the young actors had to have an on-camera rapport with both actresses, Garrett believes that Vance had a say in the casting.

"They brought in all the kid actors in town to read for the roles," he notes. "We actually went in with Lucy and Viv and did a breakfast scene around the table. I'll never forget them coming out and saying, 'Everybody can go home except Jimmy Garrett and Ralph Hart.' Apparently, they had trouble casting the daughter. That wasn't done until the last minute."

Garrett adds that Vance and Ball "were there along with the director and, I believe, a couple if not all the writers. I think [our selection] was more of a committee choice."

He goes on to describe Vance as "absolutely adorable, the kindest, sweetest woman." And he notes that both Ball and Vance "were absolutely warm, kind ladies. They were very interested in us, and in making sure we were taken care of and treated well.

"These were great women, terrific and talented ladies. And this is from somebody who was there," he enthuses.

However, actor Rhodes Reason, who appeared with Vance and Ball a number of times on *The Lucy Show*, has a completely different story to tell. When he notes, "Unfortunately, working with Lucy was a total pain in the ass for everybody," he emphasizes the word "everybody."

"And so consequently, everybody was kind of on pins and needles [around] Lucy," Reason declares. "You had to just hang out and do what she told you to do and that was the end of that. I don't know of anybody who speaks kindly of Lucy. I mean people who've worked with her—including her daughter and her son."

Reason describes Vance as "a real trouper. Always prepared—but totally in the background because of Lucy. She dealt with her the same way we all did. We just, you know, smiled a lot, and whatever [Lucy] said [to] do we did. Lucy ran the show, and that was it. If you wanted to work her show, you just did what she told you to do and that was it."

After quitting *The Lucy Show*, Vance occasionally returned to the series for a guest appearance. One such episode was aptly titled "Viv Visits Lucy," and aired on January 9, 1967. This particular installment is reflective of its time for its skewed depiction of young people. During the course of the story Lucy and Viv end up impersonating hippies—or, at least, a middle-aged person's view of a hippie. They visit the Sunset Strip, where they describe everyone they see as "kooks" and "weirdos."

More to the point, despite her *Lucy Show* contract clauses and her desire to bury the character of Ethel Mertz, Ball still subjected Vance to age- and weight-related humor. In this episode, Viv is the target of age wisecracks, however tired. Her character (who had since remarried) has flown in from the East to the West Coast, and proudly declares, "Now that I'm in California, I'm three hours younger."

Viv asks Lucy, "Oh, say, did you notice I've lost a lot of weight? I'm down to a size twelve—and that's without my girdle." Lucy responds that she had noted the change on the way home from the airport, adding, "We never had that much room in the cab." Viv also declares that, ever since remarrying, she has stopped snacking between meals. "I just eat my six meals a day now, and that's it." If she dines on anything less, "I get so weak that I can't eat."

One simply cannot imagine self-conscious Vance relishing having to speak these lines. But she had to play along. As Reason observes, Lucy was the boss.

Upon being asked if he felt any sense of camaraderie between Viv and Lucy, Reason's response is, "I never sensed any camaraderie [with] anyone [from] Lucy. It was only when Lucy wanted to be a comrade with you. I did about ten shows with her during the 60s and 70s. It was just a job, and I kind of dreaded working with her every time after my first experience. My first show I did was with Lucy and Carol Burnett. I played an airline executive. Even Carol [played] second fiddle, and [laid] back and [was] cooperative.

"You can't assert yourself on Lucy's show," Reason continues. "You can't be too funny. You can't be too anything, because you'll be edited out or you'll be dismissed. I've seen actors dismissed from the show because they've offered suggestions. This even was true of Gale Gordon [who was a regular on *The Lucy Show* and *Here's Lucy*] . . . . [S]he treated him as if he were a novice actor . . . . I couldn't believe how Gale would put up with her. When you think of the zillions of shows he's done with her, and she doesn't treat him any differently than if it's the first time on the show and you don't know what you're doing.

"[Lucy] blew hot and cold. She'd run around smoking her cigarettes and drinking her vodka and whatever, just being the dictator telling everyone what to do and how to do it as though they didn't know anything."

Even though she admits that Ball was a "hard taskmaster," Sheila MacRae declares, "I know that [Lucy] liked Vivian very much. Everybody did. Vivian was a good egg—and perfect with Lucy, perfect. They couldn't have gotten anybody better [to play Ethel Mertz and Vivian Bagley]."

At the same time, MacRae notes, "I don't think they were that close [in the 1960s]. I really don't. When I'd go over [to *The Lucy Show* set], Lucy never seemed to be with Vivian. I never had the feeling they were that close.

"When she got Gary [Morton, Ball's second husband, whom she wed in 1961], I think she pulled away. I think maybe if Lucy hadn't married again, they'd have been closer."

Rhodes Reason's view of the Ball-Vance relationship is far more cynical than MacRae's. He believes that Ball's declarations of, "Hey, Vivian's my old pal," were nothing more than "the public face."

However, Reason and MacRae concur about Vivian's personality. Reason emphasizes that Vance "was just a very sweet person, very professional," while MacRae notes that "Vivian was like a regular dame, I would say." Whenever she would stop by a Lucy set, MacRae would sit and chat with Vance, and, further, describes her as "a charming lady. She had a lovely, open face. She was friendly, and had a lovely bearing and a lot of energy. Lucy's mother was a lot like that. [Vivian] easily could have been Lucy's sister in real life."

Nevertheless, Reason is quick to note that Vance "was there to do whatever Lucy told her to do—beginning and end of story. [Viv] was a consummate professional. She came prepared and she deferred one thousand percent to Lucy. So her own personality really wasn't able to shine through—nor was anybody else's, for that matter."

Reason reports that even Richard Burton had a difficult time with Lucy when he and his wife, Elizabeth Taylor, guested on her show in September 1970. "God, he despised every moment of it," Reason notes. "In fact, he told one of the extras sitting in the bleachers, 'Don't *ever* agree to do anything when you're drunk.'

"They [had been] at a party, and Lucy was talking to Liz and Richard and she said, 'Love to have you on the show.' And they said, 'Oh, that's great, Lucy, give us a call anytime.'

"She treated Richard like he was a novice actor. She would say, 'Mr. Burton, would you mind standing a little more to your right? And your TelePrompTer . . . look into the camera left over here. Don't look at me.' That kind of thing. And Richard is going, 'Oh, who needs this.'"

Reason's story is corroborated by Burton's own commentary. In his biography of the late actor, Melvyn Bragg reported that Burton wrote of Ball in his notebook, "I loathe her today but now I also pity her. After tonight I shall make a point of never seeing her again. . . . [She] can thank her lucky stars that I am not drinking. There is a chance that I might have killed her."

Other performers have their stories to tell regarding Ball. Back in the
1950s, Sylvia Miles appeared on a TV comedy special that featured Ball and
Dinah Shore. "There was a sketch in front of a tenement house, and they
were leaning out the window," Miles recalls. "I was this very young character comedienne, and I was playing this fortune-teller who was telling them
not to do something. People were laughing hysterically at the rehearsal.

"I came out of the rehearsal and somebody, I think it was one of the
ADs [assistant directors] on the show, came over and said, 'Well, you're
very young, you're not supposed to give your all and be that funny in a
rehearsal because, you know, they'll cut that sketch out.' Within about fifteen seconds [someone] came over and said, 'The sketch has been cut out
of the show.' That was Lucille Ball's [decision]. I'll never forget that Dinah
Shore came over to me, and commiserated with me."

Marjorie Lord adds further insight into Ball's personality on the Desilu
lot. "Lucy I worked with about three times," she notes. "Working with
Lucy was fascinating because she was so creative and brilliant. But she was
hard to work with . . . she wanted you to rehearse and rehearse with her. I
was used to Danny [Thomas], who might change a line in the middle of a
scene. I liked the spontaneity of that. But Lucy was such a perfectionist.
She knew exactly what she wanted. I'm sure that Viv had to deal with that.

"Lucy was not easy," Lord continues. "She could be very outgoing one
day and maybe [because] of her home problems would be very closed-off
another day. I would go into makeup and she'd be telling me about her
kids. Another day I'd go in and she wouldn't speak. I'm sure Vivian understood that and dealt with that very well."

Adds Sheila MacRae, "For all Lucy's toughness, I found her very soft
inside. She really wanted to let a man tell her what to do, to rely on a man.
Except on the set. . . ."

♥

In a public forum, Ball, predictably, was ever appreciative of her co-
workers. Near the finale of the 1954 *Toast of the Town* TV tribute to *I Love
Lucy* hosted by Ed Sullivan, Ball thanked "everyone who's helped make *I*

Love Lucy a good show." First, she cited CBS and Philip Morris, the show's
network and sponsor. Next came "the one and only" Jess Oppenheimer, "our
head writer and producer—love that man!" Then she credited writers
Madelyn Pugh and Bob Carroll Jr.; William Asher, "a great little guy, our
director. . . . We call him William the Conqueror or Billy the Kid, depend-
ing on the mood we're in"; and Karl Freund, "our Academy Award–winning
photographic genius. Thank you, Papa."

Before concluding by thanking Desi, "the greatest producer of all
times—and I have two little Arnazes at home to prove it"—Ball generously
toasted her supporting players: "And, of course, Vivian Vance and William
Frawley," she declared. "Everyone should be fortunate enough to work with
these two. They're blessed with an unfailing sense of humor, a wish to do
their best at all times, from first rehearsal on, an understandable pride in
their work that has without a doubt been a top contributing factor to the
success of *Lucy*." Ball then struggled to keep her emotions in check as she
added, softly, "Thank you, Viv and Bill. Ooh, you get so emotional up here."

As the years passed, Vance developed a fondness for Lucy and was concerned about her well-being. Actor/director Gene Reynolds reports that,
during his Connecticut visit with Vivian and John Dodds, "She was talking about Lucy, and about how Lucy was in love with Gary Morton, and
how feminine that had made her, and how she had changed, and how it was
such a wonderful experience for her. She was just thrilled for her friend."

Despite their physical separation after Vance exited *The Lucy Show*, the
two frequently would speak on the telephone. "We'll always talk," Vance
declared in 1976. "We've been through so much together. . . . I can't think
of any family that could possibly be closer."

Audiences also viewed Ball and Vance as old friends. On one occasion
in the late 1960s, Lucy (along with Ozzie and Harriet Nelson) was appearing on *The Mike Douglas Show* (1963–82) taped in Philadelphia. At one
point, Douglas announced his next guest: a female stilt-walker. The curtains separated and out came Vivian, to a chorus of exclamations and
approval. Before the hour concluded, she and Ball reminisced about the old
days, viewed photos from the shows, and even sang and danced together.

In April 1984—more than four and a half years after Viv's death—as Ball spoke of Vance at the Museum of Broadcasting seminar, the standing-room-only crowd applauded when she declared, "No one could take the place of Vivian Vance in my life." Ball added, "[Vance] was the greatest partner anyone could ever have."

Lucy also noted, "Nobody ever enjoyed their work more than *we* did. . . . Vivian and I had an absolute ball . . . [and] it showed, I think. . . . We did everything together happily. We used to have so much fun on the set. Seriously—not just the two of us giggling. I'm not talking about that. [We had fun] by making things evolve, making things work out, making what the writers had written come to life.

"We would love it so much that if we had a social engagement for the evening, which we many times did, she said, 'I am so exhausted from laughing, and working, and I have to go out tonight.' I'd say, 'I'm supposed to go there, too.' [She'd say,] 'It's going to be anticlimactic. I don't want to go anyplace. I've had the most fun I've ever had in my life. I'm going home and go to bed.'

"Viv was something," Lucy concluded. Then she looked up to the heavens and exclaimed, "God bless you, kid!"

Rhodes Reason may be correct when he declares that such all-out appreciation of Viv was little more than public posturing. Perhaps, when Lucy would offer emotional declarations about Vance (as well as Frawley), she was only acting.

But the truth of the Vance-Ball relationship is not one of dominance/subservience. Nor is it one of bosom-buddy equality. The true nature of their complex friendship lies somewhere in between. Lucy could be a taskmaster, for sure, but her fondness and respect for Vance were genuine.

Perhaps the final word on Ball-Vance should go to one who was around long enough to fully comprehend the layers of nuances existing between the two women.

"[Viv] and Lucy were very friendly," Bob Weiskopf observes. "They got along very well together. Lucy wasn't that easy to get along with, but she and Vivian were very close."

Chapter Twenty-seven

A COMPLETE HUMAN
BEING

Leaving *The Lucy Show* did not necessarily mean that Vivian Vance was retired. "Now show business is just one part of my life," she declared in 1965, "along with my home and my community and my mental-health work. I want to be a complete human being." Apparently she was, for a year later the East Coaster happily observed, "My life is absolutely one hundred percent perfect. I wouldn't improve on anything."

Vivian may have been content to pass the days digging into an engrossing book or laughing with friends or attending one of John Dodds's literary events. When he had to travel to London to meet with his writers, she accompanied him and would spend her evenings seeing the shows on the West End. Yet she also continued her career, albeit at a slower pace.

Vance made one last screen appearance: a cameo in the Blake Edwards slapstick comedy *The Great Race* (1965), which starred Jack Lemmon, Tony Curtis, and Natalie Wood. Vance filmed her part while on hiatus from *The Lucy Show*, right before her last season. She harkened back to her wardrobe limitations while playing Ethel Mertz when she noted, "A cameo part is what used to be called a small part. I play a woman suffragette, the wife of a newspaper publisher. I loved the clothes and the full skirts. I have more clothes than lines."

In the mid-1960s, Vance had several Broadway projects in the works, including a musical based on William Inge's *Picnic*, but none came to fruition for her. By this time, the Great White Way that she knew so well from her pre–*I Love Lucy* years had changed altogether. For one thing, there were fewer plays coming to New York. During the 1950–51 season, 81 productions premiered on Broadway; in the 1969–70 season, all of 62 shows opened—15 of which were revivals. (These figures may be contrasted to the 264 and 187 productions that opened during the 1927–28 and 1930–31 seasons, respectively, which were during Bill Frawley's Broadway heyday.)

Unfortunately, the plight of Broadway was destined to only worsen. By the early 1970s, the midtown Manhattan theater district had become seedy. It now was populated by druggies, runaways, and hustlers. A tourist could not walk through the city's theater district without being subjected to pornographic peep-shows, saloons featuring topless dancers, and unsavory types passing out handbills to the men in the crowd, inviting them to sample a strip club.

This was a Broadway Vance professed to want no part of. "I'll never go back to New York. . . . I've tried it, I'm glad I did, but I think there is much more interesting theater all over the country," she declared in 1967, adding, "Theater is not New York anymore. Good theater is coming from summer stock and community groups such as the Albuquerque Little Theater.

"I'd like to get my own acting company together and tour summer theaters. They are located in the most wonderful communities across the nation—in the mountains, by the seaside, or in Florida. Summer theater audiences are always so eager and appreciative. . . ."

Despite this declaration, Vance did return to the New York theater scene one last time, in a new play written by Phoebe and Henry Ephron, titled *My Daughter, Your Son*. It opened at the Booth Theater in May 1969 and was her first Broadway appearance in twenty-two years, since the revival of *The Cradle Will Rock*.

My Daughter, Your Son (which originally was called *I Giveth and Giveth*) is an amiable situation comedy about the impending marriage of the son of a dentist (Robert Alda) and the daughter of a scriptwriter. Box office was lackluster, and soon after its premiere the newspapers ran an ad for the show, designed in the form of a memo from Vance to "every person who has ever laughed." "Just in case you missed some of our reviews," began the ad copy, "here they are. . . ." In them, Vance was lauded for "her perfect timing, her complete naturalness, her warmth and her charm," "her sparkling comedic talents," her "breezy style," and for being "completely fetching" and "split-second perfect."

Despite this hype, *My Daughter, Your Son* closed after only forty-seven performances. Vance followed this up with a stint on *You're Putting Me On*, a short-lived daytime game show—it premiered in May 1969 and folded that December—in which celebrity guests would act out the role of a prominent person, and their teammates would guess who was being portrayed.

Mainly during this period, Vance appeared in summer-stock and dinner-theater productions—which, then as today, were a refuge for middle-aged movie and TV stars. Among her many vehicles were *Barefoot in the Park*, *The Time of the Cuckoo*, *Butterflies Are Free*, *Arsenic and Old Lace*, and John Patrick's *Everybody Loves Opal* and *Everybody's Girl*. The latter, a comedy about an unmarried mother of five who becomes a Mother of the Year candidate, was written with Vance in mind. She performed it over the course of several years and, in 1967, even starred in it at the Albuquerque Little Theater.

Vance was not one to forget her roots, and the manner in which she had been supported by the Albuquerque Little Theater. Years before, when the theater was experiencing financial difficulties, she arranged for her friend Edward Everett Horton to become its very first celebrity guest star. She worked without a salary in *Everybody's Girl*, donating her time to raise funds for the construction of a new theater balcony.

Beyond the Albuquerque Little Theater, one of her favorite venues was the Cherry County Playhouse in Michigan. In 1965, she starred in *Over 21* there. The following year, she was in *Everybody's Girl*. In 1970, she appeared in *My Daughter, Your Son*. When Vance came to the Cherry County Playhouse, her popularity ensured sold-out houses—and a flurry of requests for tickets from adjoining states.

Despite her various public declarations in the 1930s and early 1940s regarding her dreams of Broadway stardom, her breakdown and years in analysis had given her a solid perspective on her life and career. And so, in 1976, Vance professed, "My ambition never was to be a big star. I never felt that I was being held back. What I wanted was my identity and I got that by going to a good analyst and doing summer stock.

"But I wouldn't have sold out those theaters if I had not been Ethel. I've just had to make a compromise with myself. I had a hell of a time adjusting to the identity of Ethel, especially being thought of as the wife of someone I wouldn't have married in a million years." So despite her displeasure over being forever linked to Ethel Mertz, Vance was smart enough to know that the role, ultimately, had been her meal ticket.

"I was a very lucky lady," she continued. "I've seen very few happy stars and I was determined that that wasn't going to happen to me. The plums hang so high and the vampires beckon and I knew that if I fell for it I'd be as unhappy as the other ladies in Hollywood." Vance then pointedly referred to her advancing years and her place in the world as the wife of John Dodds when she added, "Ambition doesn't go too well with age or companionship."

♥

In the latter stages of her life, Vance also did occasional guest shots on television. Most significantly, she made appearances on *The Lucy Show* (in 1967 and 1968) and *Here's Lucy* (between 1968 and 1972). In January 1970 she played Mrs. Grant, the prospective mother-in-law of ace reporter Hildy Johnson, in *The Front Page*, Ben Hecht and Charles MacArthur's classic 1928 newspaper comedy-drama. The program originated onstage in October 1968 at the Plumstead Playhouse in Mineola, Long Island, which was co-founded by Vance's friend Martha Scott. Robert Ryan starred as the conniving editor Walter Burns. The production then made it to Broadway for a limited run in May 1969 with Ryan; it reopened in October with Helen Hayes added to the cast as Mrs. Grant. Scott arranged for a syndicated television version in which Vance replaced Hayes (who narrated the show).

In 1975, Vance appeared on an episode of TV's *Rhoda* as Maggie Cummings, the urbane neighbor of Rhoda and Joe Gerard (Valerie Harper and David Groh), whose budding friendship with Rhoda makes Rhoda's mother, Ida (Nancy Walker), envious. "With such a hit show, what better way to make a comeback?" Vance remarked before the episode aired. "I'm tickled to death. Being asked to do *Rhoda* was a joyous surprise."

Vance also had supporting parts in two made-for-television movies: *Getting Away from It All* (1972), which was similar to *Guestward Ho!,* in that it was a comedy about two couples who abandon their urban lifestyles for rural living; and *The Great Houdinis* (1976), a biography of the fabled illusionist.

By now, Vance was a veteran television performer whose costars had grown up watching her on *I Love Lucy*. Her professionalism and bright personality were appreciated by her fellow cast members. While not having any specific anecdotes to share about her, Paul Michael Glaser, who played Harry Houdini in *The Great Houdinis*, refers to Vance as "lovely." Gary Collins, one of the stars of *Getting Away from It All*, recalls, "We were on location at Morro Bay [California] for several days and between takes most of us, including Vivian, would relax together and exchange stories, jokes—anything to kill the boredom that off-camera waiting seems to nurture.

"During one of these exchanges I asked Vivian about the *Lucy* days and she told one story after another, which were wonderful. And then, since we were doing a picture entitled *Getting Away from It All*, we began to talk about how we relieved the stress and pressures that each of us felt. Vivian said whenever she felt overwhelmed she simply thought of Portugal."

"Portugal, why Portugal?" Collins asked her.

He continues: "She looked at me with a wonderful sparkle in her eyes and said she and her husband had a getaway place on the ocean there. She began to describe the setting, the colors, the nearby coastal town, the Atlantic seashore . . . just everything about this fabulous getaway."

Collins and the other cast members were terribly envious of Viv's "second home." Collins recalls, "One of us then asked how often the two of them spent time there and she answered that she had never been there! They had purchased it from a brochure and had never visited the place."

According to Collins, Vance realized that her audience was perplexed. So she explained, "I know it sounds funny, but all I have to do is think of that place and know I could go there if all goes to hell in a handbasket, and I'm okay!"

In these last years Vivian Vance found a special contentment that had eluded her throughout her past. In the mid-1970s, she became Maxine the Coffee Lady in an ongoing series of television commercials hawking Maxwell House coffee; in them, Maxine would be forever brewing coffee— the aroma of which would entice anyone within nose-length of her—and pronouncing that "every cup" of Instant Maxwell House "tastes fresh like your first cup in the morning."

"So here I sit feeding the cat and watering the flowers and doing my commercial," Vance observed in 1976. "If I had a little part in a series that ran every so often, that would be fine because it's good to keep working. What helped me was that I knew what I wanted, and very few people do. That's how I've ended up on TV—selling coffee and loving it."

Of her years on *I Love Lucy* and even *The Lucy Show*, Vance declared in 1976, "My life is so far removed from all that, I can't begin to tell you. [*I Love Lucy*] has nothing to do with me now. My life has gone on."

Vance's final appearances with Lucille Ball came on two television specials: *CBS Salutes Lucy: The First 25 Years*, a two-hour show broadcast on November 28, 1976; and the hour-long *Lucy Calls the President*, which involved Ball and President Jimmy Carter and was aired on CBS on November 21, 1977. On *CBS Salutes Lucy . . .* , shown in conjunction with the quarter-century anniversary of the *I Love Lucy* premiere, Ball was offered testimonials by Bob Hope, Danny Kaye, Milton Berle, Carol Burnett, John Wayne, and other entertainment legends, and was reunited with several Lucy sitcom alumni, including Gale Gordon, Mary Wickes, and Mary Jane Croft. The show was penned by Bob Carroll Jr. and Madelyn Pugh Davis, the original *I Love Lucy* writers, and directed by Marc Daniels, who helmed the show during its first season.

On *CBS Salutes Lucy . . .* , Vance was introduced and sat demurely as she recalled the time when Desi asked her to be on *I Love Lucy*. "Well, I thought it was just another job so I took it," she said. "Never in my wildest dreams did I imagine what would happen to us. We became two of the best-known families in America."

Without grimacing, Vance continued. "I went out on that stage as Vivian Vance, and do you know to this day some people still think of me as Mrs. Fred Mertz?" Next, she introduced a clip of Lucy in action. "It was marvelous," she said at its conclusion, and then she went on to talk about "the great love and chemistry that was between us" and how on the show she and Ball got to "live out every childhood fantasy we ever had."

While promoting the show, Vance explained that "shooting it was just a riot. The audience was so responsive you could hardly hear the lines for the laughs. And it was just wonderful working with that dear Gale Gordon again. And with the rest of the gang."

A month before *CBS Salutes Lucy . . .* aired, Vance joked, "I sure would like to get back with Lucy. Maybe we could get a TV series called *The Grandmothers*. Of course, I don't know how Lucy would feel about the title."

Yet around this time Vance also observed, "Lucy and I live so differently. She is still in show business. I say that like I wasn't in it, but it's funny, I don't feel that I am."

♥

Across the years, Vance and John Dodds frequently changed residences. At the beginning of their marriage, they lived in Connecticut and maintained a New York apartment. They also loved spending time in New Mexico, and in 1967 settled in Santa Fe. They moved into temporary quarters on Circle Drive and eventually purchased a home on Hillside Avenue. At the time, Dodds was a vice president at G. P. Putnam's Sons. However, the couple had become tired of the pressures of New York City life. He resigned his position and purchased Travel Service Everywhere, a Santa Fe travel agency.

"And this clean air!" Vance exclaimed upon her arrival. "It's so great to be back here where the air is clean and fresh and you can breathe!"

It was during this period that Vance became an early advocate of preserving the environment. She declared, upon her relocation to Santa Fe, "If you had lived where I have and been driven out [by the dirt of New York and the smog of Los Angeles], then you would know how necessary [it is for] us to keep the air clean.

"Do you know why Hawaii is so popular for tourists—why it's so beautiful?" she asked. "There are no signboards in Hawaii. It is lovely and beautiful and you can see it." Ever so perceptively, she added that "if you clean up [New Mexico], you'll have the tourists," and that it was imperative "to make [New Mexico] beautiful and rich instead of rich and dirty."

Albuquerque and Santa Fe were favorite spots for Vance and Dodds. Yet while appearing on *The Merv Griffin Show*, Vivian described Taos as the "most beautiful place in the world."

While in the Southwest, Vance maintained her charitable commitments. She and Dodds were guests at a gala benefit for the Santa Fe County Chapter of the New Mexico Heart Association; she joined the Tiffany Players theater group for a special performance of the melodrama *Only an Orphan Girl*, held as a benefit for the Santa Fe County Mental Health chapter.

And the Dodds were local celebrities. The housewarming of their Hillside Avenue abode brought out a stellar list of New Mexicans, including then governor David Cargo, former governor Jack Campbell, state Supreme Court Justice David Chavez, and other government dignitaries, artists, and businessfolk—along with Rosalind Russell, Mary Wickes, director James Neilson, and producer Bill Fry, who were then filming *Where Angels Go . . . Trouble Follows* (1968) in Santa Fe.

When Vance and Dodds moved to Santa Fe, Vance declared that she never would go back to New York. However, she did return to Broadway that one last time in 1969—and, the following year, she and Dodds purchased a 250-year-old schoolhouse in North Salem, New York, just across the Connecticut border in the wilds of northern Westchester County. When they eventually decided to sell the property, Roslyn Targ was considering purchasing it. According to Targ, Vance "was a darling. She said, 'Roslyn, don't buy it. It's more trouble than it's worth!'"

In the mid-1970s, Vance and Dodds made one final move together, to the San Francisco area. The couple settled in a Victorian-style shingle house in the San Francisco suburb of Belvedere. Dodds opened his own publishing house, which he named for his new community, while his wife occasionally made summer-stock and dinner-theater appearances around the country. She also acted in local productions; for example, in 1976, she starred in a revival of *Marriage-Go-Round* at Cabrillo College in Aptos, California.

Mostly, Vance was satisfied to putter around the house, frequent local cultural events, cook Mexican dinners, and savor the company of her husband and close friends.

"We love it here," Vance declared in 1977, as she described her house as "just darling" and her furniture as "the same that I've had for years with new slipcovers. But it's all so pretty."

Teaching was an avocation she especially loved. Ever since the 1960s, whenever Vance would be performing in a city, she often could be found speaking with students at a nearby university. "People say that no one can be taught comedy, but that's not true," she once declared. "Experience is best, but a teacher can provide students many tricks of the trade, and techniques can be learned to overcome a poor sense of timing in doing comedy."

Upon moving to San Francisco, Viv would give acting seminars to Bay Area college students. "They all grew up with me, so it's not difficult for us to talk," she explained. "I'm like a good friend or an aunt or older sister."

Vance's confidence in psychoanalysis was ever apparent as she added, "I try to teach them that we all go through such unnecessary fright and fear that hold us back. I tell them it should be a joy to act and not to be afraid.

"Nobody was more frightened than I was, so I know what I'm talking about."

Chapter Twenty-eight

FINAL APPEARANCES

For the most part, Vance lived a contented life with John Dodds. Unfortunately, their time together was shortened by her failing health. In 1973, sixty-four-year-old Vance discovered a cancerous tumor on her breast. She had a mastectomy, performed at Columbia Presbyterian Hospital in New York.

"I saw her on the night before she had her breast removed," recalls Roslyn Targ. "It was both my husband and I. We both were very surprised that, of all their close friends, they wanted to have dinner with us. We never understood it."

For a while it was believed that all of the cancerous tissue had been removed. This was not the case. The cancer spread through Vivian's system and eventually would lead to her death. Additionally, in 1977 Viv's health deteriorated further when she suffered a stroke, which left one side of her face partially paralyzed.

Through her ordeal, Vivian still was able to occasionally travel, appear onstage, and socialize with friends. Marjorie Lord reports that, around this

time, she met Vance and Dodds in Dallas. "I was playing there, and Vivian
I think had been playing there. We all went out one night. [Dodds] was
charming that night. Vivian had been a little bit ill—I think she'd already
had a bout with cancer—and he was very solicitous and very sweet to her.
And she was better, and things looked good at that time."

Vance was fighting the disease when she made her guest appearance on *Rhoda* in 1975. Originally, the scuttlebutt was that she would
become a regular on the show, as a replacement for Nancy Walker, who
had been signed to an ABC contract and was having a TV series fash-
ioned for her.

In the end, Vance's *Rhoda* appearance was a one-shot. Even if she were
seriously considered for the show, she would have had the same problem
Bill Frawley had with regard to passing the insurance physical.
Furthermore, in the scenes shared by the two actresses, Nancy Walker is
intensely funny while Vance's character barely registers. Vivian clearly no
longer had the pep to shine in a sustained comedy role—and from here on
in, her future would be limited to brief TV guest spots.

It was two full years after the *Rhoda* spot that Vance made her final
appearance with Lucille Ball on the *Lucy Calls the President* special. "Vivian
was very brave," recalled Gale Gordon, who also was on the show, "because
she knew she had cancer and never said anything to anybody."

"The last time I saw her was in San Francisco," adds Roslyn Targ. "[By
then], she was using a walker. I knew it was curtains."

"When she was very ill," remembers Marjorie Lord, "I was up there [in
the San Francisco area] visiting friends and I tried to see her. I talked to her
on the phone. She said, 'Oh, Maggie, I've just had chemo. It takes me four
or five days to get over it. So let's do it next week.'

"I couldn't stay that long and had to go back to Los Angeles. I know
she wanted to see me, but my life was topsy-turvy. I'd just been widowed
and people were trying to take care of me. But we had a long talk on the
phone and I felt she was not going to be with us for too long. So I said my
good-byes, and how much I appreciated knowing her, and what a great
talent she was. What a dear person! I was very fond of her."

Lord laments that she and Vance had not spent more time together through the years. "I felt very close to her when we first knew each other," she explains. "And I always loved her. But our lives and work didn't allow us to see that much of each other. But [when we did get together], it was like seeing an old chum or sister after many years. I remember meeting her in Dallas, and we felt very close to each other. I just enjoyed being with her that night so much, and I think she enjoyed being with me, too."

While undergoing chemotherapy, Vance lost her hair. She dispatched several photographs to hairdresser Irma Kusely. "Vivian asked me to have a wig made that looked like the pictures she sent," Kusely recalls. "But she never got to the point where she needed it. She passed away before it was ready."

Vivian Vance died on August 17, 1979, in her Belvedere home. Shortly before her demise, she was visited by Lucille Ball, who was accompanied by Mary Wickes. For two hours, the trio—three of the funniest women in television history—giggled and reminisced. Finally, Wickes suggested they leave, so as not to tire Vance. Afterward, Ball and Wickes consoled each other with tears.

"It's bad enough to lose one of the great artists I had the honor and pleasure to work with," noted Desi Arnaz on Vance's passing, "but it's even harder to reconcile the loss of one of your best friends."

Ball responded similarly. "I lost one of the best friends I've ever had and the world has lost one of the great performers of the stage, films, and television," she declared, adding, "I shall miss her terribly." Bob Schiller corroborates Ball's statement. When Vance died, he notes, "Lucy felt that she lost her best friend."

Vance's remains were cremated. Upon her request, donations in her memory were to be made to the National Mental Health Association and the Society for the Prevention of Cruelty to Animals.

During her later years, Vance had become pals with stage producer Charles Forsythe, who mounted a number of her summer-stock and dinner-theater productions. "After she died," Forsythe recalls, "her husband and Josh and Nedda Logan threw this fantastic party up at the River House on Fifty-second Street [in New York]."

Forsythe notes that John Dodds—who also was fated to die of cancer, just about seven years after Vance—"got the [guest] list together, and everybody who was anybody was at that party. It was a sit-down dinner. It was huge. There might have been 150 people there. It was all to celebrate Vivian."

He concludes his remarks about Vance by noting simply, "I loved her."

"She was a very sharp, very bright gal," stresses Marjorie Lord. "She was very amusing, and very motivated." Adds Bob Schiller, "Vivian was a good egg. She had a pretty good career. She didn't like being typed as a frowsy housewife, but she made a lot of money and she made a lot of friends and everybody loved her."

On several occasions during her April 1984 talk at the Museum of Broadcasting, Lucille Ball noted how much she missed Vance. At the outset of the seminar, she described herself as being "traumatically bored . . . for several months after I quit work and Vivian died and my mother passed away [all] at the same time."

An audience member asked her if she ever would revive her Lucy character. "I doubt it," Ball responded. "Well, I don't know. Viv's gone. And Bill's gone, you know. Gale's [Gordon] around, thank God. God bless him. But without Viv . . . ."

She then paused, and gasped for air. Her words came slower, and she looked genuinely pained. "It's hard to even think of doing anything like that. . . . Nobody knew like Viv and Bill and Desi. . . . Even when I worked with my kids, that was still fun. Viv and I still had fun with that. But after Viv . . . ."

She then shook her head, and concluded that she could not ever again "try to do a Lucy character, not without them."

Two years after the Museum of Broadcasting appearance, Lucille Ball starred in one last, disastrous sitcom: *Life with Lucy*, which premiered on September 20, 1986. She was cast as newly widowed Lucy Barker, who comes to live with her daughter, husband, and their children in Pasadena,

California. Lucy has inherited half the hardware store operated by her late spouse and his partner, whose son is wed to Lucy's daughter.

Even though Gale Gordon was on hand as the on-camera business partner, there was no Desi, no Bill, no Viv. Plus, when *Life with Lucy* premiered, Ball was one and a half months past her seventy-fifth birthday and could no longer really do physical comedy. The show's various components did not mesh and, after eight painful weeks, *Life with Lucy* faded into the TV heavens.

In March 1989, Ball made her final public appearance, at the Academy Awards ceremony. When she and her old friend Bob Hope walked onstage, they were greeted by an extended ovation that befitted their status as entertainment-industry legends.

One month later, on April 26, after undergoing open-heart surgery at Cedars Sinai Medical Center in Los Angeles, Ball died of heart disease. Desi Arnaz had predeceased her, losing a bout with lung cancer and passing away at age sixty-nine on December 2, 1986.

So now, even though they will live on in perpetuity as Lucy, Ricky, Fred, and Ethel, the four actors who gave life to the Ricardos and Mertzes now survive only as shadows on a small screen.

In 1991, twelve years after her death, Vance was honored with a star on the Hollywood Walk of Fame. It is located at Hollywood Boulevard and Orange Drive. More than one hundred people attended the ceremony for the star's unveiling. The concrete-and-bronze tribute was sponsored by the Vivian Vance Memorial Foundation, an organization formed by *I Love Lucy* fan David Hildebrand. In 1989, while touring the famed Walk with a friend, Hildebrand noted that Vivian had no star. He was determined to rectify the situation, and organized the foundation to raise the $4,800 needed to cover the cost of the bronzed star, as well as continuing Vance's charity work.

Bill Frawley also has a star. His is on Hollywood Boulevard between Vine Street and Ivar Avenue, approximately eight-tenths of a mile away.

One could not imagine his and Vance's stars ever being placed side by side.

Appendix

WILLIAM FRAWLEY'S AND VIVIAN VANCE'S PROFESSIONAL CREDITS

From the late 1900s through early 1920s, Frawley worked in vaudeville; from the early 1960s through mid-1970s, Vance acted in summer-stock and dinner-theater productions. Both also toured in road productions of Broadway plays—Frawley in the 1920s and Vance in the 1930s and 1940s. Their New York City appearances include the following:

STAGE
William Frawley and His Roles

The Gingham Girl. Opened April 30, 1923. Central Theater. Jack Hayden. Limited run.

Merry Merry. Opened September 24, 1925. Vanderbilt Theater. 176 performances. Horatio Riggs.

Bye Bye Bonnie. Opened January 13, 1927. Ritz Theater. 125 performances. "Butch" Hogan.

Talk About Girls. Opened June 14, 1927. Waldorf Theater. 13 performances. Henry Quill.

She's My Baby. Opened January 3, 1928. Globe Theater. 71 performances. Meadows.

Here's Howe! Opened May 1, 1928. Broadhurst Theater. 71 performances. "Sweeny" Toplis.

Sons O' Guns. Opened November 26, 1929. Imperial Theater. 295 performances. Hobson.

She Lived Next to the Firehouse. Opened February 10, 1931. Longacre Theater. 24 performances. Harlan Smith.

Tell Her the Truth. Opened October 19, 1932. Cort Theater. 11 performances. Mr. Parkin.

Twentieth Century. Opened December 29, 1932. Broadhurst Theater. 154 performances. Owen O'Malley.

The Ghost Writer. Opened June 19, 1933. Masque Theater. 24 performances. Joe Gordon.

Vivian Vance and Her Roles

Music in the Air. Opened November 8, 1932. Alvin Theater. 342 performances. Chorus.

Anything Goes. Opened November 21, 1934. Alvin Theater. 420 performances. Reno Sweeney.

Red, Hot and Blue! Opened October 29, 1936. Alvin Theater. 183 performances. Vivian and a reporter.

Hooray for What! Opened December 1, 1937. Winter Garden Theater. 200 performances. Stephanie Stephanovich.

Skylark. Opened October 11, 1939. Morosco Theater. Imperial Theater. 256 performances. Myrtle Valentine.

Out from Under. Opened May 4, 1940. Biltmore Theater. 9 performances. Clair James.

Let's Face It. Opened October 29, 1941. 547 performances. Nancy Collister.

It Takes Two. Opened February 3, 1947. Biltmore Theater. 8 performances. Bee Clark.

The Cradle Will Rock. Opened December 26, 1947. Mansfield Theater. 21 performances. Mrs. Mister.

My Daughter, Your Son. Opened May 13, 1969. Booth Theater. 47 performances. Maggie Gordon.

FILM

While Frawley's prolific career lasted almost fifty years, Vance only appeared in three feature films.

William Frawley

Lord Loveland Discovers America. 1916. American Film Mfg. Co. Tony Kidd.

Persistent Percival. 1916. American Film Mfg. Co. Billy.

Turkey for Two. 1929. Pathé. Supporting player.

Fancy That. 1929. Pathé. Supporting player.

Moonlight and Pretzels. 1933. Universal. Mack.

Miss Fane's Baby Is Stolen. 1933. Paramount. Captain Murphy.

Hell and High Water. 1933. Paramount. Milton J. Bunsey.

Shoot the Works. 1934. Paramount. Larry Hale.

The Lemon Drop Kid. 1934. Paramount. The Professor.

Here Is My Heart. 1934. Paramount. James Smith.

The Crime Doctor. 1934. RKO. Fraser.

Bolero. 1934. Paramount. Mike DeBaere.

The Witching Hour. 1934. Paramount. Jury Foreman.

Ship Café. 1935. Paramount. Briney O'Brien.

Hold 'Em, Yale. 1935. Paramount. Sunshine Joe.

College Scandal. 1935. Paramount. Chief of Police Magoun.

Car 99. 1935. Paramount. Sergeant Barrel.

Alibi Ike. 1935. Warner Bros. Cap.

Welcome Home. 1935. Fox. Painless.

Harmony Lane. 1935. Mascot. E. P. "Ed" Christy.

Three Married Men. 1936. Paramount. Bill Mullins.

Three Cheers for Love. 1936. Paramount. Milton Shakespeare.

Strike Me Pink. 1936. United Artists. Copple.

It's a Great Life. 1936. Paramount. Lieutenant McNulty.

Rose Bowl. 1936. Paramount. Coach Soapy Moreland.

The Princess Comes Across. 1936. Paramount. Benton.

The General Died at Dawn. 1936. Paramount. Mr. Brighton.

F-Man. 1936. Paramount. Hogan.

Desire. 1936. Paramount. Mr. Gibson.

Something to Sing About. 1937. Grand National. Hank Meyers.

High, Wide and Handsome. 1937. Paramount. Mac.

Double or Nothing. 1937. Paramount. Peterson.

Blossoms on Broadway. 1937. Paramount. Francis X. Rush.

Touchdown, Army. 1938. Paramount. Jack Heffernan.

Sons of the Legion. 1938. Paramount. Uncle Willie Lee.

Mad About Music. 1938. Universal. Dusty Turner.

Professor Beware. 1938. Paramount. Snoop Donlan.

Persons in Hiding. 1939. Paramount. Alec Inglis.

Stop, Look and Love. 1939. Twentieth Century-Fox. Joe Haller.

St. Louis Blues. 1939. Paramount. Major Martingale.

Night Work. 1939. Paramount. Bruiser Brown.

Grand Jury Secrets. 1939. Paramount. Bright Eyes.

Ex-Champ. 1939. Universal. Mushy Harrington.

Ambush. 1939. Paramount. Inspector Weber.

Huckleberry Finn. 1939. Metro-Goldwyn-Mayer. "The Duke."

Rose of Washington Square. 1939. Twentieth Century-Fox. Harry Long.

Untamed. 1940. Paramount. Les Woodbury.

Sandy Gets Her Man. 1940. Universal. Police Chief O'Hara.

Rhythm on the River. 1940. Paramount. Mr. Westlake.

The Quarterback. 1940. Paramount. Coach.

Golden Gloves. 1940. Paramount. Emory Balzer.

Opened by Mistake. 1940. Paramount. Matt Kingsley.

One Night in the Tropics. 1940. Universal. Roscoe.

The Farmer's Daughter. 1940. Paramount. Scoop Trimble.

Those Were the Days. 1940. Paramount. Prisoner.

Dancing on a Dime. 1940. Paramount. Mac.

Six Lessons from Madame La Zonga. 1941. Universal. Chancy Beheegan.

Public Enemies. 1941. Republic. George "Bang" Carson.

Footsteps in the Dark. 1941. Warner Bros. Hopkins.

Cracked Nuts. 1941. Universal. James Mitchell.

Blondie in Society. 1941. Columbia. Waldo Pincus.

The Bride Came C.O.D. 1941. Warner Bros. Sheriff McGee.

Wildcat. 1942. Paramount. Oliver Westbrook.

Treat 'Em Rough. 1942. Universal. "Hotfoot."

Roxie Hart. 1942. Twentieth Century-Fox. O'Malley.

Moonlight in Havana. 1942. Universal. Barney Crane.

Give Out, Sisters. 1942. Universal. Harrison.

It Happened in Flatbush. 1942. Twentieth Century-Fox. Sam Sloan.

Gentleman Jim. 1942. Warner Bros. Billy Delaney.

Whistling in Brooklyn. 1943. Metro-Goldwyn-Mayer. Detective Ramsey.

We've Never Been Licked. 1943. Universal. Traveling Salesman.

Larceny with Music. 1944. Universal. Mike Simms.

Lake Placid Serenade. 1944. Republic. Jiggers.

Going My Way. 1944. Paramount. Max David.

The Fighting Seabees. 1944. Republic. Eddie Powers.

Lady on a Train. 1945. Universal. Sergeant Christie.

Hitchhike to Happiness. 1945. Republic. Sandy Hill.

Flame of Barbary Coast. 1945. Republic. Smooth "Wolf" Wylie.

Rendezvous with Annie. 1946. Republic. General Trent.

The Inner Circle. 1946. Republic. Webb.

The Crime Doctor's Manhunt. 1946. Columbia. Inspector Harry B. Manning.

Ziegfeld Follies. 1946. Metro-Goldwyn-Mayer. Mr. Martin.

The Virginian. 1946. Paramount. Honey Wiggen.

My Wild Irish Rose. 1947. Warner Bros. Billy Scanlon.

Mother Wore Tights. 1947. Twentieth Century-Fox. Mr. Schneider.

Miracle on 34th Street. 1947. Twentieth Century-Fox. Charles Halloran.

I Wonder Who's Kissing Her Now. 1947. Twentieth Century-Fox. Jim Mason.

Hit Parade of 1947. 1947. Republic. Harry Holmes.

Down to Earth. 1947. Columbia. Police Lieutenant.

Blondie's Anniversary. 1947. Columbia. Sharkey.

Monsieur Verdoux. 1947. United Artists. Jean La Salle, the Police Inspector.

Texas, Brooklyn and Heaven. 1948. United Artists. The Agent.

Good Sam. 1948. RKO. Tom Moore.

The Girl from Manhattan. 1948. United Artists. Mr. Bernouti.

Chicken Every Sunday. 1948. Twentieth Century-Fox. George Kirby.

The Babe Ruth Story. 1948. Allied Artists. Jack Dunn.

Joe Palooka in Winner Take All. 1948. Monogram. Knobby Walsh.

Red Light. 1949. United Artists. Hotel Clerk.

The Lone Wolf and His Lady. 1949. Columbia. Inspector Crane.

The Lady Takes a Sailor. 1949. Warner Bros. Oliver Harker.

Home in San Antone. 1949. Columbia. O'Bleery.

East Side, West Side. 1949. Metro-Goldwyn-Mayer. Bill the Bartender.

Pretty Baby. 1950. Warner Bros. Corcoran.

Kill the Umpire. 1950. Columbia. Jimmy O'Brien.

Blondie's Hero. 1950. Columbia. Marty Greer.

Kiss Tomorrow Goodbye. 1950. Warner Bros. Byers.

Rhubarb. 1951. Paramount. Len Sickles.

The Lemon Drop Kid. 1951. Paramount. Gloomy Willie.

Abbott and Costello Meet the Invisible Man. 1951. Universal. Detective Roberts.

Rancho Notorious. 1952. RKO. Baldy Gunder.

Safe at Home! 1962. Columbia. Coach Bill Turner.

Vivian Vance

The Secret Fury. 1950. RKO. Leah.

The Blue Veil. 1951. RKO. Alicia.

The Great Race. 1965. Warner Bros. Hester Goodbody.

TELEVISION
William Frawley and Vivian Vance

Frawley and Vance made a number of non–*I Love Lucy* television appearances together, including:

Stars in the Eye. CBS, 60 minutes. Broadcast November 13, 1952.

Dinner with the President. CBS, 60 minutes. Broadcast November 23, 1953.

The Milton Berle Show. NBC, 60 minutes. Broadcast May 4, 1954.

Toast of the Town. CBS, 60 minutes. Broadcast October 3, 1954.

Shower of Stars; episode titled "High Pitch." CBS, 60 minutes. Broadcast May 12, 1955.

The Bob Hope Chevy Show. NBC, 60 minutes. Broadcast October 24, 1956.

The Desilu Revue. CBS, 60 minutes. Broadcast December 15, 1959.

William Frawley

Frawley was a regular on *My Three Sons,* broadcast on ABC. The show premiered on September 29, 1960, and Frawley remained on it until midway through the 1964–65 season. Frawley played Michael Francis "Bub" O'Casey.

He also appeared on numerous variety and novelty shows, including *The Alan Young Show* (CBS), *The Mickey Mouse Club* (ABC), *The Swift Show Wagon* (NBC), *The Bob Hope Show* (NBC), *The Patti Page Show* (ABC), *The Tennessee Ernie Ford Show* (NBC), *The Red Skelton Show* (CBS), and *This Is Your Life* (NBC).

Other Frawley television appearances include:

Your Show Time; "The Lady or the Tiger." NBC, 30 minutes. April 15, 1949.

The Silver Theater; "Papa Romani." CBS, 30 minutes. January 9, 1950.

The Silver Theater; "The First Hundred Years." CBS, 30 minutes. May 1, 1950.

Demi-Tasse Tales; "Wedding Morning." CBS, 30 minutes. March 3, 1953.

The Loretta Young Show; "Dear Midge." NBC, 30 minutes. May 16, 1954.

Summer Night Theater; "Room for Improvement." DuMont, 30 minutes. September 8, 1954.

Damon Runyon Theater; "Bunny on the Beach." CBS, 30 minutes. July 16, 1955.

Desilu Playhouse; "Comeback." CBS, 60 minutes. March 2, 1959.

The Gale Storm Show; "The Card Sharp." ABC, 30 minutes. October 8, 1959.

Summer Playhouse; "The Apartment House." CBS, 30 minutes. September 5, 1964.

The Lucy Show; "Lucy and the Countess Have a Horse Guest." CBS, 30 minutes. October 25, 1965.

Vivian Vance

After appearing on *I Love Lucy*, Vance reteamed with Lucille Ball on *The Lucy Show,* which premiered on CBS on October 1, 1962. She played Vivian Bagley through the end of the 1964–65 season.

Among the variety and novelty shows on which Vance appeared are *I've Got a Secret* (CBS), *The Arthur Murray Party* (NBC), *The Red Skelton Show* (CBS), *Candid Camera* (CBS), *The Jack Paar Show* (NBC), *Calendar* (CBS), *The Mike Douglas Show* (Syndicated), *The Dick Cavett Show* (ABC), *The Merv Griffin Show* (Syndicated), *Everybody's Talking* (ABC),

Jeopardy (NBC), *You're Putting Me On* (NBC), *Dinah!* (Syndicated), and *Over Easy* (PBS).

Vance also played Maxine the Coffee Lady on Maxwell House coffee commercials.

Other Vance television appearances include:

The Deputy; "Land Greed." NBC, 30 minutes. December 12, 1959.

The Lucy Show; "Viv Visits Lucy." CBS, 30 minutes. January 9, 1967.

The Lucy Show; "Lucy and Viv Reminisce." CBS, 30 minutes. January 1, 1968.

The Lucy Show; "Lucy and the Lost Star." CBS, 30 minutes. February 26, 1968.

Here's Lucy; "The Matchmaker." CBS, 30 minutes. December 16, 1968.

Love, American Style; "Love and the Medium." ABC, 60 minutes. December 29, 1969.

Here's Lucy; "Lucy and Lawrence Welk." CBS, 30 minutes. January 19, 1970.

Here's Lucy; "Lucy and Viv Visit Tijuana." CBS, 30 minutes. January 26, 1970.

The Front Page. Syndicated, 90 minutes. January 31, 1970.

Here's Lucy; "Lucy Goes Hawaiian, Part One." CBS, 30 minutes. February 15, 1971.

Here's Lucy; "Lucy Goes Hawaiian, Part Two." CBS, 30 minutes. February 22, 1971.

Getting Away from It All. Made-for-television movie, ABC, 120 minutes. January 18, 1972.

Here's Lucy; "With Viv as a Friend, Who Needs an Enemy?" CBS, 30 minutes. February 14, 1972.

A Dean Martin Roast: Lucille Ball. 60 Minutes. Frebruary 7, 1975

Rhoda; "Rhoda's New Neighbor." CBS, 30 minutes. November 24, 1975.

The Great Houdinis. Made-for-television movie, ABC, 120 minutes. October 8, 1976.

CBS Salutes Lucy: The First 25 Years. CBS, 120 minutes. November 28, 1976.

Lucy Calls the President. CBS, 60 minutes. November 21, 1977.

Sam. CBS, 30 minutes. April 18, 1978.

Bibliography

BOOKS

Abbott, George. *Mister Abbott.* New York: Random House, 1963.

Andrews, Bart. *The I Love Lucy Book.* Garden City, NY: Doubleday and Company, 1985.

———. *Lucy & Ricky & Fred & Ethel: The Story of I Love Lucy.* New York: E. P. Dutton and Company, 1976.

Arnaz, Desi. *A Book.* New York: William Morrow and Company, 1976.

Atkinson, Brooks. *Broadway.* New York: MacMillan Publishing Co., 1970.

Beverage, Richard E. *The Hollywood Stars: Baseball in Movieland, 1926–57.* Placentia, CA: The Deacon Press, 1984.

Bloom, Ken. *American Song: The Complete Musical Theater Companion.* New York and Oxford, England: Facts on File Publications, 1985.

Bordman, Gerald. *American Musical Theater: A Chronicle.* New York: Oxford University Press, 1978.

Bragg, Melvyn. *Richard Burton: A Life.* Boston, Toronto, London: Little, Brown and Company, 1988.

Bronner, Edwin J. *The Encyclopedia of the American Theater, 1900–1975.* San Diego: A. S. Barnes and Company, 1980.

Edelman, Rob. *Baseball on the Web.* New York: MIS: Press, 1998.

———. *Great Baseball Films: From* Right Off the Bat *to* A League of Their Own. New York: Citadel Press, 1994.

Edelman, Rob, and Audrey E. Kupferberg. *Angela Lansbury: A Life on Stage and Screen.* New York: Birch Lane Press, 1996.

Goldberg, Lee. *Unsold Television Pilots, 1955 through 1988.* Jefferson, NC: McFarland and Company, 1990.

Harris, Warren G. *Lucy & Desi: The Legendary Love Story of Television's Most Famous Couple.* New York: Simon and Schuster, 1991.

Laurie Jr., Joe. *Vaudeville: From the Honky-Tonks to the Palace.* New York: Henry Holt and Company, 1953.

Lawrence, Jerome. *Actor: The Life & Times of Paul Muni.* New York: G. P. Putnam's Sons, 1974.

Maney, Richard. *Fanfare: Confessions of a Press Agent.* New York: Harper and Brothers, 1957.

Merman, Ethel, with George Eells. *Merman—an Autobiography.* New York: Simon and Schuster, 1978.

Milland, Ray. *Wide-Eyed in Babylon: An Autobiography of Ray Milland.* New York: William Morrow and Company, 1974.

O'Connor, Kathryn Kennedy. *Theater in the Cow Country.* Albuquerque, NM: The Albuquerque Little Theater, 1966.

O'Neal, Bill. *The Pacific Coast League, 1903-1988.* Austin, TX: Eakin Press, 1990.

Oppenheimer, Jess, with Gregg Oppenheimer. *Laughs, Luck . . . and Lucy: How I Came to Create the Most Popular Sitcom of All Time.* Syracuse, NY: University Press, 1996.

Paris, Barry. *Louise Brooks.* New York: Alfred A. Knopf, 1989.

Parish, James Robert, and Vincent Terrace. *The Complete Actors' Television Credits, 1948–88.* Metuchen, NJ, and London: The Scarecrow Press, 1990.

Sanders, Coyne Steven, and Tom Gilbert. *Desilu: The Story of Lucille Ball and Desi Arnaz.* New York: William Morrow and Company, 1993.

Slezak, Walter. *What Time's the Next Swan.* Garden City, NY: Doubleday and Company, 1962.

Spehr, Paul, with Gunnar Lundquist. *American Film Personnel and Company Credits, 1908–20.* Jefferson, NC: McFarland and Company, 1996.

Voss, Ralph F. *A Life of William Inge: The Strains of Triumph.* Kansas City, MO: University Press of Kansas City, 1989.

Walsh, Raoul. *Each Man in His Time.* New York: Farrar Straus Giroux, 1974.

PERIODICALS

"Actor's Wife Gets Divorce AND 35%." *New York Daily News,* May 12, 1941.

"Actor's Wife Sues; Names Blonde Star." *Chicago Sun-Times,* March 2, 1941.

Anderson, John. "'Let's Face It' Opens at Imperial Theater." *New York Journal-American,* October 30, 1941.

Anderson, Nancy. "Vivian Vance Enjoys Specials." *Warren* (Ohio) *Tribune Chronicle,* November 18, 1977.

Archibald, John J. "'I Love Lucy': 'Ricky' Recalls Uptight Times on the Set." *Chicago Tribune,* September 4, 1989.

Arnaz, Desi. "'Okay Cuban, We Have a Deal." *TV Guide,* January 31, 1976.

"As to Bill Frawley, from the Song and Dance." *New York Journal-American,* March 12, 1933.

"At Home with Vivian Vance." *New York Sunday News,* October 13, 1963.

Atkinson, Brooks. "The Play: Ed Wynn Returns in 'Hooray for What!' with Songs and Jokes at the Winter Garden." *New York Times,* December 3, 1937.

———. "The Play: Gertrude Lawrence Appears in Samson Raphaelson's Drawing Room Comedy Entitled 'Skylark.'" *New York Times,* October 13, 1939.

———. "The Play: Saluting the Summer." *New York Times,* May 2, 1928.

———. "Routine Musical Comedy." *New York Times,* January 14, 1927.

Baldwin, George S. "Benefit Play Gave Vivian Her Chance." *Albuquerque Tribune,* August 30, 1962.

Bell, Arthur. "Bell Tells." *The Village Voice,* April 5, 1976.

Bourke, George. "Plenty of Laughs in Marriage-Go-Round." *Miami Herald,* March 1, 1961.

Brown, John Mason. "Season Has a Hit at Last as Let's Face It! Arrives." *New York World-Telegram,* October 30, 1941.

———. "'Skylark' Opens with Gertrude Lawrence." *New York Post,* October 12, 1939.

Burton, Ron. "Baseball Is Frawley's Frolic." *New York Journal-American,* April 16, 1961.

"Chan." "My Three Sons." *Variety,* October 5, 1960.

Coleman, Robert. "'Out from Under' Not Enough Out for Top Rating." *New York Daily Mirror,* May 6, 1940.

Crouse, Russel. "An Author's Heart-Rending Tale of a Girl's Fight to Make Good." *New York Herald Tribune,* December 26, 1937.

D. W. B. "Tunes, Girls, and Gusto." *Boston Transcript,* April 27, 1926.

"The Dear Old Speakeasy Days Are Recalled in Song and Story." *New York Herald Tribune,* May 7, 1939.

"The Double Life of Vivian Vance." *TV Guide,* March 30, 1957.

Dudley, Bide. "Merry Merry." *New York Evening World,* September 25, 1925.

"Elie." "It Takes Two." *Variety,* January 29, 1947.

Esty II, William C. "Lord Loveland Discovers America." *Motion Picture News,* January 29, 1916.

Finnigan, Joseph. "Vivian Vance Plans to Quit Lucy Show." *New York World-Telegram and Sun,* September 9, 1964.

"'Forty-one Standees!' say Mr. and Mrs." *New York Herald Tribune,* no date.

Frawley, William. "Off Stage Views of Stage People." *New York Evening World,* November 5, 1925.

Gardella, Kay. "'Nothing Like a Dame,' says TV's Bill Frawley." *New York Daily News,* August 17, 1961.

Gillette, Don Carle. Untitled. *The Billboard,* October 3, 1925.

Green, Tom. "Bill Frawley Long Identified with Theater, Both Stage and Screen." *The Burlington* (Iowa) *Hawk-Eye,* June 27, 1953.

Gysi, Chuck. "TV's Fred Mertz Had Burlington Roots." *Burlington* (Iowa) *Hawk-Eye,* April 17, 1994.

Hammond, Percy. "The Theaters." *New York Herald Tribune,* January 14, 1927.

————. "The Theaters." *New York Herald Tribune,* January 8, 1933.

Harris, Radie. Untitled. *Hollywood Reporter,* June 3, 1965.

Harrison, Louis Reeves. "Three Mutual Masterpieces." *Moving Picture World,* February 5, 1916.

"He Wasn't the Type: That's What Somebody Said About Bill Frawley, Who Finally 'Arrived' the Hard Way." *Brooklyn Daily Eagle,* March 5, 1939.

Hochstein, Rollie. "TV's Favorite Comedy Team Breaks Up." *Good Housekeeping,* October 1965.

Holland, George. "Boston After Dark." *Boston American,* October 20, 1941.

"Hollywood Loses 2 Top Comedians." *New York World-Telegram and Sun,* March 4, 1966.

Hopper, Hedda. "Fewer TV Shows for Vivian Vance." *Los Angeles Times,* April 14, 1964.

Humphrey, Hal. "Flattery Gets Pat Nowhere." *Los Angeles Mirror,* January 21, 1961.

Hyams, Joe. "Hard Luck Gal!" *New York Herald Tribune,* September 25, 1960.

"John Dodds" (obituary). *Variety,* October 15, 1986.

Jordan, Jack. "'Marriage-Go-Round': John Baragrey, Vivian Vance, Sylvia Miles Make Big Hit." *Nassau Guardian,* February 22, 1961.

Klein, William, and Frank Livia. "Personalities in the News." *New York Sunday News,* February 27, 1955.

Kupferberg, Audrey. "Fannie Brice." *Film Fan Monthly,* September 1973.

Lax, Eric. "Vivian Vance." *Esquire,* April 1976.

Lefkowitz, Bernard. "Two of TV's 'Good Neighbors' Die." *New York Post,* March 4, 1966.

"Les." "My Three Sons." *Variety,* September 5, 1963.

"M. A. Frawley Dead." *Burlington* (Iowa) *Hawk-Eye,* June 27, 1907.

Maffitt, Lloyd. "Hawk-Eyetems: Bill Frawley Caught Stage Fever Here." *Burlington* (Iowa) *Hawk-Eye,* March 4, 1966.

Mantle, Burns. "Gertrude Lawrence and 'Skylark' Off to a Happy Season's Start." *New York Daily News,* October 5, 1939.

————. "Hooray for What!" *New York Daily News,* December 3, 1937.

"Mary Frawley Here for Visit after 20 Years." *Burlington* (Iowa) *Hawk-Eye,* October 10, 1955.

"The Mertzes—And How They Got That Way." *TV Guide,* December 12, 1954.

Morehouse, Ward. "The Cradle Still Rocks, but —. " *New York Sun,* December 27, 1947.

————. "'It Takes Two' Is Just a Thin and Shaky Comedy about Our Housing Shortage." *New York Sun,* February 4, 1947.

Mosby, Aline. "Vivian Vance Will Wear Glamour Clothes on Show." *Albuquerque Tribune,* May 12, 1955.

Muir, Florabel. "Just Like the Folks at Home." *New York Sunday News,* February 27, 1955.

Nachman, Gerald. "Vivian Vance: Sidelight on a Star." *New York Post,* January 10, 1955.

Ormsbee, Helen. "Words Concerning the Three Merry Wives of West Forty-fifth Street." *New York Herald Tribune,* December 14, 1941.

"Pathé Sound Act Releases." *Exhibitors Herald-World,* September 21, 1929.

"Philip Ober" (obituary). *Variety,* September 22, 1982.

Preston, Ruth. "Vivian Vance: No More Housedresses." *New York Post,* April 17, 1969.

Raddatz, Leslie. "Vivian Vance Can Now Laugh Off-Camera, Too." *TV Guide,* February 9, 1963.

"Radio-TV Scene." *Kansas City Star,* December 28, 1952.

Rathbun, Stephen. "Summer Season Starts: 'Talk About Girls,' a Jazz Music Comedy, Has Andrew Tombes, Funnier Than Ever." *New York Sun,* June 15, 1927.

Ray, Terry, "Across the Footlights." *New Mexico,* September 1951.

"Rose." "I Love Lucy." *Variety,* October 17, 1951.

Ruhl, Arthur. "The Theater." *New York Herald Tribune,* June 30, 1933.

Schumach, Murray. "William Frawley: Housekeeper of 'My Three Sons.'" *New York Times,* May 14, 1961.

Schweitzer, Wilma. "Anna Ingleman Could Foresee Bright Stage Futures for Such Stars as Vivian Vance and William Inge." *Independence* (Kansas) *Reporter,* January 29, 1956.

Scott, Vernon. "Frawley's Mean Even with Apron." *New York World-Telegram and Sun,* October 15, 1960.

————. "Tale of a Horse." *Newark Evening News,* March 2, 1964.

"Shan." "It's a Great Life." *Variety,* February 5, 1936.

"She Cashes in on Her Town's Faith in Her." *New York Herald Tribune,* November 5, 1939.

"She Wouldn't Quit Trying." *New York Journal-American,* March 20, 1938.

Stein, Ruthe. "Does Ethel Mertz Still Love Lucy?" *San Francisco Chronicle,* June 11, 1976.

Stump, Al. "The Pacific Coast Baseball Rebellion." *American Legion Magazine,* February, 1949.

Taylor, Zuma. "William Frawley Not the Cook Some Viewers Take Him to Be." *Hollywood Citizen-News,* August 2, 1961.

Thomas, Bob. "Vivian, Lucy Are Pals Again." *New York World-Telegram and Sun,* September 1, 1962.

"TV Star of the Week: He's Mr. Mertz." *Des Moines Sunday Register,* no date.

"TV Talk." *Hollywood Reporter,* February 20, 1991.

Van Horne, Harriet. "Lucy's Pal Enjoys Being Anonymous." *New York World-Telegram,* May 4, 1954.

Vance, Vivian, with John Maynard. "I Don't Run Away Any More." *McCall's,* May 1955.

Villella, Lynn Buckingham. "It All Started 'With This Thing Called Love.'" *Albuquerque Magazine,* August 1978.

"Vivian Vance" (obituary). *Variety,* August 22, 1979.

"Vivian Vance, Actress, Dies at 66; Co-Star of 'I Love Lucy' TV Show." *New York Times,* August 18, 1979.

"Vivian Vance Dies of Cancer." *Daily Variety,* August 20, 1979.

"Vivian Vance Plans More Comedies at Little Theater." *Albuquerque Journal,* March 5, 1967.

"Vivian Vance, TV Actress, Is 'At Home' in Albuquerque." *Albuquerque Journal,* February 18, 1953.

Vreeland, Frank. "Not Too Bonny." *New York Telegram,* January 14, 1927.

Whipple, Sidney. "Gertrude Lawrence Liked In Skylark, a New Comedy." *New York World-Telegram,* October 12, 1939.

"Wife of Actor Tells of Raid." *Pittsburgh Press,* March 2, 1941.

"Wife Sheds 'High Living' Mate." *Los Angeles Examiner,* April 27, 1959.

"William Frawley, Actor, Dead; Played Lucy's Landlord on TV." *New York Times,* March 4, 1966.

"William Frawley, TV's Perennial Man Next Door." *New York Herald Tribune,* March 4, 1966.

Winchell, Walter. "Musical Farce Meek Show at the Cort." *New York Daily Mirror,* October 20, 1932.

Zimmermann, Katharine. "Taking 'Here's Howe!' in Diluted Doses." *New York Telegram,* May 2, 1928.

Index

About the Authors

Rob Edelman is the author of the acclaimed *Great Baseball Films* (Citadel Press) and *Baseball on the Web* (MIS: Press) and co-author of *Angela Lansbury: A Life on Stage and Screen* (Birch Lane Press) and *The John Travolta Scrapbook* (Citadel Press). He is a contributing editor of *Leonard Maltin's Movie and Video Guide* and *Leonard Maltin's Movie Encyclopedia*. He has written essays and entries in several other books (including *A Political Companion to American Film, Total Baseball, The Total Baseball Catalog, International Dictionary of Films and Filmmakers, Women Filmmakers and Their Films, St. James Film Directors Encyclopedia, International Film Guide*); and his work has appeared in dozens of periodicals (from *American Film* to *Variety* and the *Washington Post*). He is the Director of Programming of Home Film Festival (which rents select videotapes throughout the country), offers weekly film commentary on WAMC (Northeast) Public Radio, programmed film series at the American Film Institute, and has taught film courses at Iona College, Sacred Heart University, and the School of Visual Arts.

Audrey E. Kupferberg is a film and video consultant, archivist, and appraiser. She has been the director of the Yale Film Study Center, Assistant Director of the National Center for Film and Video Preservation at the American Film Institute, and Project Director of the American Film Institute Catalog. She is the co-author of *Angela Lansbury: A Life on Stage and Screen* and *The John Travolta Scrapbook*, and has written for *Women Filmmakers and Their Films* and *International Dictionary of Films and Filmmakers*. She teaches film at the State University of New York at Albany (SUNY), and works as archivist at the Peary-MacMillan Arctic Museum at Bowdoin College. In her role as appraiser, she evaluated the long-lost, sole surviving kinescope of the pilot show that predates *I Love Lucy*. She and Rob Edelman are married and live in upstate New York.

Frawley and Vance as Fred and Ethel. (PHOTO COURTESY OF GLOBE)